Looking Glasses
and Neverlands

KAREN COATS

Looking Glasses and Neverlands

Lacan, Desire, and Subjectivity

in Children's Literature

UNIVERSITY OF IOWA PRESS 🄿 IOWA CITY

University of Iowa Press, Iowa City 52242
Copyright © 2004 by the University of Iowa Press
All rights reserved
Printed in the United States of America

Design by April Leidig-Higgins

http://www.uiowa.edu/uiowapress

Printed on acid-free paper

Library of Congress Cataloging-in-Publication Data
Coats, Karen, 1963–.
Looking glasses and neverlands: Lacan, desire, and
subjectivity in children's literature / by Karen Coats.
p.   cm.
Includes bibliographical references and index.
ISBN 0-87745-882-0 (cloth)
1. Children's literature—Psychological aspects.
2. Children's literature—Social aspects.   I. Title.
PN1009.5.P78C63   2004
809'.89282'019—dc22   2003066270

04 05 06 07 08 C 5 4 3 2 1

For Will, who listens

CONTENTS

Acknowledgments ix

Introduction:
The Subject of Children's Literature 1

1 How to Save Your Life:
Lessons from a Runt Pig 15

2 A Time to Mourn:
The Loss of the Mother 37

3 Mourning into Dancing:
Recuperating the Loss of the Mother 59

4 Looking Glasses and Neverlands:
Beyond the Symbolic 77

5 "I Never Explain Anything":
Children's Literature and Sexuation 97

6 Blinded by the White:
The Responsibilities of Race 121

7 Abjection and Adolescent Fiction:
Ways Out 137

Conclusion:
Postmoderns at the Gates of Dawn 161

Notes 173

Bibliography 179

Index 187

ACKNOWLEDGMENTS

Throughout the writing of this book, I have been blessed with many good friends, good colleagues, and good critics who have helped refine and shape the final product. J. D. Stahl and Bob Siegle introduced me to the possibility of studying children's literature and Lacanian theory together. Marshall Alcorn, Inez Azar, Peter Caws, Meena Khorana, Judith Plotz, Bob Samuels, and Gail Weiss read and critiqued an early version of the manuscript. Prasenjit Gupta met with me to discuss the proposal, and he and Holly Carver of the University of Iowa Press have been enthusiastic throughout the entire project. I'd also like to thank Rod McGillis and jan jagodzinski for their generous readings, Bobbe Needham for her inspired copyediting, and Charlotte Wright for making the whole process run smoothly. Finally, Roberta Seelinger Trites—my friend, my mentor, my sister of the heart—has been unfailingly supportive of my work.

Many of the ideas in these chapters have been presented at meetings of the International Children's Literature Association, the Association for the Psychoanalysis of Culture and Society, and the Modern Critical Approaches to Children's Literature conferences. I would like to thank the members and officers of those organizations for the work they do to keep our disciplines vibrant. Time and financial support for work on the manuscript was provided by Illinois State University's University Research Grant program and the Calvin College Summer Seminars for Christian Scholarship, the latter reminding me that my scholarship, rightly regarded, can be an act of worship.

Most of all, however, this work would not have been possible without my family. My parents, Joe and Dawn Moser, have never denied any request for babysitting or a free meal, and their generous and loving support has been an unfailing constant in my life. My husband, Will, is an amazingly intuitive philosopher; I need only talk to him and my world is made larger and more beautiful. And he seems to have passed this happy gift along to our girls. In most acknowledgments one reads, the writer thanks and apologizes to his or her children, who gave up time together so that the writer could finish the book. My children, thankfully, would have none of that. Much of this book was written with a child on my lap. Their persistent and entirely legitimate demands for time and attention, their veritable assaults of love, taught me more about the theories of desire and subjectivity than any published study, and for this I am truly indebted to them. Thank you, Emily. Thank you, Blair. You are brilliant.

The Subject of Children's Literature

Stories, it has been said, are as old as bread. I like that image, because it links stories to something as indispensable to our survival as food. It also reminds us that, as each culture takes a few simple ingredients and produces its own favorite forms of this "staff of life," usually simple for everyday use, more complex and textured for special times, so too our stories are created from simple ingredients readily available but transformed according to the occasion, the teller, the listener. Recipes for stories are passed across cultures and generations. In industrialized countries, they can become standardized and bland in their mass production or even fortified with things that we have been told are good for us.

It's an apt connection, surely, with rich metaphorical implications, but we must beware, I think, of a false binary embedded in its image, namely, that bread feeds the body and stories feed the mind. Instead, we need to remember that just as good bread can often nourish and fortify the soul even more than it does the body, so stories have a profound effect on the growth, the image, and the perceived needs and desires of the body, indeed, of the whole person. From our very first beginnings, we are fed stories, embraced by stories, nourished by stories. The only way we come to make sense of the world is through the stories we are told. They pattern the world we have fallen into, effectively replacing its terrors and inconsistencies with structured images that assure us of its manageability. And in the process of structuring the world, stories structure us as beings in that world. We begin to tell our own stories, fashioning a self out of the stories and narrative patterns we have received from our culture. As one nineteenth-century commentator put it, "There is a drop of ink in the blood of the most natural of us; we are all hybrids, crossed with literature, and Shakespeare is as much the author of our being as either of our parents" (Zangwill, qtd. in Dusinberre, 106). By offering substantive representations for words and things to the child, stories, especially those found in children's literature, provide signifiers—conventional words and images—that attach themselves to unconscious processes and have material effects on the child's developing subjectivity. Thus we could say that the stories we read or are told as children have as much to do with shaping our subjectivity as do our primary existential relationships.

Lacan and the Subject of Children's Literature

Why this should be so is most convincingly formulated by psychoanalyst Jacques Lacan in his theories of desire and subjectivity. According to Lacan, the subject is an effect of language, suggesting that there can be no subjectivity without language. And while language is the system of symbolic representation that Lacan most privileges, I think it is important to remember from the outset that visual or graphic representation is also an integral part of structuring who we are, as is evidenced in Lacan's most famous concept, the mirror stage, the importance of which we will explore in great detail throughout this book. Although we are born with what is called a proprioceptive self—a self that is perceptually aware of its place in space and can judge, to a very minimal extent, the physical properties of the things around it—we have no cognitive centering principle to organize that perception. It is not until we begin to use the processes of representation, both visual and verbal, that we are able to make those sensory perceptions have meaning and consistency. That part of us which is distinctly human does not preexist linguistic and visual representation. Our project is not to find words or images that will express more or less precisely who we are or even what we desire in some essential way. Instead, representation is what causes the subject to come into being. But insofar as a representation is not the thing itself, we sense that something has been lost, and we desire to get it back.

We might think of a baby surrounded by a swirl of language and image —his parents' voices, the radio, the TV, brothers and sisters, reading voices, talking voices, disembodied voices, bits of color, pictures, patterns on clothes and walls, and so on. This undifferentiated continuum *means* little to him but is nonetheless actively structuring him with its rhythms, its music, its play of light and shape. He begins to get a sense of cause and effect, of how noises seem to make things happen, his own noises as well as those of other people. He becomes adept at imitation, taking on first the cadences of language, but soon the words. Finally, he begins to generate more or less meaningful utterances. Likewise, he adjusts his facial expressions to the images he sees, first in a pattern of imitation, then in spontaneous and meaningful play and communication. He studies visual images and begins their assignation of value and meaning by clearly indicating preferences and by recognizing pictorial representations of real objects in his world. Sometime before he turns eighteen months, he even recognizes himself as an image in a mirror.

Hence the infant-child becomes a subject, according to Lacan, with his entry into language or, more specifically, culturally encoded representational systems. But despite the fact that he can now recognize and express himself as a subject in a system of representation, it is still the Other's system, something external to him that he has taken on. So the word "subject" has resonances of both agency and subservience. When I introduce the concept of subjectivity to my students, I have them brainstorm definitions of the word "subject." We generally begin with the definition of the subject as some discrete entity under study. Under this definition, a subject is complex enough, and definite enough, to stand alone as an object of investigation. We then come up with other definitions—the grammatical definition of the subject as the actor in a sentence, the thing or person performing the action of the verb; the political definition of a subject as someone under the rule of law; and a more naturalistic definition that implicates all bodies as subject to laws of gravity, thermodynamics, the limits of physical space and properties, and so on. There are contradictions in these pictures of the subject, and I encourage my students to hold those contradictions in unresolved ambiguity. The subject is both active and passive; it has agency and responsibility, but at the same time it is bound by rules and laws outside itself and constrained by its own unconscious processes. It is also, I emphasize, beholden to the forces of its environment and in many ways limited by the possibilities of its time and culture, though it has some power to change and expand those possibilities. Hence the psychoanalytic subject of Lacan is different from the psychological notion of the ego or the individual, with its emphasis on choice and individual autonomy and its universal and ahistorical nature. Lacan's subject is differentiated by his emphasis on the linguistic, and hence transindividual and historically and culturally situated, nature of the unconscious. It is therefore within the language and images of a specific culture that the subject must both *find* and *create* himself. Lacan's theory of the subject examines the way that dual process is negotiated. His primary focus is the way the subject situates itself with respect to the Other in language and the Other as language.

Much of that "Other" language comes to the subject in the form of stories. Children are especially vulnerable to being structured by stories because they are still in the process of collecting the experiences that will shape and define their relation to the Other. According to Lacan, a person's relation to the Other determines her psychic or clinical structure, be it neurotic, psychotic, or perverse. This structure develops in the early years of a child's life and remains fixed thereafter, regardless of any obvious symptoms. Hence it would seem important for a Lacanian poetics to focus attention on the stories of childhood as formative of that relation. I would hesitate to say that texts such as *Heart of Darkness* or *Bleak House*, important as they are to our literary and cultural heritage and to the vibrancy and dynamic nature of language itself, constitute formative encounters for the average person. Books like *Charlotte's Web*, on the other hand, or *Green Eggs and Ham* are more likely to generate such encounters, not only because more people are likely to actually read them, but also because they will probably be read at a time in the life of a person when she is less structured, or, if you like, when her boundaries are more porous, her mental architecture less crowded or filled in with images that define and stabilize her sense of reality and the self. In *Seminar I*, Lacan asks: "This child, we see that he is prodigiously open to everything concerning the way of the world that the adult brings to him. Doesn't anyone ever reflect on what this prodigious porosity to everything in myth, legend, fairy tales, history, the ease with which he lets himself be invaded by these stories, signifies, as to his sense of the other?" (SI 49). The child is easily "invaded," suggesting an as yet unformed or unfixed relation to the Other that will not in the future remain so open, but that indicates that the child is formed in large part by the representations provided by and of that Other. What we get from children's literature are the very patterns and signifiers that define our understanding of and our positions with respect to the Other and, in so doing, structure our sense of self.

The literature we encounter as children, then, should be seen as central to the formation of subjectivity. Most studies of children's literature that explore this connection focus on the formation of identity, which is only part of subjectivity, which in turn is only part of what I would call the self. Identity in psychoanalytic parlance refers to the more public, social presentation of the self—the part over which we have the most control. Our identity is the outcome of a series of identifications; in large measure it is performative, meaning that we take on the gestures and language of those whom we identify as desirable and ideal in order to craft our own self-presentation. By an ideal representation, I don't necessarily mean one that is conventionally positive, but rather one that offers the perfect picture of a certain characteristic, as in the ideal expression of sadness, or the ideal figure of teen rebellion. These ideals are formed, culturally speaking, through repetition. Hence racial and gender stereotypes become a kind of ideal, and a child's identifications with these images thus become problematic and worthy of critical attention. But such attention does not go far enough, for what drives these identifications, what makes us view a representation as ideal or desirable, is very complicated and is in large part unconscious to us even as it is embedded in the aesthetic productions of a culture. Remember, for instance, in *Little House on the Prairie* when a young Laura Ingalls desires to possess a Native American baby. Her attraction to the baby is so strong that it makes her ache, and the only explanation she can offer is: "Its eyes are so black" (Wilder, 309). It's an enigmatic moment in an otherwise straightforward text, and it points out the fact that identifications and desires are often driven by forces that we can neither understand nor articulate.

Subjectivity, then, is more than identity—it is a movement between that which we control and that which controls us. To locate specifically the importance of the literature we encounter as children to the construction of a social identity, as well as to the constitution and patterning of the unconscious, both of which are implicated in the notion of subjectivity, I have undertaken to read certain canonical children's texts and genres in light of Lacan's theory of the subject. Connections between narrative and subjective structure have been fruitfully and productively explored in many studies over the years, but these studies have focused on adult readers and texts.[1] The implications of these connections seem even more urgent to the child subject. While some important children's literature critics, including Roderick McGillis, Perry Nodelman, and Hamida Bosmajian have undertaken Lacanian explanations and interpretations of children's texts, most psychoanalytic criticism in children's literature focuses on the more familiar models of Freud and Jung, which offer categories that are less implicated in historical and cultural variations that form the mirror images to which children are subject.[2] But unlike the traditional view of mirror images as passively accurate reflections of what *is*, Lacan's understanding of the mirror image is that it is an anticipation that structures a subject.[3] The child looking into a mirror sees an idealized image of his potential. This image, in its specular completeness, is at odds with how he *experiences* his body. His trajectory of becoming is toward the image; he takes its completeness, fantasized as it is, as his goal. Though he may experience himself as fragmented and incomplete, he can imagine himself as whole, and it is toward this imaginary ideal that he moves. But he does not experience this imaginary ideal only in an actual mirror. Other people provide ideal images for him to mirror, but more significantly for this study, novels and picture books also present images and worlds that the child reader takes as Lacanian mirror images.

Modernist Subjectivity

The paradigm of subjectivity that I have been explaining is, historically speaking, a modernist one. Unlike a traditional or premodern model which posits an essential, knowable individual who develops her inborn potentials more or less organically, the modernist model figures the subject as split, a construction of both natural and cultural influences, of conscious and unconscious processes. Part of her operates consciously, negotiating roles and positions with respect to others in the world, as well as with respect to her own idealized images of herself. But another part of her operates outside of her conscious control. Her unconscious is just as active, if not more so, as the conscious part of her in shaping the movements and decisions of her everyday life, but she has no idea how it does so. It is unknowable, beyond her conscious understanding. Under Lacan's reading, it is not even intrinsic to herself, not something she is born with, even as a potentiality. As we shall see, the unconscious is deeply implicated in the Other; its verbal and visual representations come from culture, from outside the subject, so that what is most uniquely "ours" is in fact not native to us at all. Modernist novels by writers such as Dostoevsky, Woolf, and Lawrence take up the task of representing that split between consciousness and the unconscious to the subject. For the children's book, however, I think the task goes far beyond representation of the split. "Prodigiously open," the child (unconsciously) uses his books to precipitate or activate his split, to fill his unconscious with representations and images, shape his reality, and define the parameters of his possibilities. As I indicated earlier, this process depends on repetition—both the repetition of the same book, and the repetition of structures, images, and values across books. Hence, as her books have a definable structure, so structure becomes a psychic necessity for the child. As her books depict a whole world, the child seeks nothing less than a whole world. As her books operate under an oedipal configuration, the child will become structured under an oedipal configuration. As her books value closure, the child comes to desire closure. The child takes an adult fantasy, manifested in a story, as his ideal image, and undertakes to enact it as his own subjective structure.

In the first chapter of this book, I use Lacan's theory of subjectivity to explore exactly how the book and the child interact on this level—how the book articulates the child's development into a subject in such a way as to help actually structure that subjectivity. It offers an overview of the key aspects of Lacan's theory of how the subject comes to be through the characters of Fern and Wilbur in E. B. White's *Charlotte's Web*.

In addition to structure, modernist subjectivity, especially in children's literature, has content. It is avowedly patriarchal and understands Whiteness and heterosexuality as sites of privilege and desire. Wordsworth's famous maxim "The child is father to the man" is instructive here. In one sentence he predicts some of the key insights of psychoanalysis. Most obviously, he indicates that our childhood experience is vital to our adult personality. But more subtly, we see in his words that the child, an ungendered signifier, grows into the masculinized subject of adulthood. And interestingly, he passes through the "father" to get there. In Lacanian terminology, the child must come under the "Law of the Father" in order to take up a position in the Symbolic; he must, paradoxically, become his own cause. I will explore both these processes, explaining what they mean and how they are distinctly modernist in their conception, throughout the book. We will see how, in a modernist context, growth *means* separation from the mother and the taking up of a position with respect to the Law of the Father. Closure *means* heterosexual marriage, secure gender roles, and father-led families. These define happy endings and thus create desire that runs along specific channels. Even in literature that attempts to celebrate diversity on a conscious level, there is often the unconscious acknowledgment that deviance from white, masculine heteronormativity is a problem to be solved, to be lived on top of, so to speak, rather than to be rethought or challenged at the level of unconscious fantasy. To maintain the hegemony of its conceits, the modernist subject operates under a sacrificial logic of abjection.

The subject must abject, that is, define and exclude, those things which threaten it and must build strong defenses against their return. She must take up a position with respect to difference and must learn what her culture values as ideal in terms of bodies and behaviors. This education often begins through picture books and early readers, which are the subjects of chapters 2 and 3. Using Lacan's model of developmental time, I explore precisely how picture books participate in our growing sense of subjective awareness. For most characters in children's books, growth begins with a separation of some kind from the mother, which is metaphoric for our awareness of the other as Other, as different from ourselves. Since our encounters with difference are always linked to the grief of separation from the mother, our imaginary constructions of race and gender are fraught with sadness and fear, as is evidenced in works such as *The Story of Babar*, *Curious George*, and *Stellaluna*. An understanding of the structural time and specular logic of the Lacanian Imaginary allows us to grasp how Whiteness and heterosexuality become normative master signifiers in some texts, and how that view is challenged in others. I then link these responses to difference to the three psychic structures of psychosis, perversion, and neurosis, which, in Lacan's schema, are positions taken up with respect to the Other.

But how, then, might we imagine a departure from, or at least the potential of a challenge to, the hegemonic discourse of modernity? Chapter 3 turns from the specular logic of the Imaginary to the more verbal logic and elastic play of the Symbolic. Because our subjectivity depends on a fantasy structure based on tenuous exclusions, and because the subject does have an active but unknowable unconscious, the child is able to imagine other structures, to take on other representations, to move through narrative's totalizing images to a creative beyond. His encounters with poetry and nonsense fiction, by taking language's limits and its arbitrary connection to its referent as their object, point to this beyond without filling it with the contingent contents of his culture. In other words, modernism has always contained within itself the seeds of its own challenges, which we have come to call postmodernity. A specular image, especially a mirrored one, seems a pretty reliable, stable indicator of its referent. But linguistic representation is less organically connected to its referent, and thus it has the ability to destabilize the child's trust in representation itself, opening the door to all sorts of possible writings and rewritings of the self. What surrealism did for art, nonsense and nonrealistic fiction has done for literature, and the combination of the two, especially in the genres of early reading experience provided by the likes of Dr. Seuss and *Sesame Street*, has rendered it almost impossible for the contemporary American child to undertake a subject position that does not hint at some sort of postmodern irony or at least fluidity of representation within the Symbolic.

Chapter 4 helps us understand the persistent residue left over when the child enters the Symbolic by focusing on the nature of desire itself. By exploring Lacan's notions of the *objet a*, the cause of desire, and *jouissance*, that toward which desire always tends, we can begin to understand the persistence and infinite cultural variations and repetitions of two iconic figures of Western childhood—Alice and Peter Pan. A close reading of *Through the Looking Glass* situates Alice as that impossible nonspecular object that causes us to desire but also ensures the perpetuation of that desire precisely because it is impossible to attain, and not merely prohibited. Likewise, woven throughout the text of Peter Pan are metaphoric representations of the four different kinds of *jouissance* that alternately drive each of us in our quest to recover the lost pleasures of an unmediated embodiment.

The modernist Symbolic order has some fairly strict rules about gender, especially for children. Children's literature critics have been exhaustively critical about the portrayal of restrictive gender roles at least since the landmark Weitzman study in 1972 of the depiction of gender in North American picture books. We all know the problems—boys are depicted as active, girls as passive; boys are valued, girls devalued.[4] But a psychoanalytic understanding of gender must go beyond the roles we play or are expected to play in the Symbolic, and account for gender in the Imaginary and the Real as well. Thus I turn to gender in chapter 5, looking at its structural formation rather than at the cultural contents with which we fill that structure. For the most part, constructionist theories, such as those developed by Michel Foucault and Judith Butler, can account for gender only in Imaginary ways, or even in a dialectic relationship between Imaginary ideals and Symbolic mandates. But a psychoanalytically inflected queer theory, which situates the subject in relation to the heterogeneous realm of the Real and is illustrated most eloquently in characters such as Mary Poppins and Pippi Longstocking, allows us to move beyond gender in productive ways.

Just as the modernist Symbolic order requires the subject to be gendered, it also requires the subject to be racialized. As with gender, I attempt in chapter 6 to look at race psychoanalytically, focusing on Whiteness as a master signifier that functions to ground a racist system. By looking at how secondary signifiers attach themselves to this master signifier, we can begin to get at ways to destabilize Whiteness as a master signifier and bring it into the chain of signification as one signifier among many.

Chapter 7 takes us back to the Symbolic and the Imaginary, but with a difference—the exploration of the Real. In chapter 7, I look at adolescence as a time when the oedipal work accomplished in early childhood is revisited. That which had been coded as abject in the initial configuring of the body, both individual and social, returns and has to be dealt with all over again. The body itself has to be remapped; many things that were considered gross and unacceptable have to be reconsidered for their erotic potential. The process of situating the self with respect to the Other is continued, but with the difference that the self is now a much less permeable space; the invasion by the Other is much more violent, both actually and figuratively. Hence it becomes imperative to explore the possibilities of a positive ethics in light of modernist subjectivity, comparing and contrasting an ethics located in the Imaginary with an ethics of the Real.

Becoming Postmodern?

These pages tell a developmental story in which children's literature is vitally important in the construction of the subject both in its structure and content. They also offer what I hope will be a lucid but nonreductive introduction to Lacan's theories of desire and subjectivity. I pursue close readings of texts as manifestations of psychoanalytic structures and show how the child subject is interpellated into the position of modernist subject through them. Though I focus on specific examples, children's texts seem to have family resemblances that make my assertions more broadly generalizable. So, one may ask, isn't this project dated? Aren't we all postmodern subjects now? I suppose the answers to those questions depend on how one conceives the project of postmodernism. If one defines postmodernism as a necessary critique of the conceits of modernism, as I do, then this project provides one such critique even as it identifies its specific sites of complaint. But in that sense, there can as yet be no such thing as a postmodern subject, since he or she would exist only as a critique, a negativity, or a subversion of something definably modern. If my theories about the way children are constructed by the texts they encounter are correct, we can identify trends in contemporary literature for children that may have the effect of redefining unconscious fantasies, both in terms of what we fantasize about and the ways in which we fantasize at all. It is important to keep in mind that Lacan's theories are structural in nature, and that individual subjects as well as cultures fill in those structures with the sum of their unique experiences in time and space. My intent is to outline the general structural features of subjectivity within which we currently operate. But since they are structural features, their content may indeed change through the intervention of postmodern ideological critiques found in some contemporary children's texts. I conclude, then, by identifying some of those trends and providing some speculations on how they may alter subjectivity as we know it.

Looking Glasses
and Neverlands

How to Save Your Life

Lessons from a Runt Pig

When Fern Arable realizes that her father is headed out to the barn to kill a runt pig, she is immediately engulfed in identificatory existential angst: "'But it's unfair,' cried Fern. 'The pig couldn't help being born small, could it? If *I* had been very small at birth, would you have killed me?'" (*Charlotte's Web* [CW], 3). In a flash of horror and insight, she articulates the truth of Lacan's assertion that all humans (and some pigs) are born prematurely, and she understands that it is the task of someone else to save their lives. Her appeals to justice indicate further just how ideologically overdetermined that task is for humans: We are not simply about practical considerations or survival of the species, we are about love and fathering and mothering, we are about the transcendence of a mere brute existence where weaklings are more trouble than they are worth. So in a supreme moment of fathering, John Arable makes his daughter a mother, and a runt pig begins his existence as Fern's "baby," Wilbur.

Written in 1952 by E. B. White, *Charlotte's Web* is a homely, comforting story about friendship. It is often, as noted by Perry Nodelman, the first "chapter" book adults choose to read to children; it has all the elements that make a story feel right for the very young—a main character with whom the child can identify, a wise and loving mother figure, villains that are not too fearful, and a triumphant story line, all woven together with gentle humor and carefully crafted language that emphasize the glories of the natural world. More than that, the story is empowering for the young child; it offers a vision of what most parents want for their children (and themselves) in that it can be read as a "consoling fantasy in which a small Everyman survives and triumphs over the pathos of being alone" (Griffith, 111).

Not only does Wilbur triumph over his fundamental isolation, but also he triumphs over the terror of his being-toward-death. He is saved not once, but twice, by women who act as mothers to him, and who use language to intervene in his destiny and to turn him into something that, by any objective standard, he should not be. In order to save Wilbur, first Fern and then Charlotte have to convince Mr. Arable and Farmer Zuckerman that Wilbur is worth saving, that he is more than simply a runt pig, good for nothing and a lot of trouble besides. The way they do that is by speaking for him, by connecting him to the world of language. In a sense, they do what the Lacanian (m)Other does—together, they provide the conditions for him to have a "voice," at the expense of their own erasure.

The story of Fern, Wilbur, and Charlotte, then, is one of love, death, and the role of language in the formation and transformation of the self. Approaching it from the perspective of Lacan's theory of the subject allows us to situate it in terms of its own preoccupations, for Lacan's theory, like White's tale, is informed by existentialist concerns regarding the relations between language, meaning, and being. This is not to say that Lacanian theory is existentialist. Rather it is *informed by* existentialism, but also by structuralism, two philosophies that are at some points radically irreconcilable. For instance, Laurence Gagnon's Heideggerian reading of *Charlotte's Web* centers on what he calls the characters' "various personal struggles to live authentically" (Gagnon, 61). Wilbur and Charlotte "find themselves thrown into existence together, inescapably confronted with the task of truly becoming what they can be—even unto death" (63). At the heart of this type of reading of the human, there is an interior sort of "unique identity proper to oneself" (62) that must be found and cultivated. The words that appear in Charlotte's web regarding Wilbur are read by Gagnon as temptations for the pig to live inauthentically—to be what Gagnon calls a "people-self," one defined by what others have to say about him rather than what he somehow *is*, essentially. The only word that Gagnon finds appropriate to Wilbur's true self is the word "humble": "Only with the last, prophetic message is there a genuineness in Wilbur's attitude—he has finally become more of himself, a humble pig" (65). But what Gagnon's strictly existential reading does not take into account is the role of language in the creation of that self. Lacan's particular blend of structuralism and existentialism dismantles the notion of an "authentic" self, relocating it as the subject of language; in fact, for Lacan, *the subject is the effect of language*, a concept that I shall explain further in what follows. But for Gagnon, the power of language is descriptive rather than constitutive; Wilbur is under threat of inauthenticity because "[a]s a young pig, he does not have an especially strong personality" (65) and hence cannot ward off identifications that Gagnon sees as inappropriate or inaccurate. But if we see the subject as the end product of those identifications, as actively structured by them rather than merely corresponding to them or not, we see that the notion of the subject as an interiority seeking words that suit it is not tenable.

Certainly, the subject comes to invest its world with its own meanings, with what could be called in existentialist thought its own idiosyncratic "calls of concern." Despite the fact that Fern and Charlotte speak for him and in many ways call him into being, Wilbur must develop his own projects; he must find ways to nominalize his idiosyncratic desires. Ultimately, he must approach his life, and his death, differently than does Charlotte or Fern. Nonetheless, there are laws that regulate those meanings, structures that contain and constrain the production of (meaning in) the subject. Those structures are not organic or idiosyncratic to the individual, as a sort of innate ego. Instead, they are located in language, which is a public order in which we always already find ourselves. The identifications that Gagnon condemns as temptations toward inauthenticity are in fact the necessary linguistic positings of the subject by the Other. This Other we understand in its multivalent dimensions: It encompasses the others that surround us as parents, siblings, teachers, and so on, as well as the societal structures, both formal and informal, that provide the racial, cultural, and gender markers through which we are defined. Wilbur teaches us that in order to develop any sort of self whatsoever, one must first be recognized by an Other in language, which implicates the Other, and the Other's words, in the construction of the self. In fact, White's story is exemplary of the ways in which language functions to constitute subjectivity in its structural dimension. It also offers us a way to look at the substantive aspects of a specifically modernist subjectivity. In what follows I will be looking at *Charlotte's Web* through a Lacanian poetics that explores how "literature operates a magnetic pull on the reader because it is an allegory of the psyche's fundamental structure" (Ragland-Sullivan, "Magnetism," 381).

Fern Enjoys Her Symptom

The first two chapters of *Charlotte's Web* are not really Charlotte's story at all, nor are they Wilbur's. They belong to an eight-year-old girl named Fern.

She is the "cause" of the story, so to speak, in that it is her dramatic reaction to her father's intended action that brings Wilbur into existence in the first place. Without Fern, the runt pig is of no importance whatsoever. Interestingly enough, as a pig, he is not especially important to her either. He is simply a symbol with whom she narcissistically identifies. Her father, John Arable, exercises absolute authority over his pigs, just as he exercises absolute authority over his daughter. When he threatens the life of a small pig, Fern, a small girl, decides to challenge his authority. She does so in the way that is most threatening to the symbolic male power structure—she loses control and grabs her father's, um, ax.[1] It is not so much that she cares about the life of this particular pig as it is her desire to impose her will, to be recognized as having a voice and a vote in the affairs of her world. Her father, although admonishing her to control herself, nevertheless reasserts his control over her by giving her more than she asks for. He turns her into something more than an object of his and his wife's affection. It is a loving gesture, but one implicated in power nonetheless. John Arable is acting at this moment as the primordial Freudian father, exercising complete control over who may or may not acquire the phallus in his wee tribe. Significantly, Arable's son, Avery, "heavily armed" with pretend versions of his father's weapon ("an air rifle in one hand, a wooden dagger in the other" (CW, 4), is excluded from his father's bequeathal of phallic authority. He is then and remains throughout the story (until the end, where he acts as Wilbur's fool) a threat to Wilbur's well-being, and Arable is not about to let him assume a role for which he is not yet ready.

Fern, on the other hand, has received her father's authorization to mother the pig. In the confrontation between Fern's desire and the Law of her Father, Wilbur is precipitated as an object. He is a narcissistic object-choice, according to Freud, who first defined this type of object-choice in his discussion of homosexuals, but who later integrated it into the stages of development of the ego. The narcissistic object "is chosen on the model of the little child or adolescent that the subject once was, while the subject identifies with the mother who used to take care of him" (Laplanche and Pontalis, 259). The pig is connected to Fern through the characteristics of smallness and dependency, and their positions under her father's authority. Her father encourages the narcissistic connection, and hence helps to foster Fern's psychic development, by emphasizing her role as mother: "'I'll let you start it on a bottle, like a baby'" (CW, 3). The constitution of Wilbur as an object is crucial to the constitution of Fern as a subject. Together, they form an Imaginary dyad, with Fern (presumably) replicating her own mother's desire when she herself was a narcissistic object for her mother. Hence the mother's desire is the first cause in the inauguration of the subject. But no less critical is the replication of that desire in the subject herself. For it is only when one stands on the side of the mother, so to speak, that one is able to pass through to the other side of the Lacanian mirror stage.

The mirror stage is probably the most well-known concept in Lacanian thought. The story goes as follows: At some point very early in the child's life, she looks into a mirror and apprehends the fact that her body is a distinct and coherent entity unto itself, that there are boundaries between what constitutes herself and what constitutes Other. Of course, this image is just that—an image, and an idealized image at that. The image has control of its body; the baby does not. The image is autonomous; the baby is "still sunk in his motor incapacity and nursling dependence" (Lacan, *Ecrits: A Selection* [E], 2). Thereafter, however, the baby will be in a position to know him/herself, but only in a fictional way, because the Imaginary register of ideal images has come into being and has determined the only way in which we can know anything—through alienation (knowing oneself through an external image), duality (the result of a deep ambivalence caused by the alienation between the subject and its ideal image), and identification (the attempt to dissolve the subject into the ideal image and say, "This is me"). The baby has entered the world of signifying transactions, and image has displaced being; the subsequent and inevitable entry into language represents a further displacement or alienation, a further aphanisis, or fading, of the Real in favor of the Symbolic, by way of the Imaginary.

Of course, it would be disingenuous or naive to suggest that these transactions are not mediated—the apprehension of the image by the baby is probably never spontaneous, as it is almost always interpreted for the baby by someone else, usually the mother, who tells the baby what he is looking at. And until the baby can make the conceptual distinction of what "I" means and then identify himself with that "I," the baby is not a full subject. Interestingly enough, children tend to learn the personal pronouns in the order "mine," "me," and then "I," suggesting a grammatical progression from knowing what bounds them, to recognizing their object status, to finally assuming a subject position. Because the mother (or her surrogate) mediates the entire experience, because the child encounters first in her voice those shifters ("I" and "me") that will come to stand for himself, it would seem inevitable that the mother will always stand alongside any Symbolic representation the child makes for himself. And indeed this is the case— the Imaginary acts as a support for the Symbolic. Mothers and babies, under ideal circumstances, form an Imaginary couple, a unity that predisposes the child to look for such a couple relationship later in life, but also predisposes the child to form other Imaginary relationships, including the one between himself and the mirror. These Imaginary relationships are characterized by a complete coincidence of self and other, which is, of course, an illusion, but a necessary one. If for some reason a child does not make that initial Imaginary mirror-stage identification (as is suspected to be the case in some instances of autism—see Lefort), then it is impossible to enter into the Symbolic network of relations, with its substitutionary logic of the signifier. If on the other hand the Imaginary fusional relationship remains primary, the child's relation to the Symbolic is compromised in ways that can result in neurosis or perversion. This is what worries Fern's mother with regard to Wilbur. When Fern's teacher asks her what the capital of Pennsylvania is, she is so locked in her dream of mothering that she says, "Wilbur," which, in a sense, is appropriate, because Wilbur has filled up her entire psychic geography. Obviously, this is a potentially dangerous situation for Fern. But as it turns out, Fern's mother's fears are unfounded, because the necessary intervention of the third term has already begun to have its effect.

The "third term" in Lacanian theory is the position of the Law, or the Name of the Father—that which breaks the dyadic logic of the mother-child connection. Shoshana Felman explains:

> The triangular structure, crucial to Lacan's conception, is not the simple psychological triangle of love and rivalry, but a socio-symbolic structural positioning of the child in a complex constellation of alliance (family, elementary social cell) in which the combination of desire and a Law prohibiting desire is regulated, through a linguistic structure of exchange, into a repetitive process of replacement—of substitution—of symbolic objects (substitutes) of desire. (*Jacques Lacan and the Adventure of Insight,* [JLAI], 104)

Just as Fern's father mandates the mothering relationship between Fern and Wilbur, so he also mandates its termination. What breaks the dyadic relation between mother and child is the intervention of the Name of the Father. This third term effectively bars the mother's desire, inaugurating a chain of substitutions that come to signify and replace the mother's desire. Bruce

Fink points out that it doesn't matter whether you read "mother's desire" as the child's desire for the mother, the mother's desire for the child, or the whole thing in its totality (*The Lacanian Subject* [LS], 57). The point is that it is dangerous to the child and the mother, because it is built on an impossibility. In the dyad, there is an illusion of totality. But with the triangle of (maternal) desire, (paternal) law, and (child) subject comes a hole in the middle that continually needs, not filling up, but covering over as the child seeks to regain the unity with the mother that was always already lost. The substitution of signifiers for that desire inaugurates the subject as a *desiring being*, which is what is considered normal and healthy in modern subjectivity.

Thus the Name of the Father (alternately called the paternal metaphor or the phallus) separates the subject from the mother's desire by means of a sort of redundant prohibition—redundant because it prohibits that which doesn't really exist—that eventually serves to normativize the subject's desire. Fern's father requires Fern to sell Wilbur, thus effecting the initial separation. Seeing how much that separation will hurt Fern, her mother intervenes, suggesting that Fern sell him to an uncle who lives nearby. Farmer Zuckerman, Fern's uncle and hence once removed from her father, puts Wilbur in a pen with certain prohibitions: "Mr. Zuckerman did not allow her to take Wilbur out, and he did not allow her to get into the pigpen" (CW, 15–16). Still, he allows her to visit every day, which she does, causing her mother to worry that the prohibitions are not working to normativize Fern's desire. She consults Fern's doctor (whose depiction by illustrator Garth Williams bears an uncanny resemblance to Freud himself), who reassures her that the substitution will eventually take hold in the form of a boy, namely Henry Fussy. Of course by the end of the book it does in fact do just that, and Fern voluntarily separates herself from the moment of Wilbur's triumph in order to ride the Ferris wheel with Henry. Presumably, since Fern is only eight, Henry is merely the first in a series of signifiers for Fern's desire, indicating that she has been successfully triangulated (in other words, oedipalized) and is a full member of the Symbolic.

But it must not be forgotten that it is the psychic work performed through Wilbur that makes this happen. As the representational nexus of Fern's narcissism, her desire, and her relation to the Law, he cannot simply be sold and forgotten, no matter what a Symbolic authority says. Instead he is repressed. The lovely imagery that White provides is of Wilbur being put in the cellar of a barn where he becomes a Real pig, rather than an Imaginary baby. Repressed representations function in just that way. They take on the status of the Real for the subject. The Real is one of the most difficult concepts to grasp in Lacan, much debated and little understood. It helps, I find, to consider the Real in two veins—a pre-Symbolic Real and a post-Symbolic Real of the subject (Fink, LS, 27). The pre-Symbolic Real is the subject's absolute Other. It is unsymbolizable and hence has no effect whatsoever on the subject as such. What does have effects is the post-Symbolic Real, that is, those repressed representations that create our material conditions.

For something to exist in the Real of the subject, it must be conceived of as having slipped the boundaries of symbolization. What we can conceive of symbolically is what makes up our reality, but implicit in that conception is the idea that since we have conceived it, and since we know that signifiers slide endlessly and substitute one for another in an endless chain, there must be some outside of signification where the sliding stops. Joan Copjec says it is the very duplicity of language that points to an outside which is the Real; hence the Real is an effect of language's inability to be self-identical (Copjec, 56). Bruce Fink phrases the same idea another way, positing "a real after the letter which is characterized by impasses and impossibilities due to the relations among the elements of the symbolic order itself. . . , that is, which is generated by the symbolic" (LS, 27). We have already seen how Wilbur-as-baby was generated by Fern's encounter with the Law; when he is excluded as a baby by that same Law, he has nowhere to go, structurally speaking, but into that register of the Real which is post-Symbolic. Re-pressed representations, in that they are unavailable to us, form independent relations among themselves and create material effects in our realities —take on the status of this post-Symbolic Real—just as Wilbur becomes a pig in the midst of other animals in Zuckerman's cellar / Fern's unconscious.

The story of Charlotte, then, can be read as Fern's symptom. Despite the fact that both Fern's father and her uncle have introduced a bar of sep-aration between Fern and her Imaginary other, she still has work to do to effect her own separation from him. In fact she does not separate from Wilbur until Charlotte is certain that Wilbur is safe. When Wilbur's special award is announced, Charlotte "was sure at last that she had saved Wilbur's life, and she felt peaceful and contented" (CW, 153). Immediately, Fern asks for some money so that she can be off in search of Henry Fussy. Rather than join in the general excitement surrounding her pig, she insists on being allowed to leave, having no interest at all in sharing in the accolades of her surrogate child. Because we know the end of the story, how Fern is free to separate from Wilbur at his moment of triumph, we can retroactively posit that when she sells Wilbur, she still fears for his life. And since we have seen how interconnected his life is with her coming into being as a subject, we can also posit that the entire story of Charlotte and her web is Fern's attempt to save herself. As long as she (and Wilbur) are not full subjects, they are under threat. The Imaginary is a wonderful place to visit, but the child subject mustn't continue to live there. At the same time, the sense of loss that would be generated by the death of Wilbur as Fern's Imaginary other would be too traumatic. Fern is at an impasse until Wilbur can be dialecticized, brought out of both an Imaginary relation and a Real that cannot be symbolized into a network of signifiers. Until that happens, or more precisely until Fern is sure of Wilbur's place in the Symbolic network, she is unable to break the Imaginary dyad that is holding them both in place. As a result, she develops a symptom. She unaccountably (to her mother at least) "hears" the voices of all the barnyard animals as they go about their business.

Charlotte's web-words function to dialecticize Wilbur and free Fern from her fixation and the symptom that results from it. Fixation indicates a trauma. In Fern's case, I think we can safely posit that the trauma of realizing that her father would kill a harmless creature in cold blood acted as the cause of her being unable to get over Wilbur, especially in light of her identification with him. Fern's connection to Wilbur and her subsequent symptom of believing that animals talk send her mother scurrying to the doctor, who says in effect that eventually Fern will find a substitute that will relieve her of her fixation. But in order to do that, the fixated object needs to be drawn into the dialectical movement of the signifier. Fern's father, her uncle, and Henry Fussy set the stage for this process to occur by excluding Fern's maternal desire and introducing a hole in the structure of Fern's relationship to Wilbur. But it is finally Charlotte who realizes that words are the way to unlock Wilbur from his position as Real object in Fern's unconscious (and, as such, unsymbolizable) and constitute him as a substitutable entity (that is, bring him into the Symbolic). Paradoxically, the words that "kill" him in the Real save his life symbolically for Fern. The words, by signifying Wilbur, free him from the kind of "authenticity" or Realness that he has come to embody for Fern, and that ultimately is a fantasy of the Imaginary. The words in Charlotte's web become "a Real manifestation of an Imaginary use of Symbolic-order language, whose 'first cause' is [Fern's] unconscious" (Ragland-Sullivan, "Magnetism," 405).

Some Pigs

Thus far we have looked at Wilbur as a part of Fern—her ego, or in Lacanian terms (as well as in the terms of Miss Piggy herself), her *moi*. But more can be learned about the construction of subjectivity by looking at Wilbur as a subject in his own right. Structurally speaking, Wilbur's emergence as a subject is fairly straightforward in Lacanian terms. The Lacanian subject is alienated from its own desire from its very inception. It is not Wilbur's desire that brings him into existence, but Fern's. None of us asks to be born; parental desire, in whatever form it may take, causes a child's presence in the world. And that desire continues to function in the child's life, creating the space in which the child will come to exist as a subject within language. Inasmuch as the child subject is caused by the desire of an Other, he or she is always already alienated. In fact, such alienation is the necessary condition for any subjectivity whatsoever. If Fern's desire had not been mobilized in Wilbur's direction, there would have been no Wilbur.

But Wilbur, like all subjects, doesn't immediately jump from nothingness into subjectivity. As I have pointed out, the first two chapters of the book don't belong to Wilbur, even though he is certainly there. But he is there as some *thing* to be loved, fed, talked about, and ultimately, sold. His continuing existence is not at all a surety. In fact, it is almost assuredly the case that unless something happens, he will remain ontologically questionable, filling a place in the world only until he is fat enough to fill a place, so to speak, in the Other. Alienation (understood in terms of Wilbur's existence as Fern's desire) has opened a space for him, but it is an empty space in terms of subjectivity. Wilbur has a thereness, but not a whoness. Gagnon says that Wilbur didn't have a "strong personality"; as a Lacanian subject, he has no pregiven personality at all. Fink points out that this empty space, this lack, is the "first guise" of the subject. "To qualify something as empty is to use a spatial metaphor implying that it could alternately be full," says Fink (LS, 52); that is, a runt pig now occupies a place that has been set aside in the Symbolic order for Wilbur to come to be as a full subject.

Fern chooses the proper name "Wilbur" as a signifier for the pig, because it is "the most beautiful name she could think of" (CW, 7). Already we can see alienation working—this name, connected in Fern's mind to absolute beauty, designates what her mother has called a "runt," her father has dismissed as a "weakling," and her brother has disparaged as a "miserable thing . . . no bigger than a white rat" (4–5). Wilbur as Fern's desire has completely annulled Wilbur as runt pig and has alienated him into the Symbolic order. Being has therefore been ruled out for Wilbur (thankfully so, because as a mere being, he would have been killed), and he has come into *existence*. But he is not a subject yet.

The next step in the constitution of the subject is separation. It starts with the recognition of a lack in the Other. Up until Fern sells Wilbur, he has lived under the illusion that the two of them are one, that Fern is the whole world. He follows her around, and when she is away he simply waits for her to come again so that he can follow her some more. She is his source of food, love, fun, happiness, and life itself. Under her care he has come to love the world. In one sense, we could say that the place he has been holding in the Symbolic is the space of her lack—he has covered over that lack and has produced the illusion of Fern as whole. Fern is "enchanted" by Wilbur, and Wilbur adores Fern. Williams's illustrations emphasize this relationship; the gaze—of Wilbur at Fern and Fern at Wilbur—locks out the rest of the world. But when Fern is forced to sell Wilbur, to separate from him, her position as a barred subject within the Symbolic order is made plain. Here again, both the text and the illustration emphasize the separation of the two. Fern is shown on the other side of a fence (which is on the opposite page as well), and Wilbur does not even appear to notice her, being too engrossed in his food. What has happened is that Fern has been revealed as lacking, which is the same as saying that Fern has been revealed as a desiring being, not at all coextensive with Wilbur. While her status is much more privileged than his as yet, with regard to the Symbolic, she nonetheless suffers from a lack of power with respect to its structures of authority, which have shut her off from direct contact with Wilbur and have forced her exclusion from his development. He has been turned over to the forces of the paternal metaphor, to fill out his place in the Symbolic apart from Fern.

The intervention of the third term, the paternal metaphor, as discussed in the previous section, coincides with and is the necessary condition for Wilbur's emergence into language. As long as Fern was able to speak for Wilbur, he had no need (and indeed no ability) to speak for himself. Fern's loss (read here as the loss of Fern to Wilbur, as well as the loss of Wilbur to Fern) is thus potentially Wilbur's gain. For Fern, the injunction to sell Wilbur institutes the Name of the Father, which bars the desire of the mother.

For Wilbur, it is the rule established by Homer Zuckerman that bars him from Fern and releases/forces him into the assumption of his place in language as a signifier. And while that signifier may well start out as something like "pork chops" for the Zuckermans, it is a signifier nonetheless and hence is open to contingency, substitution, displacement, and all the other operations of the signifier in the Symbolic order.

Significantly, Wilbur's entry into language is preceded in the story by a rather long introduction to the barn in which he finds himself. In Nodelman's discussion of the text, he points out that "the basic structural pattern in *Charlotte's Web* is the list" ("Text," 116). The lists encompass everything in the book; what the characters see, what they do, where they are, what they eat, what they plan, are all given to the reader in long, detailed lists. Nodelman asserts that the lists "not only evoke the qualities of barns but also imply the glorious wholeness of existence" (118). But the lists are noticeably absent in the first two chapters of the book. Nodelman notices that the first two chapters offer a vision of a "prelapsarian world, a paradise of innocence" (117). He suggests further that this paradise is a space of naive wish fulfillment. What better way to describe the mythologized place of the *infans*, the Lacanian infant before she enters into the registers of the Imaginary and the Symbolic? In this prelapsarian world, before the infant has "fallen" into language, it knows nothing of its own alienation. Here the child in its prelinguistic state is unself-differentiated, an "'hommelette'—a little man and also like a broken egg spreading without hindrance in all directions" (Coward and Ellis, 101). The child has no impression of otherness. He assimilates everything, experiencing what Lacan has called "plenitude," what Freud called the "oceanic self." Lists in such a world would make no sense, precisely because lists imply differentiation, an acknowledgment of things which are not oneself and the placement of those things within a structure. Prior to its entry into language, the subject has to learn its own boundaries, what constitutes its own body and what constitutes Other. It must be expelled from its place in the mother, structurally speaking, which creates a hole in both. And though that expulsion is registered as a loss in the Lacanian economy, it also represents a gain—specifically, the gain of a place from which to speak.

The prelapsarian world of the infant is characterized by two registers: the pre-Symbolic Real and the Imaginary. The pre-Symbolic Real for the infant might be thought of as perceptual information without a subject to organize it. Ragland-Sullivan explains:

More primordial than the *je* (the social, speaking self), the Other is created by imprinting the outside world in networks of meaning made up of images, sounds, and effects. Such concrete elements, symbolized as mental representations, have the power to constitute the *source* of meaning only because the biological and psychic infant perceives reality directly from its birth. No ego is needed to accomplish such perception. ("Magnetism," 383)

Certainly Wilbur is a perceiving being. The two lists that do appear in those first chapters (which Nodelman remarks are perceived as lists only retroactively, in light of what comes after—a nice parallel to the retroactive way any sort of analysis is projected onto this stage of infant development) are "evocations of sensuous detail" (Nodelman, 118) that seem coextensive with the baby pig. Kitchen smells are described right after the pig is brought in, and there is a description of the kind of mud Wilbur likes: "warm and moist and delightfully sticky and oozy" (CW, 11). These perceptions begin to get organized when the baby develops the capacity for mirror-stage identifications. The unity that the baby projects onto the image and identifies with himself provides the necessary fiction that holds the world together. But interestingly enough, as we have seen in the case of Wilbur, the subject himself is not the guarantor of the world's cohesion; rather it is the Other. Wilbur's world is initially put together, and held together, through Fern. Over the course of the book, there are other "ego ideal" representations that Wilbur tries to substitute for Fern, with the ultimate result that "through the identificatory and mimetic processes of introjection and projection, the *moi* is constituted from the Other" (Ragland-Sullivan, "Magnetism," 383). We don't have a single instant where Wilbur apprehends himself in any kind of mirror. This is just as well, because it clears up a common misunderstanding that the phenomenon of the mirror stage is an all-at-once, one-time event that takes place between a presubject and him- or herself. It is, instead, a process, and it may not involve a mirror at all but is rather the ability to identify oneself with an other, and *as* an other, that is, the ability to place oneself into the play of signification.

The play of signification that the child enters into when he separates fully from the mother is determined by the Symbolic order itself. Chapter 2 ends with Fern being forced to separate from Wilbur; chapter 3 begins with an extensive description of the barn, the new world they both must enter in order to stay together—the Symbolic. We know it is representative of the Symbolic because everything in it is distinct, separate, and located in terms of a structure. Smells, seasons, housing for the different animals, and tools are all represented as collections. We also know it is part of the Symbolic because of its link to the Name of the Father: "And the whole thing was owned by Fern's uncle, Mr. Homer L. Zuckerman" (CW, 14). It exists as an order apart from Wilbur in which he must nevertheless find his place. Hence White accomplishes temporally in his narrative what exists structurally for the subject—the existence of the Symbolic prior to and independent of any conscious ordering of it by any subject.

Though White presents the barn and its environs as a wondrous place indeed, Wilbur is not yet ready for it. The first two chapters that are rightfully Wilbur's are called "Escape" and "Loneliness," indicating how overwhelming and marked with loss the entry into the Symbolic is for the young child, because what is excluded in a very fundamental sense is the mother. Without Fern, Wilbur is not quite sure who he is or what to do with himself. His first reaction is to try to escape his predicament, but the cacophony of voices telling him what to do is too much for him, and he succumbs to the "old pail trick," regressing into the kind of material comfort offered by the mother. Next he tries to fit in through assimilation—he becomes a maker of lists himself. He plans out his whole day, hour by hour, but then it rains. He is undone. "Friendless, dejected, and hungry, he threw himself down in the manure and sobbed" (CW, 31). It is clearly a time of crisis for Wilbur, a time when he must come to be something or other. He is faced with a choice—he can stay in the place assigned him as an object of Zuckerman's demand, or he can come to be in the place of Fern's and Charlotte's desire.

There are four privileged objects in Lacan that relate the subject to the Other—the breast, the feces, the gaze, and the voice. The breast and the feces are on the side of demand, that is, they represent the time of the subject when he does not clearly differentiate himself as a desiring being apart from the Other. It should be noted that time here is structural as well as chronological, in that the subject often "retreats" to a relation of demand once desire has been established. To remain in this position always is the definition of obsessional neurosis for Lacan; the subject is locked in the position of always wondering what the Other wants of him and has no sense of what he may want apart from the Other. But basic appetites are taken care of in this position, and people can live this way, in a sort of infantilized position that ultimately leads to their complete consumption by the Other. This is the offer Zuckerman makes to Wilbur. He feeds him warm, wonderful slops and gives him a nice manure pile to sleep in. But it is a trap, and to accept it blithely will lead to Wilbur's annihilation. It is better for him to enter the world of desire, where the privileged objects are the gaze (provided by Fern, who sits "quietly during the long afternoons, thinking and listening and watching Wilbur" (CW, 15), and of course, the voice: "You can imagine Wilbur's surprise when, out of the darkness, came a small voice he had never heard before. It sounded rather thin, but pleasant. 'Do you want a friend, Wilbur?' it said. 'I'll be a friend to you. I've watched you all day and I like you.'" (CW, 31). Hence Charlotte begins Wilbur's substantive development as a subject. Separate from his m(O)ther, empty in his own being, he needs some other structuring relationship to give his life meaning, and to help him achieve a place outside of Zuckerman's demand. Fern can't do this for him, for many reasons. Structurally speaking, as we have already noted, she must be excluded in her maternal function. The danger is, according to Lacan, that the mother's desire is like a crocodile; you never know when the jaws might clamp shut, so you insert a stone roller, the phallus, in her mouth to prevent her from shutting down on you (Fink, LS, 57). If we think of Fern as a human who presumably eats the bacon her mother fixes for breakfast (CW, 3), we see the metaphor is not an idle one in this case. But in addition, in her position in the Symbolic, Fern is ultimately ineffectual. Certainly she wins her argument with her father to save Wilbur's life initially, but White makes it clear that it is her father's love, and not the force of her argument, that wins the case. Wilbur is in need of a spokesperson whose relation to the phallus as language is a bit less tenuous. Fern had only the phallus loaned to her by her father. Charlotte, through her connection to language, through her ability to spin her own web, possesses her own version of the phallus. She is thus a phallic mother for Wilbur. She can provide the signifiers that cover over Wilbur's lack of being and firmly implant him as a subject in his own right in the Symbolic order.

In doing this she is continuing the work that Fern began when she treated Wilbur as what Nodelman calls a "'pretend' human being." Nodelman says of Wilbur in the barn: "He *is* a person, so it was silly indeed to treat him like a pretend person" ("Text," 125). Like Gagnon, Nodelman posits a "true" Wilbur to whom Fern and Charlotte must respond. But this is not the case in a Lacanian frame. The individual personality of the subject, those qualities that fill out the structures of his subjectivity, owes its very existence to the Other's language. Hence the substantive conditions of subjectivity are time bound and culture specific, rather than atemporal and universal. Wilbur's concerns are largely modernist in composition. He is engulfed in existential angst regarding his death, his loneliness (his essential isolation), and the banality of his existence. He seeks intimacy, a person whom he can trust. He wants to know how to live. Such questions imply many things about the subject in modernity. They imply a sense of emptiness at the core of one's being. They imply a desire for unity and connectedness as a hedge against personal disintegration. And they imply a sense of choice in the way we deal with our angst.

White's "solutions" to Wilbur's problems also imply something about the modernist subject. Wilbur finds someone he can trust, and trust her he does. Charlotte proves to him that his trust is well founded, as she understands something about modernity herself. She understands the faith people have in the printed word. She understands that it is not enough to find personal meaning, but that in order to survive, you must prove yourself in ways that the world finds profitable. She understands the connection between the public self and the private one, and she understands the role and power of language in creating that self.

In a limited way, Fern understands these things too. Fern's treating Wilbur as a pretend person is never silly; it is the necessary precondition for his becoming a person. Similarly, Charlotte does not search for words that will describe the Wilbur that she somehow "finds." Rather, she chooses words, weaves them into her web, and expects Wilbur to embody, or, in other words, to perform them. It works wonderfully. When Charlotte decides to write the word "terrific" in her web, Wilbur at first objects:

> "But Charlotte," said Wilbur, "I'm *not* terrific."
> "That doesn't make a particle of difference," replied Charlotte. "Not a particle. People believe almost anything they see in print." (CW, 89)

When the web is finished, and people come to look at it, Wilbur really feels terrific, and Zuckerman confirms it: "'There isn't a pig in the whole state that is as terrific as our pig'" (96). What's more, Zuckerman improves Wilbur's circumstances in such a way that he waxes radiant. He becomes "a pig any man would be proud of" (114). Hence, in a very real way, Wilbur emerges as the effect of Charlotte's words.

Thus we see how the subject is an effect of language. If language can be said to have effects, then it must function in some way, that is, it must act rather than simply refer to something that already exists. Indeed, to understand Lacan's notion of the subject in more than a superficial way, one must have a working knowledge of and commitment to language as essentially performative. In the view of critics like Gagnon and, to a lesser degree, Nodelman, language functions in what Shoshana Felman calls a traditional, cognitive way:

> [L]anguage is an instrument for transmitting *truth*, that is, an instrument of knowledge, a means of *knowing* reality. Truth is a relation of perfect congruence between an utterance and its referent, and, in a general way, between language and the reality it represents. If it is not given to man to know truth in its totality, such absolute knowledge exists nonetheless in the word of God, in whose omniscience, indeed, language originates. Thus incarnating the authority of truth, God, or the "voice of heaven" (that is, the fact that God speaks), underwrites the authority of language as a cognitive instrument. In this view, the sole function reserved for language is the *constative* function: what is at stake in an utterance is its correspondence—to its real referent, that is, its truth or falsity. (*The Literary Speech Act* [LSA], 27)

In contrast to the constative view of language is the view that language is not about knowing, but about doing. Language is itself performative. Language has effects that are retroactively construed as knowledge—specifically, referential knowledge, knowledge of things as they exist in the world. Lacanian psychoanalysis, and runt pigs, show us that language does not simply refer but, as Felman adds, "makes itself part of what it refers to (without, however, being all that it refers to)" (77). Heidegger says "the person is no Thinglike and substantial Being" (*Being and Time* [BT], 73); Felman concludes: "The referent is no longer simply a preexisting *substance*, but an *act,* that is, a dynamic movement of modification of reality" (LSA, 77). Consider Wilbur: As a referent, he is no "substantial being," as Gagnon and Nodelman would have it, "but an *act,* . . . a dynamic movement in the modification of reality."

Charlotte saves Wilbur's life through the performance of speech acts. Indeed it could be said that she brings the Wilbur that comes to be known to the outside world into existence through speech acts. But what is significant is that these speech acts are never attributed to Charlotte. When Mr. Zuckerman explains to Mrs. Zuckerman the "miracle" that signifies to him that they have no ordinary pig, she replies, "Well . . . it seems to me you're a little off. It seems to me we have no ordinary *spider*" (CW, 80). But Zuckerman insists that the words in the web are a sign from God, completely referential with regard to Wilbur, and have nothing whatever to do with a spider. Zuckerman is here represented as actively repressing the possibility of a performative subjectivity, as well as the role of the Other in that performance. Considering his role as the Name of the Father, this move on his part is uniquely appropriate, in that it is part of his function in a patriarchal economy to delimit the possibilities of being, just as Mr. Arable decided who could mother a pig and who could not. A performative subjectivity, on the other hand, implies endless possibilities, constrained only by the unpredictable desire of the mother who channels the desire of the subject in the first place. Hence the production of subjectivity is to some degree out of his control. But Wilbur has two fine, strong, modernist mothers who offer no challenge to the authoritative role of Zuckerman, even as they subvert the natural order of things regarding the fate of runt pigs.

As for Wilbur himself, he becomes fully actualized as a subject when he becomes the "mother" of Charlotte's babies. In so doing, he "traverses the fundamental fantasy."

> The traversing of fantasy involves the subject's assumption of a new position with respect to the Other as language and the Other as desire. A move is made to invest or inhabit that which brought him or her into existence as split subject, to become that which *caused* him or her. (Fink, LS, 62)

The initial trauma that "caused" Wilbur's existence was the fear of his imminent death. By taking responsibility for Charlotte's children, Wilbur enters into a new relationship regarding death. He doesn't exactly take responsibility for Charlotte's death, but he inserts himself into it as her heir. Not only does he inherit her egg sac, but also he inherits her desire to help others, and to be a true friend. The very satisfying closure of the novel indicates a certain completeness in Wilbur's development that the traversing of the fundamental fantasy suggests.

The Child Reader of *Charlotte's Web*

Clearly, *Charlotte's Web* serves a Lacanian poetics well in its allegorical representation of the development of subjectivity. But what remains to be discussed is whether or not such a poetics might have a transactional (or in our language, performative) component as well. That is, while a Lacanian poetics figures the text as a metaphor for the subject, it may also be the case that it is not merely metaphorical. I have argued that language has effects, and that among those effects is the development of subjectivity itself, through the individual's assumption of the position ascribed to the subject in language (just as Wilbur became what Charlotte said he was). I have also argued that this process is ongoing, though it is most active in childhood, when the libidinal attachments of the subject are in the process of finding their preferred channels. Hence a Lacanian poetics specific to children's literature should take into account the relative lack of reification in the substance attaching to the structures of subjectivity. Perhaps even those very structures are less stable than psychoanalysis suggests: Just because the triangular structure of the Oedipus has held sway for so long does not necessarily mean that it will continue to do so in a less textually monolithic, more imagistically multivalent society. At any rate, however, a child in a literate society has a radically text-based subjectivity; print manifestations of the Other, as well as of Authority and the Law, are everywhere for the child, so it is quite natural for her to identify with them in relations of Imaginary fusion. Western culture has built its religious traditions, its academic traditions, and its popular culture all on the basis of the book. It should come as no surprise to think that we would construct our identities through the book as well. In that sense, books become our phallic mothers in much the same way Charlotte mothers Wilbur. They provide the signifiers that we perform. We use them in much the same way the infant uses the mirror image—to reflect back to us our own idealized image that we then identify with and attempt to become.[2]

White's rhetoric in the first two chapters is an invitation to the reader to do just that. Nodelman points out that White provides just enough detail to evoke a recognizable world and sets up a situation that will be recognizable and enjoyable for the young reader. "It is enjoyable because it describes a pleasurable fulfillment of common wishes: to have a real live doll to play with, to get your own way with your parents and feel the satisfaction of saving another creature's life in the bargain, always to be happy" ("Text," 122). But these wishes could be said to be generated in the reader by the text itself. All is dependent on the successful interpellation of the reader in an initial identification. Whereas the young reader might not immediately make an interspecies identification with a small pig who wakes up in a barn, he or she is invited to identify with a curious young girl. Nothing in the opening lines would serve to distance the reader from the scene—no physical description of Fern or her mother or their setting. Instead, the book opens with Fern asking a question, placing her in the same position as the reader

—a position of ignorance of what is about to happen. Once the reader has made that initial Imaginary fusion that covers over his own constitutive lack, Fern's concerns can become the reader's concerns in a process so seamless as to seem the other way around. She inaugurates the identificatory relationship with the pig through the characterization of him as very small and weak. Through both Fern and Wilbur, the reader's angst over her being-toward-death is first created and then relieved. Hence the reader is placed in a position to learn that the way to save your life is through the successful performance of speech acts.

The recent movie *Babe: A Little Pig Goes a Long Way* (based on the book by Dick King-Smith) produces a similar set of concerns and addresses them in similar ways. A young pig is separated from his mother, enters language —his first words in the film are in fact "Bye, Mom"—and is adopted by a wise and loving surrogate of a different species. The cast is a bit different— the threatening authoritative male is not the human male, but the dog, Rex, who supervises the activities of all the animals in the barnyard. But he, like Farmer Zuckerman, is also in charge of enforcing the status quo. When Babe and Ferdinand the duck attempt to steal the "mechanical rooster" and end up wrecking the Hoggetts' house, Rex delivers a long speech about how he was wrong to let people act as if they were something they were not. Ferdinand, for instance, knowing that humans eat "plump, attractive ducks," endeavors to keep himself unnaturally thin, and searches for ways to make himself indispensable to the farmer so that he won't be killed. He tries to emulate the rooster, and when making eggs with the hens doesn't work, he takes to crowing in the morning. But his attempts to use meaningful, important language are thwarted—Mrs. Hoggett, finding Ferdinand's efforts annoying, buys an alarm clock, which precipitates the aforementioned crisis. Rex's solution is that everyone should stay in his or her "proper place" and be happy to do so. Obviously, he can proffer this command because the system works for him. But what is interesting is that Rex is disabled— he is nearly deaf and so cannot compete in the sheepdog trials, and later, he turns violent and must be sedated, so he can't work in the fields. His only saving grace is that he is a breeding dog; his position in the life of the farm is secured, quite literally, by the "phallic function."

Despite Rex's attempt to keep the patriarchal order intact and everyone in his place, Babe's life is saved through the intervention of the new mother, who gives the pig a new identity; he becomes a sheep-pig. Language is crucial to his success. Unlike the dogs, who bite, chase, and growl, Babe uses his words to establish a relationship with an older sheep and, with her help, to herd the sheep. Later, at the sheepdog trials, the sheep Babe has to herd won't talk to or listen to Babe, so Rex must humble himself to talk to the sheep in order to get their "password." When Babe chants this universal sheep call, the sheep become immediately receptive; they figure he is one of them because he knows their most sacred language. But more importantly in terms of this analysis, the farmer's language intervenes to actually save Babe's life. In the most crucial moment of the pig's existential angst, when he is ready to die because he has learned that pigs have no purpose but to be eaten, the farmer revives Babe by singing: "If I had words to make a day for you, I'd give you a morning, golden and true. I would make this day last for all time, then fill the night deep in moonshine." Words to make a day . . . words to craft an identity . . . words to save a life. The subject is constituted, again and again, in and through language.

CHAPTER TWO

A Time to Mourn

The Loss of the Mother

In chapter 1, I looked at *Charlotte's Web* as an allegorical story of the advent of subjectivity. I suggested that it and stories like it not only show how the theory works, but also actually facilitate the process whereby the modernist subject comes into being by taking the reader, by way of identification, on a journey through what counts as the normal development of subjectivity. This chapter explores that process a bit more thoroughly and from a slightly different perspective. I will be looking at books targeted at very young children—from infants to pre-readers. These books, I suggest, go even further than chapter books in setting the stage for the advent of subjectivity, for they make a conscious effort to move a child from his position in brute reality to a position in the world of representation. Most importantly, they intervene in a process of grieving loss that can easily go awry. The child must lose his connection to his mother's body, to an unmediated relationship to embodiment and the world as such. If he can come to acknowledge these things as actually lost, or sacrificed in the service of something, then he can complete a process of mourning whereby he disentangles himself from the loved object and asserts his own ego concerns over and against it—in other words, he can individuate. But if he can't acknowledge and grieve his losses, that is, if he continues to think of these inevitable losses as failures on his part, then he may develop the melancholic stance of trying to sustain a connection with that which is always already lost.

Another way of looking at this distinction is to see in it two faces of love. The love involved in melancholy is regressive, consuming; the child seeks to reclaim the space of oneness that he feels he has lost by incorporating and cannibalizing the other. "I'll eat you up!" as Max of *Where the Wild Things Are* says to his mother. But the love involved in developmental mourning entails the birth of self-love through separation. The child posits the mother or mother substitute as ideal, the ideal inevitably fails or is lost, and the child ego takes on the characteristics of the lost ideal in order to render the loss acceptable to the desiring id. Freud says: "When the I assumes the features of the object, it is forcing itself, so to speak, upon the id as a love-object and is trying to make good the id's loss by saying 'Look, you can love me too—I am so like the object'" ("The Ego and the Id" [SE 19], 30). This distinction of incorporating the other versus taking on her characteristics seems overly subtle until we look once again at Max. His mother and he are having a fight, and he ends up banished to his room. The fact that she never appears in the book indicates that she is already lost to Max in that inevitable and fundamental way. But instead of imagining a scenario where he does in fact eat his mother or her surrogates, which would indicate a melancholic incorporation, he imagines that he himself is in danger of being eaten by these wild things that love him, and like her, he does not allow it. His process of mourning the loss of his mother as ideal involves crossing over a maternal sea on a boat, and taking up his phallic scepter to assert his own power, which, in essence, solidifies his ego position as ruler of unruly id impulses. He emerges quite self-satisfied and ready to eat proper food.

As we learned through Fern and Wilbur, the exclusion of the mother, that is, the expulsion of the child from the (m)Other, is the necessary condition for the subject to enter into the Symbolic. This process seems to take place in a tidy little chronological sequence. In the beginning, the child's cries are interpreted by the mother, and her readiness and ability to meet the child's needs cause him to feel that she is but an extension of his own body. But before long, the child begins to understand that the mother has desires other than him. This impression, which may be brought on by something as ordinary as the aversion of her gaze, causes him to desire; mostly he desires to be the object of her desire, to regain her attention. At any rate, the fact that she looks elsewhere, that she is a desiring (and hence lacking) subject, mobilizes *his* desire. Having lost the one thing that held his world together as a seamless whole, he enters into the project of human subjectivity—that of perpetuating his desire. Representations in the form of words and images rush in to fill the gap—initially to call the mother back, but soon enough to find substitutes for her and even to keep her at a safe distance, a point I take up in greater detail in chapter 3.

Although this separation from the mother exists in theoretical parlance as a moment in the subject's history, it is not really a moment at all, but more like the outcome of a series of events that occur over "time." Time here is not to be understood as chronological time, but rather as logical, or structural. For instance, inasmuch as psychic events acquire meaning retroactively, the present can affect the past. And inasmuch as the mirror-stage infant sees himself as whole or together, a future state that never in fact comes to pass, the future is anticipated in every moment of the present. But separation, in Western culture at least, is rarely allowed to happen in the subject's "own time." Hospital birth separates the baby from the mother almost immediately for checks and tests, and mothers are given the option of whether they want to "room in" with their babies, or whether they want their babies taken care of by professionals for the few short hours HMOs allow for recovery from the birth process. At home, there may be other children, and there are certainly other responsibilities for the mother to attend to that have nothing to do with the baby. In medical and legal discourse, six weeks from an uncomplicated birth seems to mark some sort of magic number for a stronger separation of the child from the mother. This is the common "release date" for the mother to resume both sex and work. In these respects, the time of the subject is from birth marked by both inevitable and authoritative mandates. Lacanian theory is very interested in the role such authoritative mandates have in the life of the subject. In his early essay "Logical Time and the Assertion of Anticipated Certainty," Lacan outlines three moments of the subject that have broad implications for understanding his theory as a whole. For our purposes, we will look at those moments as they enter into the structuring of the subject itself.

Lacan begins with a logical problem that involves three prisoners who have a chance of release if they can figure out the solution to a puzzle set for them by the warden. The warden has five discs, three white and two black. He fastens one disc to the back of each prisoner; the task is for each prisoner to figure out what color he is through logical and not merely probabilistic means. Temporal pressure is added because only the first prisoner to deduce correctly his position will be released. While the details of the solution are unimportant for this analysis, the conclusions Lacan draws from them are certainly pertinent.[1] The subjects in question come to know who they are (that is, what color the disc on their back is) through three logical moments. There is first the instant of looking, wherein each prisoner sees immediately what the other prisoners are, and hence what he himself is *not*. If each of the other two men has a black disc, in other words, then he cannot have a black disc and therefore must be white. Then follows the time for comprehending, where each prisoner uses the hesitation of the other prisoners to posit some conclusions about what he *should* be. He does this by imagining what the other prisoners must be thinking, by imputing to the others the same thought processes that he himself is moving through. In a sense, each prisoner *invents* the other in the time for comprehending, so that this moment might also be called the moment of Imaginary identification. Finally, then, the prisoners move into the time for concluding, in which the prisoner must take some action, make some move that will commit him to leaving the room and offering his account of himself to the warden. The action, Lacan reminds us, is one of precipitate, or anticipatory, certainty, because if the prisoner hesitates while doing it, he will slip back into the cogitations of the Imaginary identification stage and thus lose his chance for release. Lacan summarizes the moments in the following way:

(1) A man knows what is not a man;
(2) Men recognize themselves amongst themselves to be men;
(3) I declare myself to be a man for fear of being convinced
    by men that I am not a man. ("Logical Time" [LT], 18)

Inasmuch as these moments of the subject correspond roughly to the three registers of Lacanian theory—the Real, the Imaginary, and the Symbolic—we are reminded that each of the moments implicates the other two, that they coexist with and by turns define the others. It should also be noted here, for future reference, that three senses of the Other are at stake in the three moments. In the first, there is no small *o* other or big *O* Other, only otherness as a sort of general field. In the second, there is only the small other. This small other is, conceptually speaking, an invention of the subject, what Evans describes as "but a reflection and projection of the ego, . . . thus entirely inscribed in the imaginary order" (Evans, 132–133). Finally, in the third moment, the big Other comes into the picture, in this case as equivalent with the Symbolic order itself. It is within the Symbolic that one asserts oneself as a "signifier for another signifier," which is Lacan's general definition of the subject. One might also think of the big Other at this point as equivalent with language, for in this moment the subject assumes an "I"—a shifter that has no meaning outside of a discursive situation. Now since any "before" of language is retroactively posited through the medium of language, we are again reminded that although these stages may seem chronological, they are instead structurally dependent on one another; the third cannot be anticipated without the first two, but the first two cannot be thought without the third already in place.

I would like to concretize some of this theoretical maneuvering by suggesting that these moments of the subject correspond to three categories of children's picture books, and that the kinds of books we find in each of these categories help propel the child toward that anticipatory subjective assertion wherein the child actively assumes (as in the Lacanian sense of *assomption*—actively taking on oneself the position heretofore merely ascribed to her by the Other) her "symbolic identity-mandate" (Žižek, *The Indivisible Remainder* [IR], 136) as, say, a boy, or a girl, or a radiant pig. The first moment, the time of looking, corresponds to the type of book where the image predominates. Words are absent, or nearly so, and certainly are not necessary to understand the action, if any, of the pictures on the page. The second moment, the time for understanding, corresponds to storybooks —books where the text works in tandem with the pictures, whether in a straightforward or an ironic manner. These books are usually too difficult for the very young child to read by him- or herself, and they are not made for that. They are either openly didactic, or they belong to the genre of the artistic or literary picture book. Finally, the third moment, the time for concluding, corresponds with books that the child can read for himself, on which I will focus the next chapter. This is the moment when the child adds his "I" to the sum of "I's," so to speak, when he breaks the written code and the words of the Other fill his mouth. It is interesting to note that many, if not most, of the books in this third category participate in some type of nonsense. In the next chapter, I suggest that there are good reasons for this.

Because this study concerns itself with questions of modernity, I think it is entirely appropriate initially to categorize picture books based simply upon an analysis of the strategies of their marketing. Bookstores, book clubs, and book catalogues consistently arrange their titles under roughly the same categories—baby books, which include wordless or nearly wordless books; storybooks, which are characterized by artwork that supports a narrative; and books that the child can read by himself, including books for beginning readers and continuing through intermediate chapter books and young-adult novels. Not only do these groupings tend to correspond to the moments of the subject outlined by Lacan, they also tend to fit the categories of oral-, anal-, and phallic-stage development, which again are not temporal stages in Lacan, but structures that concern different ways of relating to the Other. Although the books are targeted for certain age and ability groups, they become important or relevant to subject formation because of their position in the subject's structural time rather than in any chronological age. In what follows, I will be analyzing what happens in the various moments of the subject as they correspond to the books that are recommended for children in those moments.

A Man Knows What Is Not a Man:
The Time for Looking

In Slavoj Žižek's discussion of Alfred Hitchcock's "phallocentrism," he differentiates between what could be called oral, anal, and phallic approaches to filmmaking. His distinctions can be instructively applied to a discussion of children's picture books, in that both mediums depend on a specular investment of the subject in the text, and in that these investments are controlled to some extent by the vision of a "director" who manipulates the images. In the kind of filmmaking that corresponds to the oral stage, Žižek contends, the montage of images "has no function in organizing narrative tension" (*Looking Awry* [LA], 89); that is, there is an illusion that we are seeing things as they would naturally transpire or occur in real life. Many picture books for very young children participate in this sort of "direct 'rendering of reality'" (LA, 89), their purpose being simply to represent the objects of the child's daily experience. Books such as Denise Lewis Patrick's *What Does Baby See?* and *What Does Baby Hear?* answer the questions of their titles with "shots" that are supposed to represent to the child the scenes of her life in a generalized way, the narrative consisting of the chronology of a "typical" day. Other books have structures that are dependent not on narrative at all, but on the grouping of objects by their characteristics, such as color or species (like "farm animals" or "trucks"). Many of these books are illustrated with photographs; the images look so real that the baby attempts to pick them up or turns the book over to find the other side of an object that appears three-dimensional.

The child is learning some important lessons about representation at this stage, lessons that precede any sense of self. There is no "I" at this stage, but there is a perceiving eye. This is the beginning stage of the "general form of the noetic subject: he could as easily be god, table, or washbasin" (Lacan, LT, 14). The *Chinaberry* book catalogue encourages the person reading to the child at this stage to "disregard the text, if necessary, and simply point to and talk about illustrations of familiar objects." The gesture of pointing begins the work of othering for the child, but if one imagines a scenario of the child being held in the caregiver's arms with the book in front of the two of them, one can see how the origin of the pointing (that is, *who* is pointing) is blurred. The origin of the look and of the pointing is outside the book, but it is unclear whether it is the gaze of the child or the gaze of the caregiver that is operative, or whether those gazes are even separate. In a sense, then, it doesn't really matter at this moment of the subject *who* is looking; what matters is the emergent sense of the not-me, which comes about (partially, of course) through the gesture of pointing away from the body.

This is a significant phenomenal gesture in the psychic life of the child, one which underscores the importance of early reading. The majority of the infant's bodily energy has to do with the taking in, the in*corpo*rating of the world into the child's body. Everything goes into the mouth. And reciprocally, the child tries to insert himself into every nook, cranny, or hole he finds—putting his fingers in the caregiver's mouth, nose, and eyes, and in bowls, electrical sockets, and so on. Rosine Lefort interprets this gesture of the child as his attempts to fill in the hole in the Other. Even books go into little mouths initially, but their tastes and textures, coupled with the caregiver's "No," make them more interesting for the eye than for the mouth. Their two-dimensional quality gives them an opaqueness that stops little fingers from filling in the holes they see.[2] A picture of a pacifier, or a rubber duck, or a cookie, then, is doing something different for the child than does the real thing. The page imposes a boundary that the child cannot cross, so he cannot assimilate the thing he sees into his own body. The pictures in books, the books themselves, are no doubt material, but they represent a materiality of a different order—the materiality, in fact, of a signifier.

While we as adults take it for granted that signifiers are arbitrary and conventional, it is important to remember that this is something that must be *learned*. The child must do the work of learning that things in the world have names, and that those names may be used to designate things in their absence as well as in their presence. But she must also learn to go beyond a univocal associational logic, where one word designates one thing exclusively.[3] Children must learn that signifiers "float" across a limited range of signifieds and vice versa. This is primarily the business of the oral stage; it is the business of the initial othering of objects in the world that occurs during the time of looking. The collection of images found in the wordless or nearly wordless books for this age group has a metonymical function characteristic of the oral stage. In this "devouring" stage, the child must make sense of the undifferentiated mass of images and sounds that surround her by metonymizing objects, taking the part for the whole. What must be emphasized for the child is the homogeneity of objects, their conceptual contiguity, so that the child may learn to sort the things in her world into manageable categories. In *How Children Learn*, John Holt cites multiple examples of children using one word to designate groups of things or activities; he stresses that it is not because they cannot distinguish a difference, but because they are, according to him, developing the abstract-thinking skill of categorizing.

But here is where the hegemony of modernist conceits begins to take effect. For instance, in the books mentioned earlier, *What Does Baby See?* and *What Does Baby Hear?*, baby and family are white; baby has a mother, a father, a sibling, and a pet; and baby lives in a nice house. All of this contingent visual information gets rendered normative because of the attachment of generic signifiers—baby, mommy, daddy, and so forth—to these particular signifiers. When this association is repeated over and over again, it becomes an unconscious ideal—the way the books look is the way the world *should* look, and if your particular world does not, then it is not the ideal that has failed, but your enactment of it, thus positioning the nonwhite subject or the subject in a nontraditional family in a potentially melancholic position.[4] This is further emphasized in children's animated film. It is not simply the fault of Disney animators and marketers that they occupy a position of cultural hegemony. Rather, it is the intellectual processing activity of the targeted audience that makes every white prince a daddy, and every white wasp-waisted princess an ideal image with which to situate a "me" (for little girls at least). Children will even go so far as to accept an animation *style* as normative and base their prejudices and expectations on whether or not a production conforms to a particular studio style. Hence cultural change would involve self-conscious parents' and teachers' making sure children are exposed not only to representations of phenotype diversity, but also to artistic and stylistic diversity, so that they don't settle into a particular norm as ideal.

Of course, it may seem contradictory to assert that these images and structures are problematic when my argument is suggesting that children view these books as part of the not-me, but in this "oral" time of the subject, the child is collecting the images that he will come to identify with in the time for understanding. Moreover, picture books in general tend to appeal to the reader in a way consistent with the oral stage. While this stage is dominated by the demand to be fed and an emphasis on those pleasures that the mouth provides, it is also characterized by the lack of a language that would determine vision and hearing through its *semantic* values. That is, although the child hears language from before birth and produces sounds from the moment of her birth, she understands very little except the phonemic quality of the utterance—its music, so to speak. By the same token, the child does not "read" the pictures he sees. He instead encounters pictures as meaningless images to be consumed. But the child's subsequent meaningful associations are dependent on this collected store of meaningless images. Once the subject has entered language, there is no art that is not graphic art (Copjec, 34), but nonetheless there is the unconscious visual imprint or memory of a time before language (just as there is the unconscious phonemic imprint of the time before understanding that language) that haunts the subject's vision and makes the picture mean more than one can ever express. Books aimed at appealing to the eye, then, also invoke a return to the indiscriminate appetites of orality.

The mother in the time for looking is still conceived of as part of the child in metonymic form as breast, voice, gaze. As Lacan points out in *Seminar I*, the other comes into (and goes out of) existence for the subject by degrees: "The ego has a reference to the other. The ego is constituted in relation to the other. It is its correlative. The level on which the other is experienced locates exactly the level on which, quite literally, the ego exists for the subject" (SI, 50). So we could say that the child's ego forms in a directly proportionate relationship to the degree to which he perceives otherness—the not-me. In the time of looking, although knowledge of what counts as otherness is being developed, it is more or less the "knowledge without a subject" (Fink, LS, 22) that characterizes the unconscious. And just as we don't talk about a personal subject in this time, we don't talk about the other in any positive sense either. Rather it emerges as a verb, a process—othering. The child at this stage is just beginning to know what constitutes a frontier, a border, but as I mentioned earlier, the border between the mother and the child is a blurry one at best. Reciprocally, the child's ego is in a nascent state as well, such that it couldn't even really be called an ego or could just as easily, as noted earlier, be called a table or a washbasin. That it is *not* called a table or a washbasin is more a function of anticipated certainty on the part of the mother. Hence it can be said that, in addition to her status as part of the child, she is also, paradoxically, playing the part of the big Other. It is she who guarantees the child's place in the world; she interprets his cries, meets his needs, and incites his desire. She provides the language that gives him meaning, and it is her voice that introduces him to the music of his "mother tongue." Her consistency, the fact that she always returns, introduces him to what will become a sense of the Real for him—that which, in a world of constant change, always returns to the same place. This is the mother's role in the time of looking, and it should be remembered that it is a structural role, capable of being filled by any consistent caregiver. Part of her does not, however, continue in that role.

Men Recognize Themselves among Themselves to Be Men

The second moment in Lacan's schema has obvious connections to the mirror stage. From pure negation (this is not-me), the subject moves into a stage of interaction with other subjects. But, like the child in the mirror stage, the subject in the time for understanding has no "I" as of yet. Instead, Lacan refers to *undefined reciprocal* subjects, "who must recognize '*one another*'" and are in a place of being introduced to "the form of *the other as such*, i.e. as pure reciprocity, since the one can only recognize himself in the other, and only discover his own attribute in the equivalence of their respective times" (LT, 14). One of the attributes that the child discovers in the other is the loss of the mother, for it is here that the loss of the mother is first figured in fiction for the child.

All along, the mother-child dyad has been on a tenuous footing, since it would be an unfortunate situation indeed for a child to consume the whole of her mother's attention and desire. Nonetheless, the unity of the mother and the child serves as a sort of operative fiction, a hedge against the child's disintegration. It is as if the recurrent face and body of the mother guarantee the unity of a world that presents itself in a sort of horrible randomness. As the child learns what is not-him, the mother nonetheless remains in tandem with the child. Their separateness is not constituted as a problem until the child enters into this second moment of the subject. Even here, when the other is constituted as such, the child, using a tactic that has always served him well in the time of looking, turns toward that other in a disidentificatory logic. The mirror-stage infant stops trying to get to the child on the other side of the mirror and instead recognizes it as an image, a not-me, a representation like those in her books. This time, however, the representation is of her. Herein lies the paradox of the mirror stage: The child has come to understand in the time of looking that representations of things make up the not-her, and yet here she is confronted with a representation that is both her and not-her. And if she can be split, that is, in two places at the same time, then she must not be wholly in either place—she must be lacking. Facing her mirror image, she must cover over that sense of lack by making an identification. Inasmuch as she is identifying the her with the not-her, she is poised to extend the identification of herself into mirroring relations with other small others, many of these others appearing in storybooks. And in many of these storybooks, the central theme, in one way or another, involves separation from the mother or her stand-in. Thus a general experience of loss or separation, a general experience of sensing one's own lack, takes on a specific signifier—that of the mother as the most profound lost object.

Let us examine a very familiar book which can be read as riding the cusp of the time of looking and the time of understanding: *Goodnight Moon*. In this book, the child is introduced to and then invited to say goodnight to various objects represented in his room, among them an "old woman saying hush." The gesture of pointing is what organizes the narrative as we move from one object to another, reminding the child of his "time for looking" books, but the fact of saying goodnight to each of these things introduces a subjective element to the text. We are not simply looking and pointing; we are *separating* from the objects. The old woman (and it is not clear whether she is the mother; more likely the mother has been expulsed from this story at the outset and the old woman is already a substitution) comes and goes in the pictures without any mention in the narrative— sometimes she is there and sometimes she is not. The child character, with whom the child subject is presumably to identify, ends the book alone in a very large room saying goodnight to a very large moon. If it is true that the child will "recognize himself in the other, and . . . discover his own attribute in the equivalence of their respective times" (Lacan, LT, 14), then what the child subject will recognize in this logical time of undefined reciprocity is his smallness and his isolation.

Books more fully embedded in the time for understanding, that is, storybooks that center around a character with whom the child subject is supposed to identify, go even further in narrativizing the loss of the mother as a problem the child must somehow solve. Despite the heterogeneity of the children's picture book industry, there seems to be a species of books regarding mother/child relationships that remains consistently popular. P. D. Eastman's *Are You My Mother?* is perhaps prototypic of the genre. A mother bird, feeling her egg about to hatch, decides to leave the nest to go get food for her soon-to-arrive baby. While she is gone, the egg hatches, and the baby goes off in search of his mother. He queries several animals as to whether they are his mother. This makes some sense, since they are animate. But then he asks an old car, an airplane, a boat, and a bulldozer if they are his mother. This strikes one as odd until we realize that the subject in a modernist world could indeed, and often does, form a self-image based on a mechanistic model. In the end, fate, in the form of a deus ex machina, returns him to his nest at around the same time as his mother returns.

> "Do you know who I am?" she said to her baby.
> "Yes, I know who you are," said the baby bird.
> "You are not a kitten.
> "You are not a hen.
> "You are not a dog.
> "You are not a cow.
> "You are not a boat, or a plane, or a Snort!
> "You are a bird, and you are my mother." (61–62)

Implicit in that series of "nots" is the realization of what the baby bird has learned about what *he* is and is not. Through his encounter with several small *o* others, he is able to retroactively recognize his mother and his connection to her through their conceptual contiguity—"You are a bird, *and* you are my mother." He does not, however, assert his "I."

Are You My Mother? has spawned any number of more or less nondescript grocery-store versions of the same story—a little animal gets separated from his mother and must move through a series of not-hers until they are finally, joyfully reunited. What the animal has gained in the process is not an individual personality, but more of a sense of who he is and where he belongs through gaining a sense of who he is not, thus illustrating the way the founding "instant of the gaze" persists into the "time for comprehending"; the second moment cannot come about without the first, but the second moment is what causes the first to have meaning. Other, more sophisticated, stories offer alternate readings of how babies go about learning their place in the world apart from the mother. For instance, in *Owl Babies*, the three siblings turn to each other for comfort while their mother is gone. In *Have You Seen My Duckling?* the story is told from the mother's point of view, and the child reader is put in the delightful position of helping the mother find her lost child, thus shifting the whole dialectic of who is in the position of knowledge; the child reader becomes the other of the baby who helps him find his way home. Most of these books end in the time for comprehending—the child is safely restored to his mother's bosom, thus reinforcing that one "solution" to the problem of separation from the mother is found in the fantasy structure. Lacan's algebraic formula for fantasy is $\$<>a$, which is read as the split subject (here represented by the baby animal separated from his mother) in relation to the *objet a* (here signifying the mother's desire). The relation is one of unity—pictorially represented by the baby snuggled up to the mother. Instead of having developed her own "I," the subject has retreated to a fantasy space of no separation. But there is a separation nonetheless—the separation within the subject herself.

One of the richest versions of this story comes to us in Janell Cannon's *Stellaluna*. Stellaluna is a baby bat who becomes forcibly separated from her mother during an attack by an owl.[5] Stellaluna falls into a bird's nest. Taking her cue from her "undefined reciprocals," she tries to become a bird. Although she is a fruit bat, she eats bugs and learns to sleep at night. Her most recalcitrant bat trait, however, is that she still likes to sleep upside down. Consciously, Stellaluna can refashion herself any way she likes, but her unconscious—which comes to the fore during sleep—is still dominated by her mother's desire. When her bird siblings imitate her, her surrogate mother becomes very angry and issues a mandate of her own: "You are teaching my children to do bad things. I will not let you back into this nest unless you promise to obey all the rules of this house" (n.p.). Stellaluna agrees in order that she might not lose this mother as well. When it comes time for the birds to leave the nest, Stellaluna is forced into the third time of the subject—the time for concluding. It is here that she must make a precipitate identification. "I'm just like them, thought Stellaluna. I can fly, too" (n.p.). This is true enough—she *can* fly. What she can't do, however, is land gracefully. After embarrassing herself by attempting to grasp a branch with her feet instead of her bat thumbs, she further implicates herself into the tenuous symbolic-mandate that she has assumed: "I will fly all day, Stellaluna told herself. Then no one will see how clumsy I am" (n.p.). It is as if she were paraphrasing Lacan: "I declare myself to be a bird for fear of being convinced by birds that I am not a bird." Of course the birds do not convince her that she is not a bird, but the bats do, and the story ends with a heroic Stellaluna rescuing her bird siblings as they try unsuccessfully to behave like bats. They ponder over their differences and their similarities and conclude that otherness is a great mystery.

Several things strike us as important in this story. First, it not only shows the movement through the logical moments of subject formation, but also it presents those moments through a modernist ideology. That is to say, it rejects as dangerous any thought of staying in the time for understanding. Rather than staying in a time of undefined reciprocity, the subject *must* assert a separate and distinct identity. In Lacan's logical problem, remaining in that time for too long means that the subject will remain a prisoner. Only the first prisoner to *act*, independently, gets freed. For Stellaluna's siblings, attempting to recognize themselves in the other results in their hanging upside down (which causes their mother to cry, "Eek! . . . Get back up here this instant! You're going to fall and break your necks!") and attempting to fly at night (which necessitates Stellaluna's having to rescue them before they crash into a tree). An assertion of individuality is necessary even within your own species—Wilbur and Babe may "recognize themselves amongst themselves to be pigs," but they have to assert themselves beyond a simple reciprocity if they are to survive (Lacan, LT, 18). So Stellaluna's attempt to be a bird among birds is destined to fail. On the other hand, it is as a direct result of Stellaluna's attempting to be a bird that she is reunited with her bat family. It is better, the story seems to say, to assume some sort of positive if provisional identity, even if it is a wrong one, than to continue to hesitate in the time for understanding.

Another important point that this story brings to the fore is something which Lacan does not elaborate in his discussion of logical moments, but which is central to it nonetheless, and that is the presence of the unconscious. In the more-or-less subjectless time of looking, the unconscious does not figure for several reasons. First, the unconscious is a function of the big Other proper, which does not exist in the time for looking. Thus, though the big Other is always there, it is not always there for the subject. That is, until the child is aware of his own lack, he has no sense of a big Other. Of course, the otherness of the time for looking, and the little others in the time for understanding, let us know that the big Other is operative in the background, so one could say that the unconscious is instantiated with the onset of representation itself, since that is the first split for the subject. But since the big Other is only recognized as such for the subject during the time for concluding, the unconscious is only really operating in that logical time. Second, the mother in her dimension as big Other is precisely what is repressed in the time for concluding. The mother gets split into many dimensions during the time for concluding. Part of her becomes a signifier in the system of signifiers set in motion by and for the big Other; this part of her can and will grow and change as her relationship with her child grows and changes. But another part of her, that part of her that was acting as the child's guarantee, gets sublimated, cut off, or foreclosed, as it were. Lacking his guarantee, the subject becomes what he always was—a void, an indeterminacy. In the time for looking, there is also no mirrored other, no consciousness of self, and hence, no splitting. But with the time for understanding comes the need to, as Žižek puts it, "take the other's reasoning into account" (IR, 135). If I am taking the other's reasoning into account, I am essentially admitting that my reasoning is not sufficient; I am experiencing lack. Hence I am experiencing my own split; I am recognizing myself in the other and *as* an other, as other to myself. The genesis of the unconscious lies in this splitting.

Significantly, the first thing that happens to Stellaluna is a momentous fall. In the clash between the mother's desire and the Law, the subject is precipitated as a sort of fallout. Structurally speaking, the same thing happened with Wilbur—in the clash between Fern's desire and her father's Law, Wilbur was precipitated as a compromise. In *Stellaluna* this is beautifully rendered in a visual dialogue between the full-color, full-page illustrations of the book, and the tiny pen-and-ink illustrations that are found as a sort of breach in the border that surrounds the text on the opposite page. In the first full-color illustration, the mother bat is shown flying with the baby bat "clutched to her breast." This picture of mother/child merging so that you can't tell where one ends and the other begins is found often in children's books. You have to look very closely, and even read the text, to see that there are two bats in the picture. On the facing page, the picture is repeated in the pen-and-ink border illustration, as if to emphasize the fact that there is as yet no division—not between Stellaluna and her mother, or between the specular version of the story and the textual one. The next full-color illustration shows the encounter with the owl. Mother and baby are separated, the mother contending with the owl while Stellaluna is in a free fall. The accompanying border illustration shows only the owl and

Stellaluna's mother. From this point on, it seems that the logic of the illustrations is to show the reader what is going on "offstage" with Stellaluna's mother in the border illustrations, while featuring Stellaluna herself in the full-color renderings. But this does not continue to be the case throughout the book. When Stellaluna reunites with her mother, the border illustrations take on a different perspective. They become Stellaluna's story.

This suggests to me that something more is going on in the border illustrations than simply letting the reader know what is happening with Stellaluna's mom. Instead, the border illustrations may be read as renderings of the emergence of Stellaluna's unconscious. At the place where Stellaluna and her mother are one, there is no disjunction between the color pictures and the black-and-white ones. This is the case not only in the initial illustration, but also in the scene depicting their reunion. In both cases, their bodies are united in such a way that it requires a close examination to ascertain that there are in fact two bats. In the first instance, the repetition of images suggests that nothing has happened to precipitate anything like an unconscious in Stellaluna. There has been no repression, or any need for repression. The primordial repression that instantiates the unconscious is the introduction of a third term, illustrated by the fight with the owl. In the next border scene, only the owl and the mother are present, suggesting the expulsion of Stellaluna. This illustrates further an important concept in Lacan that has not translated well into popular understanding: The unconscious is not the place of the "real" person; it is not the seat of one's *own* innermost thoughts and feelings that a public persona somehow covers over, for better or worse. In fact, the subject doesn't exist anywhere at this point, except in a sort of mute free fall. It's a pretty dangerous place for the child to be, really. The fight is between the mother's desire and the Law, and the mother's desire is not necessarily mobilized on behalf of the child. Stellaluna's mother, for example, is shown fighting for her own life, and in the process, she drops her baby. Perhaps the first fantasy that sustains the expulsed child, even under normal circumstances, is that of a mother who desires him. Certainly this may be read as being the case for Stellaluna, for the next eight illustrations show Stellaluna's mother searching for her. For the child reader, as well as for Stellaluna, actually believing that this is what the mother is doing is a wish-fulfilling fantasy. These illustrations occur after we see that the owl has forced Stellaluna's mother into a cave. The Law has forced her repression, sublimating her in her aspect as part of the Real of bodies, only in order for her to reemerge as a signifier of wish-fulfilling desire for Stellaluna.

As Stellaluna begins to assert herself as a bird, the border illustrations begin to prepare her (and the reader) for the reunion of mother and daughter. Against a pathetic-looking Stellaluna hanging by her thumbs, we see a serene mother bat hanging by her feet. Then we see Stellaluna's mother joining the other bats, who have found her and are questioning her about her strange habits. Finally, we have the reunion scene. Once again, there is a repetition between the color illustration and the black-and-white one, recalling Lacan's fantasy formula of $\$<>a$, and suggesting that a fantasy fulfilled covers over any split between conscious life and the unconscious. From that point on, the border illustrations depict Stellaluna herself, suggesting that she has come into her own, so to speak, that she no longer sees herself *through* her mother, or *in* her mother. Instead, she sees herself as a full subject *alongside* her mother, as is depicted in one of the illustration pairs; in the full-color version she is eating a mango by herself, while in the border illustration she and her mother are eating mangoes side by side. She has fulfilled the mandate of the modernist big Other to conclude, to achieve a more-or-less autonomous identity, with her Imaginary identification with her mother relegated to unconscious support for her Symbolic subject position.

Stellaluna shows how the subject, as the fallout in the encounter between the mother's desire and the paternal metaphor, is set adrift in the field of the big Other. The big Other mandates that the subject project some sort of stable identity, but it takes the interaction of many small others, as well as the continual negotiation between an internalized, repressed desire and an external, authoritative will or Law to establish that identity. This is the project of the anal stage. In the anal stage of the subject's development, instead of metonymizing objects, the subject enters into an economy of exchange. In Lacan's words, "The anal level is the locus of metaphor—one object for another, give the faeces in place of the phallus" (E, 104). It is in this stage that something must be given up by the subject, because it is here that the introduction of a Law prohibiting desire forces the subject out of her dyadic relation with the mother as her own body. The most ordinary and easy-to-understand example of this operation is to be found in toilet teaching. Will the child channel his desire away from the desires of his own body into the demands of the Other—demands to wait, to go only in a certain place, to ritualize the action in a socially acceptable way? To do this, the child must learn to be generous, to present his gift of obedience and cooperation to appease the threatening Law. (The threat, of course, as implied in the quotation from Lacan, is one of castration. The gift serves to mediate, though not completely eradicate, that threat.) Once this structure of exchange is in place, it is redeployed endlessly in the negotiations between the subject's desire and the Law prohibiting that desire.

At this stage, the child's interest is rarely held by picture books with no organizing narrative tension—the undifferentiated consumption of images has entered into the embattled dialectic of value or taste that an authoritative will is imposing on the child to channel her desire. It is no longer enough to know that this is green; now green has a set of socially determined meanings that have nothing to do with its greenness, but with a code that the child must learn, an intellectual montage that combines a positive characteristic with a contingent societal value. Metaphorical meaning, according to Žižek, emerges in the anal stage as an effect of the employment of montage. "Montage," he says, "can combine elements of a wholly heterogeneous nature and thus create new *metaphorical* meaning having nothing whatsoever to do with the 'literal' value of its component parts" (*Looking Awry* [LA], 89). This, in effect, is what happens when words are added to pictures; as Perry Nodelman points out, "Any given picture book contains at least three stories: the one told by the words, the one implied by the pictures, and the one that results from the combination of the first two" ("Words," 2). This tension replicates the structural tension that is organizing the subject. There are two lines of desire—the desire of the subject, which is structured by the mother, and the desire of the Other. The first represents idyllic wish fulfillment and the second represents a threatening prohibition. They come together to form a plane of tension on which is enacted the drama of the continual metaphoric displacements of the desire of the subject. In *Stellaluna*, while there is some tension between the border illustrations and the full-color illustrations, there is a more-or-less direct relation between the pictures and the written text. Nonetheless, we can see how the axis of the subject's desire, represented by the border illustrations, moves in and out of alignment with the axis of the Other's desire as represented by both the text and the full-color illustrations.

So what, finally, are we to make of these storybooks? On the one hand, they invite the child into the realm of signification. Rather than presenting the world as other, cutting it up into categories and labels, as the books in the time of looking tend to do, they ask the child to make an identification with the main character, most often by capitalizing on the categories and labels the child has become familiar with in the time of looking. The child has learned, for instance, that he is relatively small, that he is a child, perhaps, and that children as a general rule have a mommy and a daddy. Hence he is in a position to categorize himself as the same or different from the character in the book he is reading. Having made that initial identification, he then takes on the problems of the main character (recall the discussion of Fern in chapter 1), one of the most prevalent of these problems being the loss of the mother. The child is in an especially vulnerable position with regard to the signifier—his experiences are limited, his structures (of loss, of desire, of joy) haven't yet taken on the thick layers of coding that will increasingly become his "issues" as he grows. The signifiers that attach themselves to those structures now are those which will continue to return to him; they will be the signifiers through which he defines both his ills and their cure. In that sense, these storybooks tend to offer the world of signification as a closed narrative system. They most often provide fantasy closure as a *value,* rather than as simply an episode. The Law supersedes the mother's (and the child's) desire almost without residue, both at the level of the narrative, and at the level of the pictures.

Of course this is not the case in all picture books. Very recently, perhaps within the last ten years, picture books with a more postmodernist vision have emerged. These books use visual and verbal irony, intertextuality, and postmodern artistic techniques to violate notions of closure, to challenge a univocal and constraining Law, and hence to attempt to leave room for an anarchic desire. But for the most part (and please note that this is a contingent generalization rather than a universal rule), the storybook genre as it has emerged over the past century and a half has attempted to "capture" the child into the world of signification, and to channel that child's vision through identification into certain signifiers that mark modernist culture— the loss of the mother, with salvation coming through fantasy on the one hand, and capitulation to the Law on the other.

In addition, here is where the proliferation of white middle-class imagery, so prevalent in books for this age, becomes so dangerous for both white and nonwhite subjects. For white child subjects whose families are composed of an arrangement where the mother is the primary caregiver and the father is an intermittent though benevolent presence, all living in a detached home with no extra relatives or nonrelated people in residence, a sense of their own normality and even superiority is affirmed. They grow up into the blithely dangerous consciousness that they are the status quo, that they are racially neutral, and in fact that they are "we"—that is, that everyone either shares their values and characteristics, or desires to, or ought to desire to. Whiteness becomes a master signifier that unites economic privilege, male privilege, maternal benevolence, insularity of the immediate family, able-bodiedness, and a benevolent ownership of environmental resources as its secondary signifiers. This master signifier is no less compelling for nonwhite subjects or children whose family arrangements or embodiments don't fit the pattern. But their problem is that this distorted, narrow image becomes an ideal image; the site of undefined reciprocity with which they are invited to identify very soon reveals itself to be an impossible ideal. Unfortunately, the mirror-stage fiction has taught child subjects to trust and value and aspire to what they see more than to what they feel or experience or know to be true. The problem for subjects whose life circumstances align with normative ideals, then, is that they are confirmed in this fictional view of themselves, and when things go awry they have very few resources with which to construct a new ideal image for themselves. For the nonnormative subject (the subject who is disabled or nonwhite, or who lives in a family culture unlike the one described), the problem is more complex—how does the child reconcile the ideal images in her books with the ideal image in her mirror with the ideal images she sees in the people who surround her?

In representative terms, for instance, we take it for granted that members of a family should look somewhat alike. But even such simple representational assumptions can cause problems for some mixed-race children or those who have been adopted cross-culturally, as is beautifully demonstrated by Allen Say's book *Allison*. When Allison realizes that she looks more like her doll than like her parents, and when she realizes that this is not the case with other families, she acts out her grief by destroying her parents' precious things from their childhood. This emotional outburst is entirely appropriate because it is directed at precisely the right objects— the things that connect her parents to their childhoods are exactly what disconnect her from them. Her parents act appropriately too—they are angry and sad, but they respect and understand her anger, and they forgive her actions. Meanwhile, Allison "adopts" a stray cat, which, as Wilbur with Charlotte's babies, as Max with the Wild Things, facilitates a process whereby she takes on the characteristics of the ones she loves, rather than seeking ways to incorporate them or deny their loss. Though this story has some problems with realistic depiction, it holds psychoanalytic truth for the non-white subject who must endure the bombardment of images of white people set up as ideal images before she is even able to be a discriminating consumer of images.

The time for looking and the time for understanding mark for the subject times of loss and vulnerability. While the work of the signifier helps to name existential losses so that they can be in some way mastered, the imprint of white masculinity as a normative master signifier can lead as often to melancholia as to mourning. In the next chapter, we will look at the time for concluding, where the child asserts his identity with respect to the Symbolic and attempts to come to terms with both the Real and the Imaginary.

CHAPTER THREE

Mourning into Dancing

Recuperating the Loss of the Mother

The books that correspond to the time for concluding are the ones aimed at beginning readers. Learning to read involves certain important shifts for the child. It is as if he were making one giant step on the road to individuality; once he learns to read, reading will rarely be a situation where he is cuddled close to the body of another, receiving the words through another's voice as he simultaneously receives her smell, her touch, and a myriad of other positive limbic interactions that physical proximity makes possible. As he learns to read silently, even his own voice will be replaced by the solipsism of his eye and inner voice. Admittedly, this is a rather grim picture of reading, but I suggest it because in contemporary Western society we tend to so value literacy that we often don't direct our attention to the bodily and communal losses that accompany the acquisition of the ability to read for oneself. Whereas reading undeniably opens worlds of possibilities for the reading subject, it also closes or at least significantly interferes with the worlds with which the child has to this point been familiar. At the very least, it makes a child responsible for a whole range of things that he has not been responsible for previously. Once a child *can* read, he *must* read. He will move from being a person-read-to to being a reader and a writer, that is, to being an active participant in the authoritative structure of written language, the code that (arguably) dominates the modernist Symbolic order. This shift, which follows hard on the heels of the advent of spoken language and the precipitation of subjectivity itself, involves the realignment of desire and authority in the child and helps him "work through" the very difficult renunciation of the *jouissance* he experienced in his illusory connection with the mother's body before language intervened. Hence the Symbolic has to run a sort of PR campaign to convince the reluctant child that the space he is entering has as much if not more to offer than the space he is leaving behind. Children's picture books and beginning readers then, in their colorful, lively, humorous presentation, can be seen as ads for the Symbolic, attempts to ease the child away from an impossible connection to the mother into a slightly less impossible position as a subject.

We find a brilliant illustration of this transition in Phoebe Gilman's *Something from Nothing*. Gilman's retelling of this traditional Jewish folktale can be taken as a specimen story for anal-stage development. In the story, Grandpa makes a blanket for the baby Joseph. As Joseph grows older, the blanket becomes increasingly dirty and tattered and Joseph's mother insists that he throw it out. But Grandpa snips and stitches the blanket through various transformations as Joseph grows—from blanket to jacket to vest to Sabbath tie to handkerchief to button, each time repeating the refrain, "There's just enough material here to make . . ." Finally, when the button is lost and Grandpa can no longer make "something from nothing," Joseph himself takes up both a pen and Grandpa's refrain: "There's just enough material here to make . . . a wonderful story," transforming the entire experience, presumably, into the story we have just read and presenting it, apropos of the anal stage, as his "gift" to his family. He has metaphorically replaced his desire with a venue that preserves it at the same time it renders it socially acceptable; he has, in effect, successfully negotiated the anal stage.

Two elements help the reader negotiate it with him. First, the threatening prohibition is made less terrifying by the fact that it is his grandfather, not his father or mother, who is mutilating the blanket. The figures of the young boy and the elderly man are sexual parentheses—the threat of castration, in their supposedly presexual and postsexual positions, means less for them, as the grandfather is not the boy's rival and the boy is not yet entirely sure in what the rivalry consists. For the child reader, this translates into a less threatening negotiation; whereas the mother (or father) would simply insist on the complete withdrawal of the blanket (castration), the grandfather, as grandfathers in general are wont to do, acts as an intermediary. ("When the going gets tough, the tough go to Grandpa's.") Second, at the level of the pictures, the mouse family who lives under the floorboards of the house helps the reader negotiate Joseph's loss by preserving and transforming Joseph's blanket/desire all along. Most of the action takes place in Joseph's house, which is presented in cross-section, showing three floors and a crawl space beneath the floorboards. Every time Grandpa snips the blanket with scissors, bits of it fall through the cracks in the floor, and a mouse couple uses these bits as blankets, curtains, tablecloths, and clothes for their growing family, Joseph's successive losses becoming their boon. As Virginia Blum and June Cummins have noted in their object-relations reading of this text, Joseph could be said to be clothing and furnishing his unconscious as bits of his desire get repressed; the story he writes in the end functions as a socially acceptable integration into the Symbolic of the tabooed desire he feels for the mother/blanket. The mouse mother is always pictured smiling and giving her children the bits of the blanket, in direct contrast with Joseph's mother, whose countenance is almost always threatening, as are her words. Thus the tension between the desired object and the overbearing social taboo plays itself out in the parallel montage.

Joseph's emergence as a writer culminates a series of transactions in which each of the logical moments of the subject are visible. In each instance of prohibition, Joseph sees what his mother sees, transposes himself into her way of reasoning, and, with his grandpa, effects a preemptive solution for the problem of total annihilation. But wait, one might say, it is not Joseph who is at risk, but his blanket. True enough, but we must consider what role the blanket plays for Joseph. If it functions as an *objet a*, that is, an object not wholly distinct from oneself that covers over one's constitutive lack, and it is summarily removed before a substitutionary logic has been established, the result would be devastating for Joseph, just as a similarly preemptive separation of Wilbur from Fern would have left Fern in thrall to her symptom.[1] He has to find some way of mitigating his loss, of managing the tremendous risk of performing the assertion of anticipated certainty, for while the assertion provides him with the freedom to become someone apart from his mother, it also sets him loose from the moorings of the prior certainty of his Imaginary place in the mother.

Joseph mitigates the final loss of his blanket by writing a story. He makes something from nothing. That is, through language, in language, he undertakes to become something in the Symbolic to cover over the nothing that he is in the Real, having lost the blanket as his Imaginary bridge— $(Joseph)<>a$(his blanket as it stands in for his mother). In so doing, he accomplishes something very different from the reuniting of the baby birds, ducks, owls, and bats with their mothers at story's end. What Joseph does is negotiate for himself a position from which he can speak, rather than simply be bespoken.

Or does he? Using the same logic that we used in dealing with *Stellaluna*, we find that, in the final scene, the image in Joseph's "unconscious," that is, the scene depicting the mouse family, corresponds identically with the picture of Joseph's conscious structure. The son of the mouse family, just like Joseph, is shown presenting a story to an adoring family. Both he and Joseph are positioned in the center of their respective groups, and each face in both families is turned toward the young writers with looks of joy and approval. Such a replication in the pictures points to a renewal of the fantasy structure for Joseph—as with Stellaluna, when Joseph is reunited with his family, the discordant vision between the unconscious and the conscious disappears. Most important in this reading is the face of Joseph's mother; heretofore either cross with or disinterested in her son, she is now beaming at him, hands clasped in a gesture of happiness, excitement, and pride. She has become less like herself, and more like the mouse mother of his unconscious.

Through that replication, the unconscious as a force is closed off rather than activated, and Joseph, instead of experiencing subjectivity, experiences subjection. He has done well, of course, to choose meaning over being. In Lacanian terms, the human being must cross over from brute being into meaning in order to become a subject. This is what we've been talking about all along when we talk about the subject entering language and becoming a signifier for another signifier—as we know from Saussurean linguistics, the signifier does not refer to the thing itself, but to the idea of the thing, the signified. As a result, Lacan says, the word kills the thing—the signifier/signified combination replaces any experience one might have had of the thing in itself. Instead of slipping into the nothingness that would come of completely merging with his blanket, Joseph opts for the pleasures of complete compliance with the Other. Gilbert Chaitin formulates the two sides of the coin this way:

> On the social level, if you choose being, then you refuse the social mandate contained in the meaning imposed upon you, exclude yourself from social life, and, since subjectivity can only exist in society (through recognition, the desire of the Other), you renounce subjecthood.... When you opt for meaning, on the other hand, you become "petrified," reified in the function laid out for you by the Other. Joining society, acceding blindly to the demand of the Other, turns you into something like an inanimate object, a pure universal rather than a subject. (184)

Joseph's story has such closure that nothing whatever slips predication. We know exactly what happened to the bits of cloth, the button, the mouse family, the human family. Even though we can't read what he is writing, we know exactly what Joseph's story is about. Everything is contained within the circular vision of the story within the story, the pictures beneath the pictures, and as a result, Joseph becomes Everychild rather than a distinct subject. This reading is, of course, not the only one we could formulate, and perhaps it is not even the best one, but it illustrates the problem of the subject at the cusp of being and meaning—which side will I choose, and at what cost? This is precisely what is at stake in the time for concluding.

I Declare Myself to Be a Man:
The Time for Concluding

In the time for concluding, the subject must "set to sea in a sieve," so to speak. He has to assume, by means of a precipitate assertion, his place in the Symbolic as a signifier, mobile and substitutable, rather than as a mere product of signification. The subject will be a bird, if she pleases, or a bat with bird brothers. Or he will be a radiant pig. Or a spider who is also a writer. But whatever she will be, she will never be fully determined by the big Other. The storybooks that have attempted to capture her have had the opposite effect; they have precipitated her desire. This is partially because through storybooks, she has learned to open herself up to multiple identifications. But it is also because through the process of making these multiple identifications, she has learned that she is never quite equal to the sum of them. There is always more or less to her than she finds in her books. The sense of a boundary, reinforced by the material existence of a book that has edges to its representations as well as an ending to its narrative, creates in her the desire to transgress the boundary—to find out what happens next, or what happened before, or what happens around and beside and outside of the pages of her book. She wants a beyond of the book.

Just before the child begins to read, he is at his most vulnerable point with respect to assimilation (and subsequent annihilation) into the Symbolic order. For the preliterate child, the relationship between the child and written language is mediated through the spoken voice of someone else. This imposes a distance, even when the child is in the mode of identifying with what he is encountering. After all, it is through his mother's voice that he hears the voice of the characters he is supposed to be, and it is her voice that is doing the narration, that is, posing as the big Other. But when he starts to speak words through his own mouth, that distance is lessened. Children often learn the words of their favorite books verbatim long before they can read. Perhaps this is why the prospect of learning to read is perceived as so empowering for the child, so exhilarating. Instead of someone else being in a position to articulate the word of the Other, it will be the child himself. Hence he will be able to move more easily into identifications with the big Other, rather than with smaller, weaker others. His "I" will now be shored up by an Other- (and other-) sanctioned activity. But this does not tell the whole story. In learning to read, the child encounters rules. The phonotactic logic of his language, which he absorbed effortlessly from his birth, has been displaced into a strange symbolic logic. Letters don't sound like what they look like, and some letters have different sounds based on where they are and what they're next to. Idiosyncrasies and accents vanish in favor of rules of spelling and grammar that, even though they are presented as rules, won't stay in place, so he has to learn the exceptions as well. What a mess!

The *Amelia Bedelia* series and Dr. Seuss's Beginning Reader books are some of the many offerings of the species "beginner books," meaning that they are designed for and marketed to children who are just beginning to master those universal rules and their ever-present exceptions. So despite the fact that the beginning reader is still encouraged through text and illustration to make identifications with the characters of the stories, she is also in the position of the writer—that is, she is making the story happen through reading it, rather than simply receiving it as it is read to her. She has moved from a passive position to an active one, and she can perform that position correctly or creatively as is her whim. In this respect the act of reading is always performed in the time for concluding. By performing a reading, the child (or adult) subject is placing herself into the trauma of linguistic castration that caused her to come to be in the first place. Instead of being read (to), she learns to read. And in learning to read nonsense, she manages to hold on to that bit of outlaw *jouissance*—as it appears in the humor, music, and anarchy of the nonsense text—that has broken off from the mother and winds up circulating in language itself.[2]

In the time for concluding, the subject knows, through the processes of othering and of identifying with the other that take place in the other two moments, that she is precipitately closing off a plethora of options. She grieves the loss of those options and, more profoundly, grieves the loss of the mother that propelled her into action in the first place. She needs to mourn her loss. To successfully mourn a loss, according to Freud, one must first acknowledge the object as lost. This is precisely what the storybooks we have analyzed do—they bring to signification the loss of the mother, constituting it as a problem. But to move beyond the acknowledgment of loss into the successful working through of grief, children must introject the loss, take it on themselves in such a way that they assume the characteristics of the lost object. They do not become the object they have lost, but they work to preserve the attributes that made the object precious to them in the first place. When it comes to the mother, the child has to find a way to enter meaning, which, being on the side of the Law, is the site of the mother's exclusion, while at the same time holding open a place for her as nonmeaning. Interestingly enough, an entire literary genre exists that attempts to do just that, and it is the genre that predominates in books written and recommended for beginning readers: nonsense.

According to some critics, nonsense has been around since recorded language (see for instance, Anderson and Apseloff), but even they acknowledge that the genre as it exists for children today is a modernist phenomenon, established in the nineteenth century with Edward Lear and Lewis Carroll. Its aim, then as now, is to "capture" the child into the world of language and representation and at the same time to make the child aware of the limits of that world. Its connections to the principles and vocabulary of psychoanalysis would require a separate and involved study all to themselves, but for our purposes we will simply stick to articulating the way nonsense literature helps the child establish and maintain the proper (in modernist terms) relationship to language.

Just what is the proper relationship to language? Certainly it is not a refusal of language altogether. Nor is it a relationship structured by the fantasy that our everyday existence within the Symbolic is not somehow "it," that instead there is some beyond of language where the "real me" lives. The subject has to acknowledge that she is subject to the rules of language, that only within and through them can she hope to cast an identity. Otherwise she will be caught in a paralyzing fantasy space. Her desire to "escape" her predicament through fantasy rather than through effective precipitate action will result in her being completely subject to the big Other's mandates. She will be buying her identity off the rack and attempting to fit into it, becoming in the process "so completely identified with her social role that she loses the distance from herself that constitutes subjecthood"

(Chaitin, 184); she will lose any sense of her own lack, thinking that she has been filled in by the big Other. This type of identity construction doesn't work, because by it the subject ignores the hole in the big Other. She imagines that the apparent solidity of the Symbolic order is an actual solidity, and she feels that the only way to become solid herself is to be absorbed into the big Other. But the acknowledgment of the mother as lost preempts the possibility of such thinking. If the mother is lost, then the Other is lacking, the totality of meaning through signification is disrupted, and there is a space for the unconscious, and simultaneously the subject herself, to come to be.

Nonsense helps the child negotiate this position with regard to language in several ways. First of all, nonsense can be said to operate under a phonemic logic. Jean-Jacques Lecercle, in his excellent studies on Victorian nonsense, undertakes a linguistic analysis of the nonsense text that reveals several things. First, he emphasizes that good nonsense rarely violates the phonotactic rules of the language in which it is written. There is a music specific to each language, and certain rules of word formation that even nonce words follow. For instance, the narrator of *Dr. Seuss's ABC* is called a "Zizzer-Zazzer-Zuzz." Though this word does not exist in English, there is no reason why it shouldn't. It doesn't contain any unpronounceable combinations of consonants or vowels, and moreover, it is fun to say. This phonemic logic is one way that nonsense preserves the mother through language —the mother's voice is what is linked to the phoneme as a privileged object for the child. Meaning exists on the side of the father/Law, but the phoneme exists on the side of the mother/desire.

Just as nonsense doesn't usually violate phonotactic rules of language, it doesn't break morphological rules either, though it may certainly bend them to good effect. The Grinch "puzzled and puzzed 'til his puzzler was sore." Dr. Seuss operates under a rather strict meter; in order to preserve the rhythm of the line, he lops off a syllable from the second "puzzled" but nevertheless maintains it as a verb with a regular simple-past ending. He then morphs the word into a noun that exists but dubiously in our language, and that is rarely used as a synonym for mind or brain. Morphologically speaking, however, the -er ending is a perfectly correct ending and his meaning is never in question.

The last rule that nonsense does not violate, and in fact it maintains its strictest adherence here, is the rule of syntax. No matter how many nonce words are in play, or how many questionable morphological feats are undertaken, the text remains recognizable as a text because of its syntax. In fact, Lecercle claims that one way of conceiving of nonsense is as a dialectic movement between the excess of syntax and the lack of semantics.[3]

The trials and tribulations of Amelia Bedelia illustrate perhaps better than any other text I know the way the subject must approach semantics in nonsense. Nonsense, as Lecercle points out, refuses metaphor. Metaphor is unruly; it breaks straightforward rules of semantics. To borrow an image from Fink, metaphor creates a circuit from one signifier to another, with the subject acting as conductor. Because it requires the presence of a subject in order to have any meaning, metaphor points out the gaps in the big Other. Amelia Bedelia's troubles usually stem from the fact that she is left alone with a written text. Believing herself to be in command of a language that doesn't slip, she takes everything literally. She behaves as if there were no holes in the big Other, as if language and meaning were objective, self-identical, totalizable. As a result, she does things that strike the reader as hilarious—she dusts the furniture with dusting powder, dresses the chicken with lace and bows, puts the lights out on the clothesline. All the while, she marvels at the silly ways other people behave. She of course fixes everything with a wonderful pie—the triumph of orality, no doubt. But the reading subject is able to position himself at a distance from Amelia Bedelia, so that her foibles produce humor rather than anxiety and teach him something very important about the way signification works. Humor here is certainly regressive for the child, who has repressed such associational logic in favor of a logic of the signifier. From his advanced perspective in the Symbolic, he is able to see, through her blunders, that language cannot be taken literally. Hence the lesson of Amelia Bedelia's nonsense is that one should never be too sure of the Other's meaning—that there is a beyond of what the words on the page may seem to say. This beyond is what forgives—it substitutes the sublime experience of a good pie for the mistakes we make in attempting to measure up to the standard of the Other.

I choose my examples from Amelia Bedelia and Dr. Seuss rather than from the venerable fathers of nonsense simply because I do not think that many children today enter language via Lear and Carroll. It is a rare child, however, who does not enter language, and especially reading, through some encounter with nonsense, be it *Sesame Street*, Amelia Bedelia, or Dr. Seuss. The genre has proliferated to the point where canonical texts can be difficult to locate, with the possible exceptions of *The Cat in the Hat* and *Green Eggs and Ham*. These texts, as Tim Wolf points out, have inspired an almost cultlike devotion. In his article "Imagination, Rejection, and Rescue: Recurrent Themes in Dr. Seuss," Wolf points out the following three elements that keep cropping up: "a rejected child, the exercise of childlike imagination, and a rejecting parent whose anger seems focused against the exercise of childlike imagination" (137). The theme of the rejected child of course dovetails with the theme of the lost mother, which occurs in at least two Seuss texts that Wolf does not treat—*The Cat in the Hat* and *Horton Hatches the Egg*. Wolf notes that Seuss offers three different resolutions for the problem of rejection. In the first instance, exemplified in *And to Think That I Saw It on Mulberry Street*, the child responds to the parent's rejection by rejecting him back. In the second, the child in *The 500 Hats of Bartholomew Cubbins* finds a way to satisfy the parent and is granted a financial reward, as well as reconciliation. But in *The King's Stilts*, as in *Green Eggs and Ham*, the rejected child ends up rescuing the parent from the parent's own unhappiness. Wolf reads these last books as a "perfect resolution" to the problem of the rejected child.

Certainly Wolf's argument is compelling and thorough from the perspective of ego psychology, the aim of which is the harmonious adaptation of the inner world of the subject to the outer world in which it finds itself. The child in Wolf's analysis has a privileged access to the inner world, and the parent figure an equally privileged access to the outer world. The parent has seemingly lost touch with his inner world and hence suffers an imbalance that must be corrected by his encounter with the child. To effect this correction, however, the child must make some offering to the parent—they each have to give a bit in order to achieve balance. Under a Lacanian analysis, however, the perfect solution Wolf points out is a bit too perfect. Lacanian theory sets itself against ego psychology—it is about not adaptation, but disruption. As we saw in *Something from Nothing*, adaptation shuts down the unconscious; it petrifies the subject in signification. Lacan's complaints regarding ego psychology, and there are many, mostly stem from the fact that adaptation is merely another name for social control, subjection rather than subjectivity. Lacan requires the subject to retain his distance from the big Other—to be more like Marco and the children in *The Cat in the Hat* than they are like Sam-I-am.

Green Eggs and Ham is in many ways quite a conservative text. Although the child character is Sam, the reader will be just as likely to identify with the harried parent figure for two reasons. First, the story is told in first person through his/her voice. But second, the child subject is continually being harassed by (m)others to try things that are new. Green things are probably the most heinous. Seuss points out the absurdity of this "try it it's good for you" tactic by using something that would certainly not be good for you if it were in fact green. But he undercuts that message by having the main character cave in to the pressure at the end and actually *like* green eggs and ham. The Other succeeds in capturing the subject, luring him away from his own desire into the desire of the Other. In the end, as Wolf points out, he seems happier and more at ease than he has throughout the book. But the goal of the Lacanian subject is not necessarily happiness, especially if that happiness is bought at the price of ceding his desire.

The Cat in the Hat is arguably more popular and certainly more revolutionary than *Green Eggs and Ham*. With the mother gone, the children are faced with the problem of how they will be related to the big Other, and by the same token, their own unconscious, since that unconscious is one face of the big Other. The Cat represents the anarchic possibilities of desire, and the fish represents the Law. Having the two in such close proximity creates a sense of anxiety in the children, but they end by keeping their distance from either extreme. On the one hand, they do not fully capitulate to the fish, acting only with expediency in regard to the Law. On the other hand, they do not fully give in to the pleasures of the Cat. By asserting and maintaining their distance, they are in a position of relative autonomy; like Marco in *Mulberry Street*, they can make a genuine choice with regard to what they tell their mother or father. By putting the question to the reader, Seuss encourages the reader to place himself in the same position—a position that keeps enough distance from the Law to make a choice. This inner distance, constituted by the repression that instantiates the unconscious, safeguards the young reader against remaining an object for the big Other.

The act of reading is, in a sense, an act of anticipated certainty, in that the reader is actively attempting to master and collect unto herself the "seemingly stable units of the symbolic system" (Chaitin, 165). By connecting and reconnecting signifiers on her own, she is responding to the trauma of expulsion from the mother by identifying herself with the Law as it is represented in the written word. But she has to retain some sort of relationship with the lost mother, and she does this through the material qualities of the signifier—its phonemic quality, its brute facticity, its structure that requires relationality to constitute meaning. The fact that her early reading experiences are most likely to be nonsense texts establishes in her the sense that the "only ground of identity, of meaning, of representation, is in fact the non-ground of the play of difference which constitutes the signifier" (Chaitin, 165). As Lecercle points out, nonsense acts as both support and subversion of the rule of Law—support because it reinforces the rules it is mocking, and subversion because it introduces ways the child might use language's own rules to undermine it and preserve his own desire.

Concluding in Favor of What?

Lacan's time for concluding seems in fact to be a mere beginning, for surely the child does not assert an identity once and for all. What then is meant by "concluding" in a Lacanian sense? I would suggest that intrinsic to asserting one's position in the Symbolic order is the establishment of a way of conceiving one's relation to the Other. This relation with respect to the desire of the Other is what Lacan would call one's psychic structure. In Lacanian psychoanalytic theory, the subject can take up one of three relationships to the Other's desire—psychosis, which forecloses the possibility of otherness altogether; perversion, wherein the subject sees himself as an object-instrument of the Other's desire; and neurosis, which poses its relation to the desire of the Other as a question and continually wonders what the Other requires of him or her. These three structural configurations of subjectivity are the potential outcomes of the complex interplay between the *infans* and the Other. We can see how these relationships play out, respectively, in *The Story of Babar, Curious George*, and *Stellaluna*. The political dimensions of the first two books have been explored in compelling assessments by Herbert Kohl and June Cummins; my work here actually builds on their work by supplementing the political with the psychic operations at play in these texts. In each instance, the child is forcibly removed from his or her home environment and yet ends up demonstrating what Judith Butler, in *The Psychic Life of Power*, calls a "passionate attachment to subjection." That is, instead of rejecting the lifestyle, language, and value system of their tormentors, they strive to assimilate to them. They become libidinally, erotically attached to the prohibitions imposed on them by social constraint and seek to "serve" the cause of homogeneity and the hegemony of the dominant culture in one way or another. A gentler way of saying this would be that they learn to substitute the joys of language for the prior joys of the body.

Interestingly enough, Babar and Curious George, both classic characters of postwar Western children's literature, repeat and reinforce the theme of

a passionate attachment or commitment to the conditions of their own op-
pression, whereas Stellaluna, a contemporary, but soon to become canonical, work calls those conditions into question. So perhaps there is more
hope for subversive and active resistance than Butler's theory acknowledges. At any rate, the pattern of subject development that we have traced
is once again operative—a period of initial unity, followed by a separation,
concluded by the assertion of a singular distinct identity. In this section,
however, I want to look at the conditions under which that assertion takes
place, focusing in particular on the child's attitude toward the terms of his
or her separation and reincorporation into a community.

In books that focus on the coming into subjectivity of a child, the preoedipal stage is nearly always figured by a visual totality reinforced by large,
full-page, single-scene illustrations. The child is shown eating (an oral-stage
preoccupation) or in such close touch with the mother that there is no separation between them—they are, visually speaking, one entity. In the case
of *Curious George*, we may read the jungle as the mother's body—a place
where George is happy and at home. In the case of *Stellaluna*, the totality is
even further reinforced as a psychic unity discussed in chapter 2 as well—
the interplay has yet to emerge between the border illustrations, which we
may read here as the first inklings of Stellaluna's unconscious, and the full-
color ones, which correspond to her actual lived experience. They are simply the same illustration. The end of the preoedipal stage, as we have noted,
is marked by a separation. In children's literature, the separation is usually
not the mother's fault—she doesn't want to leave her baby but is forced to
by some external force. In many cases, it is not the baby's choice either.
Most often, the separation is initiated by a masculine force—either a male
character alone, or a male character wielding a masculine weapon. One re-
calls with poignancy the foreshadowing moment in Disney's *Bambi* where
Bambi's mother says, "Man was in the forest." Indeed man enters both Curious George's and Babar's forests, and the results are tragic indeed. Curious George is captured in a sack, and Babar's mother is shot out from
under him while he is riding on her back. We have already discussed in detail the moment of separation for Stellaluna. In each case, the shield of the
mother's body fails. To negotiate from that position of being squeezed out,
ejected, from the body of the mother, the child begins a process of imitation. What is surprising and somewhat disturbing is that the child does not
imitate the mother, the place of his or her own desire, the one place that
represents needs met and longings fulfilled. Instead, each child willfully

chooses to take on the characteristics of the *masculine force who killed his or her mother.* Babar runs as fast as he can, not back to the nurturing presence of the jungle, but toward the place where his greatest tragedy originated. Curious George, even though he does try to jump ship, nevertheless learns to enjoy life in the city of the Man with the Yellow Hat. And Stellaluna takes up residence, not with owls, but with birds nonetheless. The result is a split between what the subject desires, and what he knows he must do in order to survive—that is, to capitulate to the Law. And this is the crux of Butler's point—power is not so much "internalized" by the subject as it is assumed against the core of one's own self.

DeBrunoff, Rey, and Cannon choose to illustrate this imitation/alienation process in remarkably similar terms: They switch from full-page or almost full-page single-scene illustrations to fragmentary, multiscene illustrations. Reality no longer seems a totality so much as a series of performances, as the little animals try, through interspecies identifications, to live up to the standards of behavior and values of a society that, quite literally, threatens their very existence. The use of fragmented illustrations emphasizes the break with the preoedipal unity of the dual relation between mother and child, and also the gaps that must now exist within any notion of a coherent self. Because as Stellaluna points out, as much as one tries to identify with and imitate others, one is not completely coincident with them, and at some point, the seams will show.

Curious George and Babar demonstrate how these attachments can be called passionate. Curious George doesn't just suffer human affectations, he relishes them. He is fascinated and curious about every aspect of human behavior, and he is continually trying out how those behaviors feel in, on, and through his own body. He puts on the Man in the Yellow Hat's pajamas, smokes his pipe, and tries making a phone call. Babar not only relishes human behaviors, especially fashion and fitness (which is interesting in an animal whose species doesn't depend on color for sexual attraction, and for whom girth is a sign of robust health, not to mention a structural inevitability), but proselytizes as well. When Celeste and Arthur track him down in the city, he is put off by the touch of his friends, and he quickly dresses them, takes them to a pastry shop, and puts them in a car. And even though Curious George's versions of these behaviors land him in trouble, there is no questioning voice in these texts, no interrogation of the values themselves. We forget—or perhaps it is more accurate to say we repress—the fact, along with the monkey and the elephant, that these men they are so eager to imitate are the reason they are displaced and have to find someone to imitate in the first place. For them, the emphasis is on the passionate attachment itself, and the pleasures that can come with giving in to the power structures that oppress you. They don't just go along to get along, biding their time until they can rise up and call to account the men who murdered their mothers and appropriated their bodies. Instead, they enjoy their subjection. The bizarre pathos of Babar's situation is made stunningly clear as he drives fashionably dressed Celeste and Arthur back to the jungle, followed by their naked mothers, who run along behind, having to keep their trunks up so as not to breathe in the fumes from the car.

In Stellaluna's case, however, the emphasis is on the subjection in Butler's formula. Stellaluna does *not* appreciate the values of her new family—their taste in food, their tendency to sleep right side up, their staying awake in the daytime and sleeping at night. And yet she submits to them because of her need to survive and have some sort of community. The power dynamic at play is clearly illustrated in the picture that accompanies the mother bird's scolding of Stellaluna for endangering her children. The period of transition, which we have called the time for looking, is a liminal period during which the subject finds the tools with which to reintegrate into the larger social structure. In the case of all three of these little subjects, it is a place of alienation and fragmentation, but in Curious George's or Babar's case, at any rate, it is also a place of play and fun. Stellaluna's transition is frightening and unpleasant, a frank recognition of the conditions of reincorporation into a society that failed to protect you from the beginning.

Babar's re-incorporation, of the three, can be read as the greatest success from a traditional standpoint. He has gone away, learned some things, and returned triumphant as a sort of *über* elephant. But his exalted position masks the very conditions to which he has had to submit for his "success." He has had to accept alienation from his own species, and his denial of that alienation in his return is nothing short of psychotic in structure. Psychosis is marked by a foreclosure of Otherness proper—the psychotic doesn't deny Otherness, he simply doesn't understand it to exist and hence does not have the distance from himself that subjectivity requires. Not being able to see himself, he cannot see his world and hence does not perceive anything at all unusual about his position. It is one thing for an elephant to drive a car among other driving elephants, but when you're the only one, and you view that as a superior position rather than as a violent aberration, you have a problem. Babar sees no difference between himself and his fellow elephants, just as he saw no difference between himself and the humans in the city. It is as if the violence of Babar's mother's death prevents him from seeing it as a separation; as a trauma that he cannot assimilate, it fixes him in a place before separation could even be thought or imagined. The interesting thing is that the other elephants accept his psychotic behavior as superior to their own split condition and crown him king. Lacan reminds us that it is not the man who thinks himself a king who is necessarily psychotic, but the king who thinks himself a king. The king who sees his kingness as a feature of his subjectivity and does not recognize the place from which his kingship derives has foreclosed the Other. Because otherness has never been instantiated for him, Babar does not recognize the contingency of his position, because there is no possibility for him to be other than what he is.

Curious George, on the other hand, is regarded as a failure in his rite of passage. He never grows up, never changes his status, never becomes anything other than a spectacle for the people in his stories. What he does, however, is continually get into "mischief." This rebellion in the face of a prohibition from the Man in the Yellow Hat marks Curious George as perverse in terms of his psychic structure. According to Butler, perversion is the only possible site of resistance to the overwhelming domination of the oppressive forces of social power. But Curious George shows her reading of perversion to be misguided. As Slavoj Žižek points out, the pervert isn't really in a position to subvert the dominant order (*The Ticklish Subject* [TS], 247–249). He merely supports it by acting out its secret fantasies. Curious George acts out the child's desire to rebel against parental authority much as the pervert acts out against normative sexual practices mandated by the social order. But their actions never have the possibility of disrupting the fabric of oppressive law, because the law is what creates the possibility for its violation in the first place—it includes its own opposite. The prohibition against making false fire-alarm calls includes within it the desire to make them, and Curious George simply plays to that. He is a pretend rebel —never truly rebellious. And he ends up in a pretend jungle, where he can perform all of his monkeyish pranks for the enjoyment of the Other, which is, in fact, the clinical definition of perverse structure. The person with a perverse psychic structure sees himself as the object-instrument of the Other; he feels that he knows what the Other wants, and he offers himself as an instrument to secure the Other's pleasure and enjoyment. That this position is as never ending as it is unproductive is reinforced by the number of sequels in which George, never achieving autonomy or self-regulation, repeats the same scenario of acting as instrument for the big Other in one way or another.

But whereas the pervert acts on behalf of the enjoyment of the Other, the hysteric (a version of the neurotic) continually questions her ability to do so. She wonders incessantly who she is for the Other, and her wondering prevents her ever closing on an answer that might spell her complete subsumption into the power structure that threatens her. She wants to be wanted, but never to be claimed. Throughout the book, Stellaluna never loses her desire for her bat self—the border illustrations link her with that self as they operate as wish-fulfillment fantasies, no matter what she is being forced to do to live in bird culture. When she rediscovers her bat community, she rediscovers her favorite foods, her joy in sleeping upside down, the smell of her mother. She rediscovers the body she has lost, rather than getting to the point Babar does of sacrificing his elephant body for a clothed human one, or Curious George does of commodifying his body in exhibition. Nor does she completely abandon one communal body for another: Stellaluna sustains the communities she has made, while understanding her separateness from them. Her rediscovery of her bat relatives comes through a long detour during which her position in both communities has been called into question. She develops the proper relationship with community at two levels. On the Imaginary level, as shown in the black-and-white border illustrations, she recognizes her separateness, the singularity of her desire, and the singularity of her fellows' desires. That is, she comes to no difference—erasing conclusions about who she is, or who others are. On the Symbolic, public level, she bridges those gaps with affection and love. She and her bird friends leave the peculiarities of their relationship in the form of a question that they pose but don't attempt to answer. The structure of an unanswered question preserves an openness to change and liberation that effectively foils the clamping down of the power dynamic of the dominant order.

Stellaluna offers a way to think about the conditions for radical change by showing us how one might escape a passionate attachment to subjection and replace it with a passionate attachment to joy. In the progression of pictures that shows her finding her bat relatives, we see the disconnection between conscious waking experience and unconscious life. For instance, in the scene where she is enjoying her first mango since her life with the birds, she is alone in the color picture but accompanied by her mother in the black-and-white border illustration. Thus even in her singularity, Stella-luna holds within her the trace of a mother who is and was her site of joy. They are separate beings, even in fantasy, which indicates that Stellaluna has in fact broken free from the dual relation and completed her rite of passage. But rather than attach herself, publicly or inwardly, to the site of her subjection, her passion is reserved for her own desire.

Hence it would seem that the preferred position in contemporary culture is one of neurosis. Since we must take up a position with regard to the desire of the Other, the position that affords us the most mobility and freedom is in fact neurosis, since it prevents us from being closed off from or subsumed by the Other. And if its manifest symptoms, which include insecurity and obsessional behavior, are sometimes difficult to bear, they can at least be made manageable and open to resignification. The neurotic subject recognizes that she doesn't want her entire life taken up by the Other, that she must defend against this Other desire in order to keep open a space for her own desire to manifest itself. But since our relationships with the Other, whether perverse or neurotic, never take place without residue, we will now direct our attention to those structural elements that remain after the subject has been written into the Symbolic order—the *objet a* and *jouis-sance*. These elements play the vital role of structuring desire and keeping it mobile and active in the lives of subjects, regardless of their particular psychic structure. So whereas in this chapter I have looked at how the subject relates to the desire of the Other, especially in the face of a Law that prohibits its free play, in the following chapter I focus on what desire is and how it operates in and through language.

CHAPTER FOUR

Looking Glasses and Neverlands

Beyond the Symbolic

Inevitably, psychoanalytic readings of the Alice books and of the story of Peter Pan abound. Charles Dodgson's immense fondness for children, primarily prepubescent girls, and J. M. Barrie's fascination with the Llewellyn-Davies boys makes it almost impossible for critics to leave the *writers* off the couch. Clearly, Dodgson desired (and carefully cultivated) the companionship of children, in much the same way as did Barrie, and they each managed to create remarkably persistent signifiers of childhood. If we locate that desire in the Real of bodies, as traditional psychoanalysis tends to do, assenting to a literal appropriation of Freud's "semiotics of sex," we can only conclude, as does Gattégno in his second study of Lewis Carroll, "that, behind the conventional vocabulary and all the moral and religious attitudinizing of the age, Carroll's very denials make it clear how fundamentally sexual was the importance of little girls in Carroll's life" (96). Both Carroll and Barrie have had their desires carefully explored and dissected by critics and biographers as a means of explaining why they wrote such appealing works for children; their art is, at least on one level, read as a seduction. But this way of interpreting the appeal of their work doesn't entirely serve. It seems that nearly everyone has his or her own Alice. So bold a statement might seem reckless did it not appear to be true.[1] From Virginia Woolf to Walt Disney, from Grace Slick to the cyber generation, the adventures of Alice have woven their way into the intertext of Western lives and letters.[2]

As for *Peter Pan*, the play is one of the longest running on the English stage, attempts at sequels to his story have failed to produce closure, and his character has become a veritable leitmotif in contemporary pop psychology. To account for such broad demographics requires more than a theory of individual pathology, or yet of individual genius or facility with language. Not everyone, for example, has his or her own Lolita. Pedophilic desire named, written, becomes too local, too embodied. Even if one were to agree with Gattégno's assessment of the nature of Dodgson's feelings for Alice, one must acknowledge that some sort of alchemical process occurs in the writing of the Alice books that transforms the perversion into something evocative and joyful for all of us. Somewhere between desire and language, somewhere where desire *meets* language, or language meets desire *as itself*, Lewis Carroll and J. M. Barrie have created Alice and Peter Pan to hold a more or less permanent place as signifiers of the modernist desire to preserve the notion of a pristine childhood, marked primarily by a belief that becomes anesthetized or repressed as we grow older. In each case, the writer's commitment to language combines with his desire to create structures in which we feel at home—not a comfy armchair at-homeness, but a naughty "hand in the cookie jar" at-homeness that winks in youthful exuberance at curiosity and transgression.

All this is not to say that Barrie and Dodgson did not experience transgressive, or even perverse, unconscious desires; in fact, from a Freudian standpoint, one can say that we all have such desires as part of our repressed polymorphous sexuality. But in order for his work to evoke such a persistent fascination, the desire of the writer must in each case somehow become the desire of the reader. And in order for these works to have achieved such tremendous popularity with children, as well as such positive sanctions from adults, any scent of a perverse desire in these tales must be firmly repressed. Assuredly, the stories of Peter Pan and Alice are tales of desire. In fact, Dodgson's desire for Alice and Barrie's desire for the Llewellyn-Davies boys (and these real children are simply metonymic in this function) are the single bits of biographical trivia that resonate through the text, acting as the very condition for their existence. But for most of us, a manifest physical desire for a child is unthinkable. To get at how the reader becomes implicated in the desire of the writer, then, we must employ a critical discourse of desire that focuses on the symbolic rather than the literal uses of sex. We find in Lacan a theory of desire that is implicated more in language than in the body. It is a theory which posits desire as the organizing feature of the modern subject—not physical, sexual desire per se, but desire as an opening in the surface of the Other, that which allows, indeed compels, the traversing of distances between oneself and others, between oneself and Otherness. What these writers seem to have done is traverse the distance between the page and the unconscious as Other, creating characters that operate as bridges between the Real and the Symbolic at the level of the Imaginary (rather than the Symptom). It is in these fictional children that Barrie and Dodgson as Carroll locate the terms of desire itself; in Lacan's terms, "Le désir est désir de désir, désir de l'Autre, avons-nous dit, soit soumis à la Loi" (*Ecrits* [Ec], 852).[3] In this chapter, I address the question of where exactly Alice and Peter Pan figure in the structure of desire in their writers, and in so doing, explore how they figure in the desire of the modernist subject, or us as readers.

The *Objet Petit (a)*lice

We'll begin with Carroll. A Lacanian, as opposed to a traditional Freudian, reading of the way desire functions in *Alice through the Looking Glass* is a reciprocally rewarding investment; reading Alice through Lacan provides a new way of looking at Carroll's texts and texts in general, and reading Lacan through Alice continues to open our way into a notoriously difficult theory of the subject. *Alice through the Looking Glass* is enigmatic, linguistically skewed in brilliant and fascinating ways, and (dis)ordered along the lines of deliberate interpretive resistance. It reproduces in the reader the very desires of Alice herself—the desire to know, to understand, and most of all, the desire to know oneself, to *be* oneself. One is certainly tempted, as Hélène Cixous puts it, to "take the whole adventure for a figurative representation of the imaginary construction of self, ego, through reflexive identification, the other side of the mirror never being anything else but this side" (238), but there is something else going on in this mirror, something that suggests a dialectical motion, a repetition, even a retrogression in the movement of Alice as an emerging subject. A desire is at work in this field that is not Alice's; it is this other desire, Carroll's desire in relation to the body of language rather than the body of sexuality, that compels this reading.

Before we proceed with this reading of *Through the Looking Glass*, it will be necessary to lay a bit of groundwork in order to understand the constitution of desire. In a Lacanian scheme, desire is inaugurated with the subject's assumption of lack: "C'est donc plutôt l'assomption de la castration qui crée le manque dont s'institue le désir" (Ec, 852).[4] This lack is inherent in signification. In simplest terms, the word is not the thing, so that whenever we use words to talk about objects or experiences, there is always a gap, a mediation of the referent through language that necessarily makes the referent other than what it is. Lacan uses a bar between the signifier and the signified to symbolize this gap; think of this bar as a little guillotine that severs (castrates) being from meaning. As the subject emerges into signification, she sacrifices being for meaning, thus assuming as the condition of her identity this symbolic castration. Our physical drives get displaced into a rhetoric of desire that can never completely satisfy. The ordinary experiences of not being able to say what we mean, or of not being able to get what we want (or the sense of its being inadequate once we have it), have their roots in this immanent lack in the symbolic structuring of reality. And yet, "accession to the mediation of the symbol is . . . indispensable if the ordering of the world, of things, beings and of life is to be effected" (Lemaire, 78). So, as we have elaborated in earlier chapters, the Lacanian subject comes into being as a result of a series of inevitable losses; the intervention of language as a mediator of desire is both necessary and alienating.

The child subject seems to manage her sense of lack through an active pursuit of a subject position in the Symbolic order where she can assume and pursue her own desire. Although Lacan does not specifically explore the relations of the child to the text, those of us who study children know that the most intense energy of the child is directed toward managing the discursive relationships in her world, using them to manipulate the existential ones. Children know even before they learn to talk that the speech act is what will give them power; accession to the world of language is seen as the greatest good. Once in the Symbolic order, they achieve a sense of mastery over the object; the distance between signified and signifier is a distance that enables the speaker to exercise some control over the way in which the thing is perceived—it turns the raw material of the Real into (some pig!) the Symbolic construction of reality. Literature makes a world that is completely cut off from the phenomenal world of loss and contingency. As one children's literature critic puts it, literature

> conjures up a completely distorted world which is, nonetheless, perfectly organized and absolutely inevitable; a world where things are what they are because words make them so; where the Dong wears a luminous nose in order to find his Jumbly Girl in the dark—for the Dong only acquires his identity when he becomes "The Dong with the Luminous Nose"; once the words

have been pronounced one can no more escape from the spell than one can escape from a dream. (Jan, 58)

Lacan's formulation that "desire is the desire of the other" means, in this sense, that the child desires to enter into the discourse of the big Other, the Symbolic order, that just as the Symbolic order wants her, she wants it. She wants to have an "I."

Once that "I" has been attained, however, the subject is fundamentally nostalgic, positing and then pursuing a sense of wholeness that has been lost and must be recovered—a "pure life instinct, that is to say, immortal life, or irrepressible life, life that has need of no organ, simplified, inde-structible life" (Lacan, *The Four Fundamental Concepts of Psychoanalysis* [FFC], 198). The subject grows into the consciousness of her splitting *as a problem*, rather than as an escape from brute reality or as a grand adventure. The Real, that which escapes symbolization, begins to be courted rather than avoided, because the subject has come to realize experientially the inevitable inade-quacy of the signifiers that stand in for her desire. Since this "Real," this "pure life instinct," is what has been perceived as lost in the coming into being of the subject, the subject obsessively seeks to recover it through the introjection of certain objects that act as representatives of this wholeness. Lacan calls these "*objets petits autres*," meaning, literally, objects with a little otherness. Such an object "represents that part of himself that the individual loses at birth, and which may serve to symbolize the most profound lost object" (FFC, 198).

Let me give an example that will make the function of the *objet a* espe-cially clear. In Shel Silverstein's *The Missing Piece*, a circle with a wedge taken out of it searches far and wide for his "missing piece." He clearly enjoys the search, making up a little song about finding his missing piece, and con-versing with beetles and butterflies along the way. The first "piece" he en-counters tells him that she (the genders here are arbitrarily chosen—I dif-ferentiate only for clarity) is not a missing piece at all, but a piece unto herself, and that even if she were a missing piece, she wouldn't belong to him. After this first encounter, he meets several other pieces that won't do for various reasons—one is too large, one too small, one fits at first but once in place begins to grow and has to be left behind. Finally, he finds his missing piece. She is a perfect fit and is willing to be defined as his "missing piece," so they roll off together. But he notices that with her in place, he rolls too fast to enjoy the journey; he discovers, as Slavoj Žižek reminds us in *Looking Awry*, that desire does not have an object that will satisfy it once and for all, because its main task is to keep itself circulating:

> We mistake for postponement of the "thing itself" what is already the "thing itself," we mistake for the searching and indecision proper to desire what is, in fact, the realization of desire. That is to say, the realization of desire does not consist in its being "fulfilled," "fully satisfied," it consists rather with the reproduction of desire as such, with its circular movement. (7)

The circle decides to remove the missing piece, and he rolls lopsidedly off in the opposite direction, again singing the refrain of his search.

This example is especially apt for many reasons. One is that the *objet a* is in fact perceived as a "missing piece" of one's own body; Kaja Silverman notes that these objects "are not clearly distinguished from the self," that they "derive [their] value from [their] identification with some missing component of the subject's self" (156). So when the first piece asserts her own subjectivity, it is clear that this piece cannot function as an object; she can speak for herself and hence has too much otherness. Another useful point to take from this story is that the pursuit of the *objet a* can be read as the condition for the production of art and the enjoyment of otherness. One of the circle's complaints with the piece filled in is that he can't sing anymore. Also, as the direct result of having a piece missing, the circle couldn't move very fast. He could therefore interact with beetles and smell flowers, and butterflies could land on him. He had a reason to explore otherness through art and through contact, because he was himself lacking.

But the most important lesson from this story concerns the reality of the *objet a*. The "missing piece" is retroactively given. When we meet the figure, he already has the piece taken out of him—for all we know, it was never there to begin with; the shape we see may in fact be the shape he is. But we presume, from what we already know about circles and from what we are told about his condition, that he is really a circle with a piece missing, instead of a shape that happens to have one rounded side and two flat ones. We never see the circle as "whole" until he has "found" what was "missing"; we simply have to take it on faith that the story he tells us is the true one. In the same way, the *objet a* is a retroactive construction of the Symbolic—from the place of language we attempt to insert (though it feels like reinserting) something which "has need of no organ." Because we experience something that we call desire and because that experience of desire is bound up with an experience of lack, we posit retroactively a place where there was no lack, a place of plenitude, a Real beyond the Symbolic.

Which brings us back to Alice. We can see that Carroll sees in her one of these objects that Lacan refers to as *objets petit a*; she represents some element that he perceives as missing from himself.[5] She, like his ideal reflection, exists as a rem(a)inder of self-alienation, as a reminder of lack, but also, in the manner of the *objet a*, as a suggestion of the possibility of its amelioration. In her, lack transcends the physical and is poignantly etched in his psyche as a great aching to preserve an impossible dyadic relationship with the Other. In the Real, and in the Symbolic order, Charles Dodgson and Alice Liddell are separate, oscillating in the asymmetrical grammar and nonrelationship of subject/object, self/other, male/female, adult/child. But in the looking-glass space, in his Imaginary, Dodgson creates both himself and Alice as fictions, as signifiers in the same chain of discourse wherein each will define the other. He makes of himself her echo, the structure of his assumed name eerily echoing her own patronym. In this way, in this contiguous discursive space, he can make Alice function as an object with only "a little otherness" for Carroll, the result being that he refuses his full subjectivity to the same degree that he denies her full objectivity. And by now the reader of feminist criticism may groan, So what else is new? What is new is that Carroll does not participate in the sadistic discourse of the patriarchy in his treatment of Alice. In his "Kant avec Sade," Lacan departs from the traditional definition of the sadist in the following way:

> According to Lacan, the Sadean subject tries to elude his constitutive split, his division, by transferring it onto his other (the victim) and by identifying himself with the object, i.e., by occupying the position of the object-instrument of the will-to-enjoy . . . which is not his own will but that of the big Other. (Žižek, LA, 108)

The traditional narrative of a Daisy Miller or a Moll Flanders or a Tess does exactly this; the narrator, presenting himself as objective about or even sympathetic with his "victim," proceeds to tell her story as if he were simply the neutral "object-instrument" of a patriarchal Symbolic. These women are tormented under the guise of an inevitable "history"; the split inherent in language is passed onto them as a flaw, and they had better die. But what Carroll does with Alice as a linguistic construct must not be read as the sadistic move of the oppressor: Instead of transferring his splitting onto her so that he might tell her story as the narrative of the inevitable history of the girl-child who grows up, flowers, fades, and dies, he attempts to preserve in her the unalienated, undifferentiated self that he is necessarily unable to preserve in himself. He wants to subvert the will of the big Other; he wants to arrest her splitting. Having recognized the implications of his own Symbolic castration, he seeks to save her from hers. The great sadness of Carroll's life (and I speak here of the author-function, not the historical Dodgson) is the inevitability of the formation of Alice's ego, of the territorialization of her body apart from himself, because that will mean that she has assumed into her own body the sexual difference that is the metaphorical indicator of the split subject. *Alice through the Looking Glass*, then, does indeed function as an intricate metaphor of what happens to Alice as she becomes a subject/object, but it is colored by Carroll's increasingly desperate attempts to invert the process. The texts works like the pulsings of desire—the desire of Alice to escape, move forward, and the desire of Carroll to hold her back. He is working from the paradigm of the dyadic, setting himself and his Alice as the two foci for his elliptical Imaginary, expressing as ineffable sadness the self-alienation that allows us to become speaking subjects.

But Alice, even as a construct, insists on becoming a speaking subject, so the most obvious image to begin with in opening up the metaphor is the looking glass itself. And here we are tempted to be simplistic and think, "Ah, the mirror stage," and proceed with an interpretation that runs along the lines of the infant who experiences the joy of perceiving herself as a coherent entity and is both empowered and displaced by her ideal reflection. But this is not Carroll's invitation to Alice. Instead, we have a girl who sees in the mirror everything except herself and responds in the same way she responds to the window: She wants to go beyond it.[6] She wants to enter the Imaginary, but only as a brief step in playing her favorite game, "Let's pretend," where she may symbolize herself as woman and queen and thus enter into the whole Symbolic network of relations. Carroll, on the other hand, wishes her to stay in the Imaginary for a while, to explore that space and see what it offers. As Cixous notes, the character of the looking glass offers an inverted view of the world, where "effect thus becomes the cause of the cause" (238), and the whole miasma of images culminates with the entrance of death into the realm of childhood. This intrusion, she says, makes Carroll a "bit of an ogre" (238–239). What Cixous fails to point out, however, is that Carroll is *writing* Alice (or more precisely, as I will show later, *unwriting* Alice). Symbolic death is what Carroll is trying to save Alice from; it represents the dissolution of organic totality into linguistic fragmentation. The entry into the Symbolic, which is where death enters the story, is our collective death. Instead of allowing it to happen to his Alice, he idealizes her in a way that is painful in its impossibility; that she returns from the other side of the mirror having found nothing by way of self-recognition is the result of Carroll's desire to control her and keep her unself-conscious.

The devices Carroll uses in his attempt to control her development are legion. He mediates Alice through the locus of control that is the text, preserving his version of her in language in the same way he preserves image using his camera. Within that locus, she appears to map herself but is allowed to do so only within several more frames. There is the frame of the dream or vision, of unreality, that is the structure of the story. All action takes place within the dream; the "real" Alice stays in her armchair with her ball of yarn. There is also the frustrating frame of inversion, where effects precede causes and where she can get at a thing only by walking away from it. Within the inverted dream frame, Alice's journey is further circumscribed by the rules of a chess game that dictate her moves as a pawn who will become a queen if she reaches the eighth square.

But the most stifling frame is the elliptical space alluded to earlier, which Carroll has drawn with himself and her as its foci. If she insists on looking into the mirror, he wants to be that which she sees, "a fellow with whom [s]he merges, with whom [s]he identifies" (Lemaire, 78). If she, even as a construct, refuses to remain an object, then he desires her to be "inmixed" with himself as Other. It is primarily this relation that she wants to move beyond, and it is exactly here that Carroll wishes to keep her, almost as much for her own protection as for his desire. He tries desperately to draw her back through the mirror before she even enters the game; every path she takes leads her to the house again. For once she enters into the Symbolic, he knows what will happen. "You're beginning to fade, you know —and then one ca'n't help one's petals getting a little untidy," says a sympathetic rose, mistaking Alice for a flower (Carroll, 123); what one can't help noticing is the ambivalence in the authorial voice here. This is what happens to girl-children when they succumb to the big Other—they fade, they get "untidy," they become objects, they die. All the other flowers make disparaging remarks about Alice, and aggression, a theme which will bubble below the surface throughout the adventure, enters the story as Carroll's desire begins to be frustrated. For Alice has made her beginning—she threatens to pick the flowers if they won't be quiet, as if she were in control of the structuring of reality that they represent. She misrecognizes her position in relation to them, even as they mistake her for a flower; she has entered into the process of self-alienation that comes from knowing oneself through an external image. Carroll made his beginning long ago; he now (mis)recognizes himself as a self-different, alienated subject, and he despairs of this at times to the point of death (Taylor, 83). And even while substituting Alice as the metonymy of his desire, he recognizes that she will not (cannot) accept this position as an object; she *will* be a diacritical self. She is continually frustrated with the nonsubjectivity Carroll offers her; she desperately wants her signifiers to have a signified (cf. MacCannell, 12). There is a recognition on the part of Carroll that seven-year-old Alice is in fact already a subject apart from himself, but it is as if he were trying as hard to keep her self-knowledge repressed as she is to remember it. If he were to be successful, Alice "would be incapable of situating [her]self and other in their respective places. [S]He would be reduced to the level of animal life, [s]he would not, that is to say, have at [her] disposal the common ground through which any human 'relationship' passes" (Lemaire, 78). Carroll is the anti-analyst—trying through the poems, which are just skewed enough to be confusing, to make Alice forget the Symbolic relationships that she has formed on the other side of the mirror, relations that will eventually, necessarily, preclude Dodgson as a socially inappropriate playmate. These poems, which Alice knew so well on the other side of the mirror, are the repositories of her subjectivity; they have educated her into a subject position that will serve the enjoyment of the big Other. Leave them behind, Carroll says, and with them, yourself. Enter this bliss instead. In contrast to the fictional Alice, Dodgson's nostalgia for the dyadic Imaginary leads him to be dissatisfied with the subject positions allowed him by the culture in relation to Alice Liddell (as Humpty Dumpty refuses to be an egg, and the chess pieces refuse to behave like chess pieces), so he substitutes a textual, Imaginary relationship that calls into question both the necessity and the desirability of entry into the Symbolic order. The fact is that he prefers nonmeaning, non-sense, which he as Carroll offers in a multiplicity of voices to an impatient Alice. For Alice, obviously, the Imaginary is a wonderful and fascinating (albeit sometimes terrifying) place to visit, but for the gnat, the White Knight, and the fawn, having no existence outside the looking glass allows them to maintain the fluidity of "respective places." As a result of this tension, these conflicting desires, Alice moves in fits and starts, the pulsings of her desire hammering for signification against the pulsings of Carroll to control and subvert the signifiers, to prevent satisfaction or meaning from occurring. "'The question is . . . which is to be master—that's all'" (Carroll, 163).

Carroll has so designed Alice's adventures that she is never in control of who she is or what she does. Alice, as a pawn, may move only in certain directions and may see only what is in the squares directly adjacent to her. Carroll is showing her the work of the Symbolic, the work of the phallus, which is not the hill toward which Alice is continually drawn, as Cixous suggests, but instead is found in the Rules that govern the Game. In the Symbolic, there will be rules to follow, rules about growing up, about making sense, about what is proper and what isn't. Your movements will be circumscribed by these rules. The reader, who along with Alice is already firmly planted in her desire to function in the Symbolic, is continually confronted with the opposition between sense and nonsense, forcing the work of abandoning our traditional ways of knowing ourselves, and causing us to look elsewhere for meaning, to view ourselves with a different logic, the flattened-out logic of the Imaginary rather than of the Symbolic. On this side of the glass, we often suffer from the delusion that language is transparent; we think we can see the objects in the Sheep's shop by looking directly at them. Carroll offers a continual critique of that type of assumption by subverting the signifiers without removing the fundamental framework within which they exist.

Hence we still seek a certain kind of unified meaning, but we seek it at the peripheries of the discourse, and embedded in the images thereof. There is always a slippage in our language, and that is one of the more important locuses of control for Carroll. Like Amelia Bedelia, the White King takes everything in its strictest literal sense and so of course misunderstands everything. Humpty Dumpty claims that he is the master of words, that they mean only what he wants them to mean, no more, no less. At the same time, he fails to recognize that he is himself an egg, and then—well, we all know what happened to him. Lacan's "excess of signs" is felt throughout Carroll's work as each of Carroll's personae attempt to totalize and contain both themselves and Alice by means of a language that will not behave itself according to any rules that obtain in the Symbolic. Alice wants to use understanding as a means of passage to the next square; Carroll's attempts to stop her are always linguistic puzzles that play in the space between the signified and the signifier. That she is ultimately successful in continuing is dependent less on her decoding some hidden meaning than on her continuing to speak in a way that makes sense to her; she continues to know who she is by relating herself to who she was on the other side of the glass. There, her passage was inevitable:

> "[O]ne ca'n't help growing older."
> "*One* ca'n't, perhaps," said Humpty Dumpty; "but *two* can. With proper assistance, you might have left off at seven." (Carroll, 162)

Carroll, by writing Alice back through the looking glass without any change in herself, offers that "assistance." He wants to show her that growing and aging are not necessary or inevitable; they are merely concessions we make to the version of sanity that plays in the Symbolic.

The only trace of identity that Alice retains through the looking glass is knowing her own name. But naming, another linguistic attempt at totalizing and controlling, also becomes problematic through the looking glass. "'Must a name mean something?' Alice asked doubtfully" (Carroll, 160), prefiguring Saussure's concept of the arbitrariness of signs. Both the daisies and Humpty Dumpty say yes, and scorn Alice for not knowing any better. Later, however, Humpty Dumpty points out that things have names for the convenience of man, for the necessity, according to Lacan, of the rhetorical displacement of desire. The gnat, one of the voices of Carroll, tempts Alice to think of the convenience of going without her name, attempting to seduce her to remain out of the Symbolic, which of course is neither possible nor desirable for Alice. Without her name, she can truly function as an *objet a*, for she will have lost the last designator of her identity in the Symbolic. Hence the most poignant call that Carroll makes to Alice is when she enters the wood where things have no names. Without names, there is no fear, no separation between the fawn and the human child, and they commune like lovers, or like a mother and child. When they emerge from the forest, the fawn experiences the jubilation of once again knowing his own name, but when he realizes also the name of Alice, he flees in fear and Alice wants to cry at her loss, the whole scene echoing the experience of Carroll and his Alice.

Is Carroll an ogre, as Cixous would have us believe? Just the opposite: He wants to keep his Alice in a place that is not marked by the death inherent in the signifier. The irony of his position is that his attempts to thwart the fictional Alice's destiny only make her more impatient to attain it. His own structure, the chess game, also subverts his desire to hold her back, for it is a game that progresses. Unlike Lacan's sadist, he tempts his Alice to move in a direction that would subvert the enjoyment of the big Other. Nor does he, like a traditional "'sadist pervert' assume . . . the position of an absolute subject usurping the right to enjoy, without restraint, the body of the other, reducing him/her to an object-instrument for the satisfaction of his own will" (Žižek, LA, 108). Carroll is a realist in that he recognizes the inevitability of her splitting, but he uses all his linguistic energy to make this self-alienation, which will allow her to become a subject, as disquieting and unsatisfying as possible. Alice's entry into the Symbolic is neither gentle nor jubilant; it is apocalyptic. When she is finally seated at the head of the table as queen, when she has finally entered into the Symbolic network and makes her first demand, Carroll does not give her up. Instead, he writes chaos and frustration into her story and brings her back through the mirror unchanged, a seven-year-old trying to make her kitten, not herself, symbolize the queen. She has stories to tell, but she is not a speaking subject. Since he cannot persuade her to remain with him in the looking glass, he brings her back to a place where the whole dream might begin again. But he removes even her identity as the dreamer of her own dream, finally succeeding in confining her to be part of his elliptical space:

> "He's dreaming now," said Tweedledee: "And what do you think he's dreaming about?"
> Alice said, "Nobody can guess that."
> "Why, about *you*!" Tweedledee exclaimed, clapping his hands triumphantly. "And if he left off dreaming about you, where do you suppose you'd be?"
> "Where I am now, of course," said Alice.
> "Not you!" Tweedledee retorted contemptuously. "You'd be nowhere. Why, you're only a sort of thing in his dream!" (Carroll, 145)

As long as Carroll doesn't leave off dreaming about Alice, as long as he keeps her tucked away in his Imaginary, she will be denied otherness and subjectivity and will ever remain the *objet (a)*lice, cause of his desire.

The Neverland of *Jouissance*

Just as Alice gives us a way of thinking of the relation of the *objet a* to the subject's desire, so *Peter Pan* offers an equally vivid and sustained picture of the subject's relation to *jouissance*. Bruce Fink points out that our first impression of *jouissance* comes from our relation to the mother: "We can imagine a kind of *jouissance* before the letter, before the institution of the symbolic order (J^1)—corresponding to an unmediated relation between mother and child, a *real* connection between them—which gives way before the signifier, being canceled out by the operation of the paternal function" (LS, 60). In the course of normal development, *jouissance* as mother-child unity is renounced in favor of existence in the Symbolic. But Peter Pan is the boy who never grew up. He confides to Wendy that he ran away the day he was born because he heard his parents discussing what he would be when he grew up. "'I don't want ever to be a man,' he said with passion. 'I want always to be a little boy and to have fun'" (Barrie, *Peter Pan*, 43). Instead of existing in the Symbolic, then, he lives in Neverland, because he has refused to renounce his *jouissance*.

Because Barrie's representation of Neverland is probably one of the most successful pictures in literature of the unconscious, I will quote it in full:

> I don't know whether you have ever seen a map of a person's mind. Doctors sometimes draw maps of other parts of you, and your own map can become intensely interesting, but catch them trying to draw a map of a child's mind, which is not only confused, but keeps going round all the time. There are zigzag lines on it, just like your temperature on a card, and these are probably roads in the island; for the Neverland is always more or less an island, with astonishing splashes of colour here and there, and coral reefs and rakish-looking craft in the offing, and savages and lonely lairs, and gnomes who are mostly tailors, and caves through which a river runs, princes with six elder brothers, and a hut fast going to decay, and one very small old lady with a hooked nose. It would be an easy map if that were all; but there is also first day at school, religion, fathers, the round pond, needlework, murders, hangings, verbs that take the dative, chocolate-pudding day, getting into braces, say ninety-nine, threepence for pulling your tooth yourself, and so on; and either these are part of the island or they are another map showing through, and it is all rather confusing, especially as nothing will stand still. (18–19)

A mixture of Thing representations and signifiers, this unconscious could be said to be both Freudian and Lacanian. Two things mark it as more Lacanian than Freudian, however. One is its connection to the Symbolic. Neverlands vary with the individual, Barrie says, "but on the whole the Neverlands have a family resemblance, and if they stood still in a row you could say of them that they have each other's nose, and so forth" (19). Since the

Lacanian unconscious is made up of the discourse of the Other, it is both idiosyncratic and "public," so to speak. The signifiers contained therein are the ones provided by the child's milieu, hence children's unconsciouses could be said to have a family resemblance. The second feature that distinguishes this version of the unconscious as Lacanian is its connection to the mother. "It is the nightly custom of every good mother after her children are asleep to rummage in their minds and put things straight for next morning, repacking into their proper places the many articles that have wandered during the day" (18). Hence the mothers exercise some limited form of control in the structuring and filling in of the child's unconscious. In Barrie's formulation, the mother tidies up the child's mind, relegating unpleasantness to deep corners and making sure the "prettier thoughts" are on top. This housecleaning is how Mrs. Darling first encounters Peter Pan.

> Occasionally in her travels through her children's minds Mrs Darling found things she could not understand, and of these quite the most perplexing was the word Peter. She knew of no Peter, and yet he was here and there in John and Michael's minds, while Wendy's began to be scrawled all over with him. The name stood out in bolder letters than any of the other words, and as Mrs Darling gazed she felt that it had an oddly cocky appearance. (19–20)

The fact that Peter appears as a word in Barrie's 1911 text, rather than as an image, anticipates Lacan's assertion that the unconscious is made up of signifiers. For Wendy, Peter Pan becomes a signifier for *jouissance* itself.

As a speaking subject, Wendy has, of course, been castrated, which means that she herself has renounced some of her primordial *jouissance*. But not all of it. We find in Peter Pan a signifier that embraces several different kinds of Lacanian *jouissance*. The first kind is the mother-child unity that we have already discussed. But other kinds of *jouissance* emerge after the letter, each of them figured through Peter Pan. One, of course, is that which belongs to sexual pleasure. Wendy's attempts to seduce Peter Pan meet with incomprehension on his part. He doesn't know what a kiss is, and he doesn't understand why TinkerBell is so intensely jealous of Wendy. But that he is connected to sexual *jouissance* is made plain in subtle ways. For Barrie, the capacity for sexual *jouissance* inevitably dries up after marriage. He describes Mrs. Darling in the following way: "Her romantic mind was like the tiny boxes, one within the other, that come from the puzzling East, however many you discover there is always one more; and her sweet mocking mouth had one kiss on it that Wendy could never get, though there it was, perfectly conspicuous in the right-hand corner" (13). When she married, Mr. Darling "got all of her, except the innermost box and the kiss. He never knew about the box, and in time he gave up trying for the kiss" (14). The box and the kiss suggest two different kinds of *jouissance*. The box represents sexual pleasure, with which Mr. Darling is apparently too self-centered to even concern himself. Through Wendy's seduction attempts, we see that on at least one level, Peter is the signifier for Wendy's sexual *jouissance*. But Barrie's description of the grown-up Wendy further implicates Peter in her married life: "Wendy was a married woman, and Peter was no more to her than a little dust in the box in which she had kept her toys" (210). We can infer that Wendy's husband, like her father, knows little if anything about her "box" of sexual pleasure.

The kiss, on the other hand, represents something Lacan calls "feminine" *jouissance*. This is the *jouissance* that women have but know nothing about, according to Lacan. The reason they know nothing about it is that it is inimical to knowledge as we currently conceive it. Knowledge is a Symbolic order affair, and feminine *jouissance* is outside the Symbolic. Because of their complete enclosure by the Symbolic, men cannot access feminine *jouissance*, though they sense its presence. This is why Wendy's father cannot get the kiss and eventually gives up trying. Again, Peter Pan is connected to this form of *jouissance* in interesting and multiple ways. When Mrs. Darling questions Wendy about Peter Pan, Wendy's responses are repeatedly followed by the qualification "she didn't know how she knew it, she just knew it" (20–21). But the most compelling connection between Peter Pan and this type of *jouissance* is made through the narrator himself. When Peter Pan appears in the nursery, the narrator says, "If you or I or Wendy had been there we should have seen that he was very like Mrs Darling's kiss" (24). Mrs. Darling herself senses the connection. After Peter has taken the children, Mr. and Mrs. Darling and Nana, the Newfoundland dog who is the children's nurse, go over and over the events of the night of the disappearance, trying to figure out why the children flew away with Peter. They each blame themselves until finally, they blame Peter. "'That fiend!' Mr Darling would cry, and Nana's bark was the echo of it, but Mrs Darling never upbraided Peter; there was something in the right-hand corner of her mouth that wanted her not to call Peter names" (27).

The final type of *jouissance* that *Peter Pan* illustrates is, to borrow a phrase from Barthes, "the pleasure of the text." Renouncing one's *jouissance* does not mean that it disappears. Rather, it circulates in the Other, kind of like a sick-day pool. Some employers ask that you donate one of your paid sick days to a pool so that if someone else requires more time off than she was originally allotted, she can draw from the pool. To access the pool you must first have contributed to it. You sacrifice some of your *jouissance* in order to access it through the mediation of the Other. One difference between the sacrifice of *jouissance* and the sick-day pool is in the proportions. With the sick-day pool, you sacrifice a little to get, potentially, a lot. The exact opposite happens with *jouissance*. You sacrifice your *jouissance* and are left with a pale memory of its pleasures. Another difference is that the sacrifice is not optional or voluntary if you want to function in the Symbolic. But you can access the *jouissance* circulating in the Other through art, music, and so on. For instance, Wendy tells stories about Peter Pan, which is an attempt to reclaim *jouissance* through fantasy. But because Wendy is still a child, her fantasies come true for her and her brothers.[7] Her *jouissance* is still close enough to her to pay a visit. What's more, not only does it leave a residue behind—Peter Pan's shadow—but also Peter comes back for it. Wendy touches Peter Pan, sews his shadow, and flies with him to the land he inhabits, the land of *jouissance*.

What precipitates this flight is the bumbling intervention of her father. Having humiliated himself in front of his children, he ejects Nana from the nursery, leaving the children unprotected. Oddly enough, Nana provides a tether to middle-class respectability in the Darling household. It is she who makes sure that Michael looks his best for company, and it is she who ensures that the children get to school on time. She covers over Mr. Darling's ineffectualness as a provider—a respectable middle-class household requires a nurse and servants, but the Darlings are too poor. Nana functions quite adequately as the nurse, despite the fact that she is a dog. Part of her job in preserving respectability is to keep Peter Pan out of the house. But Mr. Darling misses her function as his support and, in expelling her, leaves his children vulnerable to captivation by their own unlawful desire. In the Disney version, which shows great insight on this point, Mr. Darling issues a direct injunction for Wendy to grow up, telling her that this will be her last night in the nursery. Mr. Darling is presented as a rather clumsy boob, but his position is nonetheless the position of the paternal function. As such, he lays down the law that would effectively drive a wedge between Wendy and her mother, between Wendy and her *jouissance*. Her flight to Neverland is thus precipitated by her rebellion against the Law of the Father. In the written text, the cause of her flight is more subtle. What she has just seen of her father is that he is a "cowardy custard." He is vain and pompous, and, when humiliated, becomes petty and mean-spirited. When she meets Peter, on the other hand, he seems gallant and brave, and he is highly complimentary of girls in general. Thus it is natural that she should choose this noncastrated boy over her castrated father. Escape with Peter to Neverland means escape from the fate of her mother.

Wendy finds out, however, that Neverland is not without its own terrors. In fact, the children's experiences in Neverland teach us much about the nature of unconscious *jouissance*. The experiences are not altogether pleasurable. *Jouissance* as such is beyond the pleasure principle; it is what is most exciting to the subject, and what is most exciting often goes beyond pleasure into pain and danger. Upon their initial approach to the island, they are shot at by pirates: "Thus sharply did the terrified three learn the difference between an island of make-believe and the same island come true" (66). The children are repeatedly faced with real danger on the island—but Peter Pan is always there to save them, despite the fact that he too is continually under threat by Captain Hook. The presence of Captain Hook in a space of *jouissance*, of precastration mother-child unity, seems out of place. Captain Hook, with his missing limb, is, after all, a castrated father. In this fantasy, it is he who is constantly trying to kill Peter Pan, while Wendy staunchly believes in Peter's invulnerability. This tension replicates the tension in the Darling nursery. Mr. Darling is a bumbling, blustering fool—castrated from the beginning. Wendy senses that he is a danger to her but nonetheless believes, perhaps because he has never gotten her mother's kiss, that he will be ultimately unable to completely stifle her *jouissance*. She is, of course, right.

Castrated though he may be, the father nevertheless is the one who imposes the prohibition of *jouissance*. But *Peter Pan* establishes our sense of the impossibility behind the prohibition. Despite the fact that Peter Pan and the Lost Boys refused to renounce their *jouissance* and hence presumably live in a state of primordial excitation and enjoyment, they still lack (and desire) a mother. It turns out that the point of reclaiming *jouissance* has never been about preserving a bodily unity, a relation in the Real, with the mother. The Lost Boys are lost precisely because they have refused to (re)find the mother in the Symbolic. They present the reader with the knowledge that the mother is always already lost. The fantasy of the father's prohibition is that if only he hadn't prohibited my union with the mother, she and I could have remained happy together. Peter Pan, in refusing the prohibition and nonetheless having no mother, shows us the impossibility that the fantasy masks.

The incest prohibition does have its compensations, however. Only the sister and the mother are foreclosed, after all, and the oedipalized subject may refind some bodily *jouissance* in the sexual union with a nonrelated female. But Peter Pan has chosen not to go through the oedipal stage. Wendy desires him sexually; upon their first meeting, she asks for a kiss and offers one, as well. In Neverland, she sees herself as the mother of the Lost Boys, with Peter as her spouse. She is seeking *jouissance* after the letter, sexually as well as textually. But since Peter Pan has refused this line of development, he doesn't understand her innuendos at all. TinkerBell, of course, does. Not at all maternal, she nevertheless inhabits the land of *jouissance* as Peter Pan's constant companion, suggesting that the sexual nature of *jouissance* is never far from its more innocent face, even if the innocent face cannot recognize it.

In the end, Peter Pan illustrates perfectly the link between *jouissance* and the death drive. *Jouissance* is that point where life and death fuse. Peter Pan can live there because he is, in Symbolic reality, a dead child. The part of the Peter Pan fantasy that Mrs. Darling remembers is about how he goes with dead children part of the way on their journey so that they won't be frightened. Peter Pan represents the loss of memory and a kind of arbitrary cruelty, both of which are linked to death. When Wendy asks if he remembers their adventures, she is dismayed to learn that he doesn't even remember Captain Hook. "'I forget them after I kill them,' he replied carelessly" (209). Wendy begins to realize the urgency of getting her brothers home when Michael shows signs of forgetting his mother. Neverland turns out to be, after all, a very violent place, a place that kills memory, a place of *jouissance* but not of joy. Ultimately, Wendy grows up. "You need not be sorry for her. She was one of the kind that likes to grow up. In the end she grew up of her own free will a day quicker than other girls" (210). Peter returns for her years later, after she has grown and has a girl of her own. Despite the fact that "[s]omething inside her was crying, 'Woman, woman, let go of me'" (214), she does not let go, because she has chosen to remain in the Symbolic, to seek her *jouissance* after the letter through the stories she tells her daughter. With some regret, she allows her daughter to go with Peter, and the legacy of the *jouissance* of Peter Pan gets passed down, significantly, through daughter after daughter after daughter.

CHAPTER FIVE

"I Never Explain Anything"

Children's Literature and Sexuation

Of the mandates issued by the Symbolic regarding identity formation, the most stringent, and the most embattled in current theoretical debate, is the assumption of a specific gendered identity. We are interpellated into gendered roles even before our birth; parental and societal expectations vary according to the pinks or blues of our layettes. These expectations seem to predetermine that our gender will be but a matter of simple correspondence to our anatomy, but as we know from experience, there is nothing simple about becoming a boy or a girl. Certainly, the call from the Other toward maleness or femaleness begins with the doctor's pronouncement, either at birth or with a prenatal test: "It's a boy!" or "It's a girl!" But the working out of that pronouncement depends on the subject recognizing him- or herself as that thing called a boy or a girl. He or she self-identifies as a gendered subject largely by taking on or rejecting the characteristics that identify boys and girls in our culture. As we have noted, such a gesture is performative—in *recognizing* myself in the role of boy or girl, I in fact engender myself thereby.[1] In other words, gender is first ascribed to the subject by the Other, and then assumed by the subject as a sort of role that comes to feel natural or essential.

The problem, socially and psychically speaking, is that the assumption of one's gender is generally thought to coincide with anatomical and genetic information and differences. People with penises are boys, and people without penises are girls. Notice that I could have positivized the distinction, saying that girls are "people with breasts," or "people with vaginas." But in our ocularcentrist culture, the perception is that little girls have neither, and given the relatively late appearance of gender markers such as menstruation, pubic hair, and breasts, girls are traditionally thought to assume their gender according to the logic of the haves and have-nots. Indeed, the popular understanding of Freud's entire theory of psychosexual development is based on the ideas that boys have something that they are afraid to lose (hence castration anxiety), and that girls lack something that they want (penis envy).

One of the key problems with Freud's schema (aside from its probable falseness in any empirical way) is that it sets up a binary opposition between the terms "male" and "female." Freud saw sexual difference almost exclusively in terms of the binary active/passive, the male assuming the active role in sex, and therefore in life, and the female assuming passive positions. As assertive subjects, both boys and girls necessarily and structurally reject the passive position, thus rejecting femininity as such. This rejection of femininity is what the Freudian system of gender is built on. Obviously, the content of this binary opposition is unacceptable as a generalization. But contemporary theory calls into question the structure of binarism itself. It is by now a commonplace of deconstruction that binary relationships really have only one term. The subordinate term is defined only in opposition to the dominant one. The binary opposition male/female should really be read male/not male. Culturally and historically speaking, male is always the dominant term: Female has no definition other than not male.[2] Lacanian theory (and children's literature, as we shall see) only accepts this stance to a certain point. While other discourses hide their phallocentrism behind words like "objectivity" and "rationalism," Lacan openly admits that "normal" is nothing more than code for "nor-male" or the norm of the male.[3] But he also insists, via Saussurean linguistics, that there are no positive terms, even in a binary opposition. That is, no term, "male" or "female" in this case, is defined or identified by its positive characteristics. Instead, every term is constructed and defined according to its relation or its position within a system. These admissions initially made Lacanian theory attractive to feminists. But many have abandoned psychoanalysis because of feminist thinkers like Irigaray and Chodorow, who cite Lacan's inevitable retreat into phallocentric discourse. On the one hand, Lacan's acknowledgment that sexual difference constitutes a (if not *the*) founding problem of the human sciences is quite a coup for feminists, because it brings to the fore an issue that is elided in other theoretical and scientific discourses. Psychoanalysis at least recognizes and poses as a problem its phallocentrism, unlike other disciplines. On the other hand, Lacan's reliance on the phallus as a key signifier continues to alienate feminists, forcing many of them to abandon psycho-analysis.[4] While Lacanian theory promises the possibility of a truly feminine position, its reliance on a signifier so closely related to the male organ makes the articulation of such a position impossible.

Recent expositors of Lacanian theory disagree with this feminist critique, mostly because they take him seriously when he says that the phallus is a signifier with only contingent links to its anatomical counterpart, the penis. Lacan *does* articulate both a masculine and a feminine position in his theoretical model, and they are not, as in Freud, opposed to one another. Nor are they in any way biologically determined. Rather they are each defined with relation to a third term. A person has a masculine or a feminine structure according to how he or she is situated with respect to the Name of the Father. Those who would seek to explicate and rehabilitate Lacan's theories of sexuation turn to discussions of symbolic logic and Kantian antinomies to make their point that Lacan has been consistently misread, ill-used, and widely misunderstood.[5] I think we can render his system of sexuation intelligible not by taking that route, but by revisiting some old textual friends, genuine male and female subjects whom we have always known, and who have, as a result of our early integration of them and interpellation by them, helped us construct our own gendered identities. Discussing Lacan's formulas alongside characters developed by P. L. Travers, Astrid Lindgren, and L. M. Montgomery has the added advantage of giving body to the theory, of helping us see what a man and a woman might look like in Lacanian terms.

Since we can't assume from cultural or anatomical markers what gender a person inhabits, we might begin by examining what masculine and feminine subjects have in common: All subjects are castrated. As we noted in chapter 1, to some degree, all subjects are under the sway of the Name of the Father, having negotiated alienation, separation, and, in some cases, traversal of the fundamental fantasy. All have been alienated in and through language, barred from the desire of the (m)Other, and brought into existence as a defense against the gap introduced by the father's prohibition. Each subject exists in a particularized relationship with three separate orders: the Real, which is the realm of what remains unsymbolized and is by definition unsymbolizable; the Imaginary, which is the realm of dyadic identification between self and other (small o) and self *as* other; and the Symbolic, which is the realm of the big Other, the Law, where the subject first asserts himself or herself as an "I" in a syntagmatic chain with other subjects. Each realm carries the other two with it, and the way they interact at any given moment constitutes the subject at that moment.

My emergence from the Real of bodies is marked by my recognition of difference; in a jarring instant, I realize that I not only see, but that I am also and always being seen by the Other. In that moment when I have a sense of the Other looking at me, I become both object and subject, annihilated as all-seeing "objective" eye at the same time I come into existence as a subjective I, which is a fanciful way of saying that my specific, particularized subjectivity is precipitated by an encounter with the Other. What I am faced with in the encounter is a hole, a space brought on by the see/being-seen dialectic. As Lacan puts it, "*You never look at me from the place from which I see you*" (FFC, 103). A subject's response to that hole is what sets the trajectory that will determine his or her gender. According to Chaitin, males and females respond to two different flaws perceived in the Symbolic order: "The incompleteness of the masculine is the lack of the referent, of a Real Presence that would act as the foundation beneath the system; the inconsistency of the feminine is the impossibility of totalizing the terms within the system due to the pure differentiality of the signifier" (Chaitin, 230). In short, the male, taking the hole to indicate the incompleteness of the Symbolic, seeks to cover over that hole, to insert himself as a sort of plug or bridge that can fill or suture it. The female, on the other hand, has no set response. For her, lack is registered as the inconsistency introduced by the fact that the signifier is not self-identical. Not only is there no referent, but also there is no agreement regarding the signified for any particular signifier. Recognizing this dimension of lack, she can fill the hole if she wants to, that is, she can act as if the problem of incompleteness can be solved. But—and this is the important distinction—she doesn't *have* to. Her fantasy isn't necessarily one of closure or of the totalization of meaning. She may leave open the hole in the Other, may occupy a space on either side of it. The impossibility of knowing completely does not represent a challenge or a site of angst for her; rather it is a space, alternately, of anxiety and play.

Lacan works out his theory of sexuation in *Seminar XX* by elaborating two different ways of relating to the Other. The masculine position maps onto the Symbolic. Thus the split subject that we have been talking about all along—that subject who has emerged completely from the Real and taken up a position within the Symbolic—is in fact a masculine structure. The Symbolic phallus is important to the construction of masculinity. It is "the signifier of that which is worthy of desire, of that which is desirable"

(Fink, LS, 102). That it is on the side of the masculine Symbolic is a cultural and historical, rather than a structural, feature. In Western cultures, those things that are desirable and hence occupy the position of the phallus (e.g., power, capital, sex) tend only to be accessible to and through the masculine position. The feminine position, on the other hand, has closer affinities with the Real than with the Symbolic. Lacan represents Woman as a generic category with the symbol *La*, but he puts a slash through it to indicate that there is no such thing as Woman, categorically speaking. Individual women exist, act, and have effects, but they are not definable as a unified category the way men are, for reasons that will become clear. The feminine position also aligns with the *objet a* and a rather confusing symbol, $S(\bar{A})$. $\bar{A}$ stands for the Other as incomplete, marked by lack; $S(\bar{A})$ is a signifier of that lack. Now, by definition, that lack in itself cannot be signified. So to say that $S(\bar{A})$ is a signifier of the lack in the Other is a bit of an impossibility, or at least a contradiction in terms. Nonetheless, as Fink points out, we do find signifiers for that lack, privileged signifiers like "God" or "art" or even "magic," that explain everything and nothing at the same time.[6]

This is not the only impossibility that we live on the surface of, according to Lacan. For if, as he says, men and women are defined by two different relationships to the big Other, then on what terms do they get together? In other words, how do men and women possibly partner with each other if they are operating in two different registers? One answer that seems borne out by his theoretical model is that they don't. The male as a split subject couples with the *objet a*, that is, he couples with a fantasized object that he projects onto an other who (or which) serves as a prop. The woman, on the other hand, partners alternately with the Symbolic phallus, which, as mentioned earlier, she has access to only through a man, and with the signifier of the lack in the Other. We shall see how these partnering relations work in our discussion of *Mary Poppins* and *Pippi Longstocking*. What is important to note is that men and women never partner with each other. This is what Lacan means when he says, "There is no sexual relation."

George Banks and Mary Poppins

To be a man in Lacanian terms, that is, to have a masculine structure, means that one is completely submitted to the phallic function, the Law that has separated the subject from his or her desire, imposing itself as the limit of that desire. He is neither master of language, nor partnered with it, but is rather its outcome or effect and, in many cases, its dupe. His partner is not Woman either, but rather a fantasized object that covers over any inconsistency or any incompleteness in that all-important big Other—the Symbolic order in which man moves and dwells and has his being. In Lacan's words, "It is through the phallic function that man as a whole acquires his inscription" (*Seminar XX* [XX], 79).

To show what that might look like, let us turn to George Banks, the father of Jane and Michael Banks and the accidental employer of Walt Disney's version of Travers's *Mary Poppins*.[7] His very name indicates the relation he has to the signifier—he is a banker, and his name is Banks. Hence his being is wholly determined by the signifier's symbolic mandate. Disney is at great pains to show how removed George Banks is from the "real" of his situation—Banks builds a wall of words to distance himself from what is really going on in his life and to position himself closer to an idealized life of peace and privilege. We first encounter Banks as he is returning from work. The success of his privileged object—capital—enables him to blithely ignore the adverse "weather report" he gets from Admiral Boom. He then exchanges pleasantries and performs a traditionally masculine function for Katie Nana, complimenting her on her appearance and helping her with her luggage, oblivious to the fact that he is helping her to leave him in the lurch after she has lost his children at the park. His first song further emphasizes the origins and directions of his fantasy structure. He relates himself to king and country: "It's grand to be an Englishman in 1910. King Edward's on the throne; it's the age of men." He then turns the relation into one of identity: "I'm the lord of my castle, the sovereign, the liege," transforming his middle-class and ultimately precarious position into one of entitlement and privilege. "I treat my subjects—servants, children, wife— with a firm but pleasant hand. Noblesse oblige." The day-to-day workings of his household are also fantasized. His wife is continually running off to woman's suffrage rallies, a cause that "infuriates Mr. Banks," while his children seem to spend most of their time torturing and escaping from their nannies. But in Banks's mind, his house runs on a precise and orderly schedule. "Consistent is the life I lead," he proclaims, while the audience winks, knowing that his life is anything but consistent. That it never has been is evidenced by the fact that the children have run away from their nanny four times in the past week, and that in recent months the Bankses have been through six nannies, who have all been "unqualified disasters."

At every turn, Banks seeks to "construct [his] phallic letter, the single trait (S_1) that endows [him] with a limited identity" (Chaitin, 224). He emphatically limits his relation to other perspectives and disavows anything that might open his identity to question, that might bring him face to face with the hole he is busily suturing. When he discovers his children are missing, he takes blustering control of the situation, trying to restore the order he so craves. His actions are of course overblown and unwarranted, but as he says, "Kindly do not try to cloud the issue with facts!" He ignores the havoc wreaked by the admiral's time-gun, insisting only that the piano be tuned, because "when I sit down to an instrument, I expect to have it in tune." "But George," his wife, Winifred, objects, "you don't play!" "That, Madam, is entirely beside the point!" He congratulates himself on taking control of the nanny situation and on delivering his children from "all this slipshod, sugary female thinking," misrecognizing that his employment of Mary Poppins has been completely engineered by Poppins herself. Banks's master signifier is "Englishman," with secondary signifiers of "provider," "leader," and "man in control." He protects these to the extreme by partnering only with his own fantasized objects, and so ignoring the otherness of the Other, here understood as the feminine embodied in Mary Poppins, the real world around him, and the otherness of his own children.

One of the keys to George Banks's existence in the Symbolic is the presence of the elder Mr. Daws. The condition that allows man to be wholly subject to Symbolic castration is that there exists one man who is wholly exempt from it. This man is Freud's primordial father. He is characterized by the fact that he is not castrated, that is, he is not cut off from any woman/pleasure/enjoyment by any social taboo. Nothing is denied him. Of course, such a person cannot really exist, for existence in Lacanian terms is a post-castration position. But the fantasy of every (castrated) male is that there is a primal father—a figure who has access to all women, mother and sister included, as well as to anything else he wants. For the man, this figure is his limit; masculine desire never goes beyond the desire of this primal father. Mr. Daws occupies this position in Banks's fantasy and reminds us once again that when we talk about the phallic function, we are speaking in structural terms rather than in "natural" or anatomical ones. The object that will not be denied Mr. Daws is not a woman, but capital itself—as we shall see in the example of Michael's tuppence. Capital, occupying the position of the phallus, is the logical signifier of desire for someone named Banks, and he who is perceived to have unrestrained access to it is of course the equivalent of the primordial father. Disney chooses to foreground the insubstantiality of this particular construction of Banks through the wondrously articulate body of Dick Van Dyke. Van Dyke's Mr. Daws appears so amazingly fragile and unstable that when Banks introduces him to Michael as a "giant in the world of finance," Michael can do nothing but scrunch up his face in disbelief. He does not see Mr. Daws through the same lens as do his father and the rest of the board members, who are constantly on the alert to keep the old man erect. When Mr. Daws seizes the unconvinced Michael's tuppence and Michael attacks him and grabs it back, George Banks's world literally erupts into chaos. In Lacanian terms, the hole in the Other has been revealed, threatening the disintegration of the Symbolic order itself.

Banks is then forced to confront the fact that his world is organized around his own fantasy. This is what it means to say that man's partner is the *objet a*. Banks's enjoyment of his position in the world, his wife, his children, is not based on them as they are, but on them as he wants them to be. He is completely consumed by his role in the Symbolic. Hence the absurdity of the ways he is taken down—turning his umbrella inside out, punching out the crown of his hat, and ripping the flower from his buttonhole—are revealed as not absurd at all, but rather as perfectly apt. His Symbolic façade is stripped away, but since that constitutes all that he is, it cannot really be called a façade. The one piece of the Real that tethers him, and that he uses his fantasy to maintain a proper distance to, returns in the guise of Michael's tuppence. Initially, Banks attempts to refuse the encounter with the tuppence as Real by insisting on its status as a signifier. When Michael says he wants to use it to feed the birds, his father joins with the other officers of the bank in dismissing such a notion as "poppycock." But tuppence wisely invested in their bank, as they sing in their big production number, leads to nothing less than the stability and preeminence of the British Empire: "While stand the banks of England, England stands. When fall the banks of England, England falls." The tuppence is linked to an entire fantasy of capitalism and colonization—railways through Africa, shipyards, the mercantile, fields of ripening tea—and as in colonization, all the guises of the *objet a* are in service of the avoidance of an encounter with the Other, which is the modus operandi of the male. But Michael's retrieval of the tuppence interrupts the process of its complete co-optation through signification. Had he not grabbed it, it would have literally disappeared and reappeared as a symbol, a statement of account; the letter would have killed the thing. But he keeps it circulating as itself. After chaos has erupted and been contained, the children offer the tuppence to their father. "Will that make everything all right?" they ask. It is as if they sense they have violated something essential to him, they have made him know what he cannot know— his own lack of being—and they, out of love, want to help him plug the hole again. But of course the unconscious has its own plans, and their reintroduction of the tuppence has exactly the opposite effect they intend. Instead of suturing the hole, the tuppence keeps it open by continually returning as Real.

Hence the tuppence functions as one of those little bits of the Real that circulate and force us to realign our position vis-à-vis the Symbolic. When it returns as he reaches in his pocket after being taken down, Banks takes into himself the hole that it formerly revealed in the bank/Symbolic and indulges in a bit of personal chaos. He begins to laugh uncontrollably, tell jokes, and talk nonsensically, effectively dissolving Mr. Daws in his function as primordial father and sole master of enjoyment. He realizes in that instant what his fantasy has been covering over: "As it turns out, with due respect, when all is said and done, there's no such thing as *you*!" he says to Mr. Daws. Words exist. But the primordial father does not. The momentary failure of the paternal metaphor/phallic function manifests itself in some Real phenomenon—in this case, the old man dies. Banks tells him a joke that effectively dispatches him to his proper place—the place of the mortal, castrated male (he dies laughing, presumably encountering humor/the unconscious/his own split for the first time in his life).

Banks's ability to encounter the tuppence results directly from his association with Mary Poppins, the Other in yet another guise. From our very first sighting of Mary Poppins, we begin to get a sense that we are dealing with something not wholly explicable. The children see her floating toward them and wonder who she is. Feminist critic Chris Cuomo discusses Mary Poppins as a failed feminist, someone who is ultimately unsuccessful in subverting or undermining the male power structure, because all she does is reinstate George, "the failed patriarch," at the head of his family. Cuomo begins her essay by observing that young Jane Banks recognizes and validates her reading by saying, "Perhaps it's a witch." Cuomo interprets this comment as exactly right. Mary Poppins is a witch—a good witch but, nevertheless, a witch. But Cuomo is precisely wrong, in her details and her interpretation of them, in a way that proves crucial under this analysis. It is not *Jane* who thinks Mary Poppins is a witch, but *Michael*. He, a little man in training, tries to place her under a traditional male-order category—witch. Jane, on the other hand, refuses that simple rendering of Mary Poppins.

"Witches have brooms," she says, by way of dismissing Michael's notion. That is, witches are witches because their power comes from a broom/phallus. They are a male fantasy, a woman with male "powers," uncontrollable and therefore menacing. Mary Poppins does not fit that category, any more than she fits any of Cuomo's definitions, and Jane, unlike Michael, is reluctant to categorize her at all. The problem is that Cuomo's particular feminist perspective actually reinscribes George's masculine perspective on events and people. Jane offers the only possible description of the female subject: "It's the person." "Person" suggests individuality, distinction. Its plural is not "people," but "persons"—a group wherein each subject retains a distinct, countable identity. Now, to be counted, each woman must have a proper name, which Mary Poppins has. But to place things or to allow oneself to be placed in a category suggests the tendency to universalize, to "judge things by their appearance," something Mary Poppins herself warns against. Even her tape measure takes the measure of individuals rather than generalizing them under the empirically verifiable category of height.

Banks, under the universalizing tendency that characterizes the male subject, always judges things by the way they appear to him. His fantasized role as master of the reality to which he is really subject is underscored by the way he handles the hiring of Mary Poppins. His ideal nanny is masculine in structure. She too must be rightly identified with England; she "must be a general; the future Empire lies within her hands. And so the person that we need to mold the breed is a nanny who can give commands." But Disney, in a particularly memorable and brilliant scene, shows the insubstantiality of Banks's fantasy by having all the nannies that correspond to his vision blow away. They lack substantiality because they are Banks's symptom, and the entire story is about to turn into the reformation of George Banks. He is about to take a major detour into the feminine. He will, of course, remain marked by masculine structure and be reintegrated into the Symbolic identity mandate that he had originally claimed as his own, but not until he has encountered a woman in her particularity, a woman who is not his symptom. His inability to change in any fundamental way suggests the stability of the structure of gender once it has been established. But what happens to George is that he is awakened to the fact that there are two genders— his own, and another that he cannot accommodate or subsume. His world depends on explanations that make sense to him, regardless of facts to the contrary. When he demands that Mary Poppins fit into his structure by explaining what he finds to be an "unseemly hullabaloo," she replies, "Let me be quite clear: I never explain anything." Offering no explanation for herself, escaping any attempt on his part to explain her, she persists as Other.

Not only is she not Woman qua symptom of George Banks, but also she is not defined by or through him at all. He offers his definition of nanny, and any number of applicants fit it. In other words, if we take George Banks as Man, then the nannies he describes would fit the category *La*, or Woman. But for Lacan, Woman is under erasure; she does not exist. The nannies defined by George Banks, in their collectivity, are blown away. Mary Poppins has to be considered in her particularity. The advertisement written by the children is very specific, and every characteristic is answered admirably in the person of Mary Poppins. "Cheery disposition . . . I am never cross. Rosy cheeks . . . obviously." And yet, she *exceeds* the definition even as she fits it. "Play games . . . I think the children will find my games extremely diverting." Her diverting games are not the ones the children were thinking of, but they do not disappoint. Nor are her "sweets" recognizable as such, taking the form of philosophy and medicine that adjusts its flavor and color depending on who takes it. In every instance, Mary Poppins particularizes an attribute in such a way as to enhance, rather than violate or fail to embody, it. In this respect, she could be said to participate in the Symbolic order, be under the umbrella of the paternal metaphor, but not be hemmed in by it.

There is a way of conceiving the Symbolic order as that which fixes reality. It states its own laws and builds it own expectations. We have been calling this its performativity; in a very real sense, the Symbolic performs what it purports to describe. Mary Poppins can in fact obey the laws of the Symbolic, the laws of reality it determines, such as laws of gravity and spacetime. But the important point in this analysis is that she doesn't have to. She can "pop through chalk pavement pictures" and have tea parties in midair. She can understand the speech of animals. She can interact with animated creatures and people just as if they were real, but when she returns to the Banks's nursery, she can become the nanny of George Banks's fantasy—the general, sharply questioning the reality of such shenanigans. She even goes so far as to invoke Symbolic authority when Michael refuses to accept her new Symbolic order persona. "A respectable person like me in a horse race? How dare you suggest such a thing?" she asks indignantly. When Michael insists, Mary Poppins counters with, "Now not another word or I shall have to summon a policeman." A bizarre, nearly incomprehensible response until one begins to realize that Mary Poppins has shifted voluntarily into a Symbolic order role where her "powers" are limited to threats and soothing lullabies.

The fact that she is free to move from one position to the other indicates the possibility of the female subject to partner alternately with the phallic signifier and with the signifier of the lack in the Other. Here is where one of the major bones of feminist contention exists regarding Lacan's theory of sexuation. The argument runs something like this: In a binary system where man is the dominant term and woman is man's Other, there is no suitable partner for woman, because there is no other of the Other. Man can partner with his own fantasized object, but woman can have no partner unless she is acting as or on behalf of a man. Here again, this is partially true. Or more precisely, it is true in the Symbolic. As a woman in the Symbolic, Mary Poppins can be either a maternal or a sexual object, partnering with her child or with her man. Both of these "partnerships" are dominated by masculine desire, and she has no real subject position in either of them. Hence it could be said that she has/is no partner, properly speaking. But Lacan does not stop there. His female subject exists in the Symbolic, but also ex-sists in the Real. To ex-sist, in Lacanian terms, is to have an existence outside Symbolic and Imaginary categories, rendering those categories untotalizable. The female subject doesn't complete relationships in those orders, filling in gaps or smoothing out inconsistencies. Instead, she disrupts them. She *exceeds* Symbolic order reckoning and can therefore, as a true female subject, enact a desire that is neither maternal nor sexual.

What then is Mary Poppins's desire? And can it be generalized to say something about the desire of the female subject? In one sense, no. The point of the crossed-out *La* is that there is no way to account for a generic feminine desire. But in another way, we can say that feminine desire, like masculine desire, is a desire to perpetuate itself. Mary Poppins appears in the lives of the Banks children because they are under threat of being co-opted into George Banks's way of being in the world. Mrs. Banks is only mildly subversive. She proclaims that "though we adore men individually, we agree that as a group they're rather stupid." So while she certainly understands the feminine logic of persons as opposed to the unitary group-think logic of the phallocentric order, she nonetheless seems to spend most of her time attempting to live up to Mr. Banks's ideal image of her. She plays on men's ideas of themselves as capable and in control in order to deliver herself from odious tasks like hiring nannies and tending children. She attempts to effect her subversion of the status quo as a man using male-defined weapons, such as force and flattery. "No more the meek and mild subservients, we. We're fighting for our rights militantly!" With the children, she is, when present, the mother, prone to emotionalism and advocacy. She covers over their flaws and insists that they be heard, even though she knows that they will be patronized. But this is one of the mother's functions in the patriarchy; she is a safe place for children while they learn to submit to their father's rules.

The children, then, have no chance without the help of a genuine female. Mary Poppins, the genuine female, refuses to fulfill any mothering function. To the contrary, she forces the children to confront the hole in the Other, and the hole in themselves. Further, she challenges them *not* to suture the hole, but instead to follow where it might take them. As one might expect, Jane is open to the possibilities, whereas Michael needs prodding and convincing every step of the way. Their initial descriptions, revealed on Mary Poppins's tape measure, are very telling. Michael is "extremely stubborn and suspicious," which he of course denies, but which works its way out in a skeptical attitude toward anything that strikes him as "tricky." Jane is "rather inclined to giggle, doesn't put things away." She is well on her way to becoming a female subject—her giggles indicate a ready acceptance of unconscious irruptions, and her tendency not to put things away indicates an openness to disorder. But Michael needs some sort of vehicle to keep him from completely succumbing to the narrow world inhabited by his father. Mary Poppins finds that vehicle in Michael's tuppence. Here she challenges his father's defining trait, his master signifier, and changes what it means, at least for the children. Her intervention changes Michael's relation to the master signifier as well, and perhaps—seeing as we don't know how Michael turned out—keeps it from being reified.

So what indeed does it mean to be female—to be a response to the "pure differentiality of the signifier" (Chaitin, 230)? It would certainly mean that you were not subjected to the signifier, in the "nor-male" sense of having to use signifiers to create "meaningful" metaphoric coverings for lack. You would be free to use nonsense words as if they made sense—words like "supercalifragilisticexpialidocious" and "chim chiminey." You would be free to hear and understand language even if it didn't sound at all like speech —as, for instance, when a dog comes to tell you of an uncle who has laughed himself into a predicament. You are free to look the Symbolic father in the face and say, "I never explain anything." While on the one hand it might be argued that Mary Poppins is herself a product of the signifier of the lack in the Other—the children "write her up" as the advertisement of an ideal person that would cover over their lack—on the other, it is as if language itself desired her as its partner. After Mr. Banks tears the advertisement up and discards the pieces, they float up the chimney and reassemble themselves of their own volition. The letter, in a Lacanian sense, doesn't fail to reach its destination; it becomes embodied in the figure of Mary Poppins. Unlike George Banks, who *is* his name, no more, no less, Mary Poppins is imagination and desire and magic, her name serving only to inscribe her in an order in which she only partially exists. Unlike the masculine subject, she is not completely under the control of the phallic function. Yet while not all of a woman comes under the sway of the phallic function, nevertheless there is not one woman for whom the phallic function is inoperative. Since there is no exception, there is no rule, no universalizable status for woman. Rather, she is indeterminate with respect to the phallic function. George Banks simply does not know what to make of her.

The Strongest Girl in the World

If Mary Poppins shows us what a subject structured as feminine might look like, Astrid Lindgren's Pippi Longstocking takes us beyond sexuality itself into that space of desire and subjectivity that is called queer. "Queer," in its current academic usage, carries with it certain politic implications regarding antinormative sexualities, in terms of both sexual behavior and sexual identity. Queer theorists distinguish themselves from gay, lesbian, and bisexual thinkers in that they resist both heteronormative and homonormative classifications; they resist norms of all kinds, including the modernist mandate that a person be one thing or another and desire one thing or another, sexually speaking. The queer subject exists in a fluid space, resisting the specificity that comes with sexed identification, and hence, resisting in some ways modernist identity itself.

"Queer" is a word often used to describe children in literature, and usually it indicates precisely this fluidity of subjective structure. For instance, Sara Crewe, of Frances Hodgson Burnett's *A Little Princess*, is repeatedly described as queer. A close reading of the incidents where her queerness is noted reveals that they are times when she seems neither young nor old, rich nor poor, male nor female, but instead a fluid admixture of nonidentifiable characteristics. Oftentimes, the queerness of a child character is temporary. For instance, Fern's queerness in *Charlotte's Web* dissipates when she meets up with Henry Fussy at the fair. Marah Gubar notes a similar resolution to Anne's queerness in her article "'Where is the Boy?': The Pleasures of Postponement in the *Anne of Green Gables* Series." Gubar locates Anne's queerness in her deferral of marriage; it takes five books for her to finally submit to the heteronormative quietude of life with Gilbert. By then, it's as if Montgomery (and arguably the reader) loses interest in her. When her fluidity as a subject has been resolved in a particular direction, her story is over, and the series turns to narratives of her children.

But of all the characters in children's literature, I would suggest that the queerest, and the one who resolutely remains queer, is Pippi Longstocking. As with Mary Poppins, our first encounter with Pippi Longstocking is a bit of a surprise, characterized by a wonder that clues us in to the fact that we are in the presence of the Other. She is an odd-looking girl, walking backward. When Tommy, a neighbor, asks her why she walks backward: "'Why did I walk backward?' said Pippi. 'Isn't this a free country? Can't a person walk any way she wants to? For that matter, let me tell you that in Egypt everybody walks that way, and nobody thinks it's the least bit strange.'" (Lindgren, 17). Her question regarding whether she is in a free country is a telling one. She is seeking out the structures of authority in her adopted home. In truth, a person cannot walk any way she wants to in the Symbolic. Bodies, postures, attitudes, behaviors are all prescribed in the male-order Symbolic, and yet until someone comes along to challenge them, these prescriptions generally do not reveal themselves as such. The female in the Symbolic may offer that challenge; the queer subject certainly does. Pippi has left life on the high seas and moved into Villa Villekula, a house "way out at the end of a tiny little town," where she has her first encounter with the conventions of the white Western world. As an orphaned nine-year-old raised in the company of sailors, Pippi has had to come into being without access to the usual identity markers that we use to position ourselves as subjects; she has no parents, no nation, no peer group that would serve to legitimate her way of being. Hence in her encounter with people who do have such markers, she is forced to make them up, to perform an identity that includes a nod in the direction of all these positions. Pippi serves as a parody of masculine identity construction with respect to the Other; she continually authenticates herself by referring to, but not quite identifying with, an exoticized, fictionalized Other. Whenever she transgresses boundaries of normal social functioning, she attaches her deviant behavior to a particular non-Western nation, which places her in the masculine imperialist position of "constructing" a mythic other to satisfy some disturbing or disruptive tendency in the imperialist.

Indeed, at first glance, Pippi seems to be a postcolonial nightmare—she rationalizes all her most outlandish behavior by exoticizing it and giving it the proper name of a nation or ethnicity. But the important thing to remember about Pippi is that she is a *pirate*—that species of being that makes its home precisely nowhere, that steals from everyone, and that respects no national law or boundary. Hence Pippi is revealed to be the *colonialist's* nightmare instead, and this reference extends to those critics who claim that children's literature is about the colonization of the child. Pippi simply refuses to be domesticated according to a modernist logic of identification, rationality, and stability. One might say that she has refused, in a psychotic way, to come under the Law of the Father, an idea that I will explore further on. But we must remember that her father, like the elder Mr. Daws in *Mary Poppins*, is the impossible father of Freud's primal horde—that is, he is by definition outside the Law, acting as its limit and support.[8] Hence her identification with him results in her resolutely antinormative existence with respect to oedipal structures. If Pippi were simply parodying the imperialist or either the masculine or feminine positions, gender theorists might suggest that her performance was akin to drag—that she is destabilizing identity by revealing its markers to be contingent and interchangeable. If she can be more Brazilian than the people of Brazil, or more boy than a boy, for instance, then such things as national or gender identity are exposed as performances or discourses that are not at all natural or innate. But Pippi is imitating nothing; she is not, like Curious George or Babar, a child "trying on" a male subject position. When she asserts that "in Brazil all the people go about with eggs in their hair" or that people from Guatemala sleep with their feet on the pillow so they can wiggle their toes, or even when she claims that lessons are forbidden to children in Argentina, who go to school only to eat caramels, she is engaging in a discourse not of power or parody, but rather of what William Desmond calls "agapeic otherness," which works itself out in "imaginative identification[s] with difference variously called love of neighbor, universal benevolence, or unstinting sympathy or compassion for all" (170). The language of power would indicate a dialectical relationship with the other in the context of master/slave, or in the effacement of difference into a monistic illusion, but Desmond asserts that agapeic otherness takes us beyond the dialectic or the monistic: "It does not entail dissolution into anonymous impersonal-ity or alternately, the fantasy that we are the all" (170). Cast in Lacanian terms, Pippi's subjective position is the position of the not-all, which she, unlike the Woman qua symptom of man, actively inhabits. It is, ultimately, a position of queerness, and one of joy.

The condition for the possibility of Pippi's subjective position is located in the family relationship. As we know, the death of the father is the essen-tial element for entry into the Symbolic—as the necessary third term, the Name of the Father as the Symbolic function necessitates the death of the Real father. For Tommy and his sister Annika, this negotiation has been successfully carried out; their subjectivity entails a knowledge not only of the rules of the social game, but also of the Law that governs the game—specifically, the Name of the Father. The essential element in understand-ing Pippi is to realize that her father *has not died*. If Pippi had been left an or-phan, pure and simple, the story would have proceeded differently—she may have been absorbed into the social fabric and patterns of Symbolic au-thority, or she would have rebelled. But Pippi's father does not die, at least not for Pippi:

> Pippi had not forgotten her father. He was a sea captain who sailed on the great ocean, and Pippi had sailed with him in his ship until one day her father was blown overboard in a storm and disappeared. But Pippi was absolutely certain that he would come back. She would never believe that he had drowned; she was sure he had floated until he landed on an island inhabited by canni-bals. And she thought he had become king of all the cannibals and went around with a golden crown on his head all day long. (Lindgren, 12)

Without the death of the father, there is no co-optation of Pippi into a white Western sensibility, which is organized around the oedipal configura-tion. Pippi's father has dimensions of orality (she casts him as a cannibal) and also of a positive presentation of the anal stage. Instead of being re-tentive, which is the usual marker of anality, he is wildly generous, having given Pippi a house, enormous shoes to grow into, a monkey, and a suitcase full of gold pieces. But without his death, he cannot embody the phallic function, and hence Pippi is positioned to embody the surplus that escapes symbolization.

This embodiment works itself out in her great strength: "She was so very strong that in the whole wide world there was not a single police of-ficer as strong as she" (13–14). But her strength should not be read as a symbol; rather, it is the residual embodiment in the Real of something that hasn't worked out—the death of her father. By "worked out" I mean two things. First, he has not died into his Symbolic function, has not become the Name of the Father, the paternal function, for Pippi. But also, he has not died when he was supposed to in the Real. That is, when most people get blown overboard in storms and disappear, we assume that they don't have much of a chance of survival. But Pippi's father miraculously survives and becomes what Pippi believes he is—a cannibal king.

Pippi's strength is, then, like Charlotte's web-words, the physical manifestation of a failed symbolization. For Fern, Wilbur had to be symbolized under the phallic Symbolic, but for Pippi, what has failed is the paternal metaphor itself: Pippi's father has not died. At one and the same time, this reveals both the status of the paternal metaphor—it has become such a reified construction as to seem a part of the Real itself—and the breakdown of the resulting patriarchal discourse of lack. What I am saying here is that our way of symbolizing the Real has become so binding as to seem necessary, but we must remember, and Pippi helps us remember, that it is what Žižek would call an *established* necessity. The failed symbolization that manifests itself in the Real is usually some failure *within* the paternal metaphor—what has failed in Pippi's case is metaphor itself. This usually suggests psychosis; indeed, one way of reading Pippi's antics would be in terms of a psychotic structure that manifests itself in delusions of invincibility. But a more positive reading suggests that as a result of this failure of the father to become a paternal metaphor, Pippi is not constructed as notmale, as a symptom or manifestation of lack. Instead, she is what Saussurean binaries would say cannot exist—a thing with positive characteristics, not defined by its difference (or in this case by its inferiority) to the privileged half of a binary. When Annika tells Pippi she can't "lick" the Mighty Adolf because he's the strongest man in the world, she responds, "*Man*, yes, but I am the strongest *girl* in the world, remember that"(99). Her queerness positions her outside of a binary that would disempower her.

Confronted with Pippi's great strength, the townspeople leave her alone —she becomes for them the one who is out of place, a subject who knows too much. What she knows is that what is holding their world together has no hold on her (and here I feel I must apologize for being a bit literal, but it's just too easy)—when the only tall building in town is burning with two little boys stuck in the top of it, she alone does not fear the fire. The collapse of the phallus does not threaten her with annihilation as it does the two boys or the townspeople. In fact, for Pippi the burning of the phallus is a sight of joy—"she thought it was fun when a few sparks fell on her" (136). As Žižek points out, there is a close connection between "Father, can't you see I'm burning?" and "Father, can't you see I'm enjoying?" (*Enjoy Your Symptom* [ES], 125). Pippi knows that the death of her father would usher her completely into the Symbolic order—the order of the phallus— which is, as Žižek notes, radically incompatible with enjoyment (22).

This radical incompatibility is important to consider, because through it Pippi teaches us something about the possibilities that proliferate only through the queer experience. It is not that Pippi threatens from the margins to subvert paternal authority, to overturn the structure and assert an anarchic subjectivity. Nor does she view her status as girl as limiting, unlike what Mukherjee-Blaise says about the experience of marginality: "The Indian writer, the Jamaican, the Nigerian, the Canadian, and the Australian, each one knows what it is like to be a peripheral man whose howl dissipates unheard. He knows what it is to suffer absolute emotional and intellectual devaluation, to die unfulfilled and still isolated from the world's centre" (151). Mukherjee-Blaise's gendered comment is apt for the subject who has accepted the male-order categories of subjective experience. Instead, Pippi's joy depends on her queer status, which is why she must keep her father alive. She dips her finger into the male-order Symbolic—she tries going to school and to coffee parties; she tries not to lie and to behave herself properly— but she knows that her subjectivity depends on her being able to construct herself in an economy of present performatives, rather than to link herself to the phallocentric, totalizing system of history that defines and holds the center in place, even while erasing its own performative origins.

It is too easy to say that she fictionalizes real events or that she exaggerates. Instead, the stories she tells conjure a past. When her monkey runs away, she says: "'Mr. Nillson certainly can be exasperating. He's always doing things like this. Once in Arabia he ran away from me and took a position as a maidservant to an elderly widow. That last was a lie, of course,' she added after a pause" (Lindgren, 83). Later, when she finds him, she says: "Well, well, so you aren't going to be a maidservant this time? . . . Oh that was a lie, that's true. But still, if it's true, how can it be a lie? You wait and see, it's going to turn out that he was a maidservant in Arabia after all, and if that's the case, I know who's going to make the meatballs at our house hereafter" (87).

"It's going to turn out that he was" represents a verb tense that is extremely difficult to conceptualize, but vital to understanding the temporality of the queer, as well as the female, subject in Lacanian terms. She is a future becoming, whose history depends on that future. Operating outside oedipal categories allows her to construct a different relationship to history —one that eludes the center and fulfills its own internal logic. Pippi's marginality is profound, and it offers us an innovative way to think of queerness as a proliferation of possibilities—a position of strength. Heigh-ho—it's not everyone who has such a stylish position! Pippi does in fact howl from the margins, but instead of dissipating unheard, her howl resonates alongside the call of the center as an interpellation to Tommy and his sister Annika, our stand-ins as we ourselves move in the shadow of the phallus, as an invitation to queer desire.

This proliferation of possibilities in the feminine and in queer desire should not be read as a "poor men—they have so few choices" position. To the contrary, masculine subjects are perfectly comfortable with and fiercely protective of their own ways of partnering with their various *objets a*, and obviously, the male system works wonderfully in terms of material conditions and circumstances. The position of the female in the system is the "one-less," the continual reminder for the man that difference really does exist, if only as something like a failure to appear. And the antinormative position of the queer subject is even more threatening, since it seems to utterly slip the oedipal noose. In a more positive light, the subtracted element must and does appear somewhere, which means that there is an order outside the phallocentric one that masculinity has established. That Pippi ends her story alone in Villa Villekulla, that Mary Poppins flies away, suggest that the female and queer cannot simply be added (back?) into the system without losing their specificity. But both characters are featured in sequels, suggesting a sort of never-ending return, a discontinuous but persistent presence of the female and the queer in the Symbolic.

Others

I have singled out Mary Poppins and Pippi Longstocking for extended analysis, but they are by no means the only characters in children's literature who embody a genuine female or a queer subject. Emily Byrd Starr, heroine of L. M. Montgomery's *Emily of New Moon* trilogy, is another such character. Her experience of the "flash," as she calls it, provides a quite lovely description of what it means to embrace or partner with the signifier of the lack in the Other:

> It had always seemed to Emily, ever since she could remember, that she was very, very near to a world of wonderful beauty. Between it and herself hung only a thin curtain; she could never draw the curtain aside—but sometimes, just for a moment, a wind fluttered it and then it was as if she caught a glimpse of the enchanting realm beyond—only a glimpse—and heard a note of unearthly music.
>
> This moment came rarely—went swiftly, leaving her breathless with the inexpressible delight of it. She could never recall it—never summon it—never pretend it; but the wonder of it stayed with her for days. (*Emily of New Moon* [ENM], 7)

She also has psychic episodes that result in her finding a lost child, solving an eleven-year-old missing person case, and communicating a message to Teddy across a tremendous distance that he should not board a ship that is destined to collide with an iceberg. But Emily is not generally "witchy"; she emphatically occupies the real world of aching cold hands, stern aunts, and editors' rejections. And she learns to partner with the phallus of social position as a member of the prestigious New Moon clan. Repeatedly she arches her back against opportunities because of the "Murray pride." But her ability to live in, know, and negotiate the world differently affirms her status as an antinormative subject. Like Anne and countless other Montgomery heroines and supporting characters, she defers marriage, preferring to keep her options open and fluid. But unlike Anne, Emily doesn't "outgrow" fantasies and beliefs held dear in childhood, because her connection to the flash and her psychic abilities represent something other than fantasy. They represent a certain access that she, as a female subject, has to the Real, an access about which she "knows" (in the male-order epistemological sense) nothing.

Emily has a beloved father who dies, but whom she keeps alive through a letter-writing campaign. When her letters are discovered and read by Aunt Elizabeth, however, we realize who the real primordial father of the Murray clan is—Elizabeth's father, Emily's grandfather. Archibald Murray possessed a fearful look that frightened everyone into submission to his will. Like the flash and her psychic abilities, the "Murray look" comes upon her unexpectedly, when some core of iron in her spirit has been touched. She has "an uncanny feeling of wearing somebody else's face instead of her own" (107). The Murray look quite undoes her stern Aunt Elizabeth: "'I saw—Father—looking from her face,' gasped Elizabeth, trembling. 'And she said, "Let me hear no more of this,"'—just as *he* always said it—his very words'" (107). Emily's transformation is further evidence of the partnership woman can have only with the primordial father, never with the castrated male. Her marriage in the end is not like the marriage of Anne to Gilbert, which represents a capitulation and a fading of Anne's particularity into the patriarchal role of mother. Instead there is the sense that Emily's marriage to Teddy has the potential to realize something of an Irigarayan ethics of sexual difference; the artist and the writer come together in a truly productive and self-productive partnership.

What Lacan holds out is a (mostly) potential view of female subjectivity, more in the realm of the possible than of the actual. As a matter of lived reality, the male Symbolic has held such cultural dominance in the West for so long as to seem inevitable. Worse, it has, for the most part, neutralized the radicality of the female position and threatens to do so to the queer position as well, which is why queer theory works so hard to resist definition and reification. Most of us walk with our feet firmly on the ground, dependent on just the five senses and a rationalized intellect to make sense of the world. The female subjects of children's literature help us understand what forms female subjectivity might take, what possibilities may be open. Moreover, many preadolescent characters in particular operate in the queer space of openness and fluidity, adopting an antinormative, anti-identitarian stance toward the structures of authority they confound and confront. As interpellative fictions by which children engender themselves, they also help structure and perpetuate a desire for such openness. Wouldn't it be fun if the world could be reorganized along the principle of a Poppins physics, or if history existed as a Longstocking future conditional? This question is not an idle one. Whether or not we can ride animated merry-go-round horses, we can reorganize the master signifiers that make up identity structures for persons in the world. In the sixties, for instance, women changed the master signifier "ladies" to a differently coded master signifier, "women." But it is important to remember that these revolutionary women were once reading girls. And chances are the books they read included texts like *Mary Poppins, Pippi Longstocking*, and *Emily of New Moon*. Books like these raise important questions about how to be in the world, and they answer those questions with characters that are genuinely female or resolutely queer. As girls and boys are interpellated by those characters, they are opened to the possibility of alternate knowledges, alternate relationships, and alternate negotiations with the natural world.[9] In tracing the genealogies of feminism, quantum physics, or the paranormal, to name but a few areas of current interest, one would do well not to forget "that Poppins woman!"

CHAPTER SIX

Blinded by the White

The Responsibilities of Race

I noted in chapters 1 and 2 how images in picture books become idealized by child readers. Children operating in an Imaginary logic read these images as metonymic representations of categorical signifiers and construct their expectations of the signifieds attaching to those signifiers through the repeated associations of image to text. Interesting to note here are the side effects of taking the part for the whole. For instance, if a child repeatedly sees a picture of a male attached to the signifier of daddy, he might make the assumption not only that all daddies are males, but also that all males are daddies. But it might not stop there. If most of the images of male daddies he sees are white with brown hair, then his expectation of the ideal daddy becomes one who is white with brown hair, and the actual daddies he sees in his life are likely to be judged against that expectation. This is even more true with imagery in books that doesn't correspond to the child's lived reality; that is, he is more likely to idealize images for which he has no actual correlates through which to correct or multiply his impressions. So if a country child repeatedly sees images of the city as dangerous, she forms her opinions and expectations on the basis of those images. Or if a child continually sees people with disabilities represented as helpless or grumpy or sinister, it should come as no surprise that he brings those associations with him when he encounters an actual person with a disability. This associative logic is the process in which multicultural children's books attempt to intervene. By increasing the kinds of representations that children encounter, authors, illustrators, publishers, parents, and teachers are attempting to expand the boundaries of what children are likely to consider normal and valuable.

However, as most educators and parents know to their frustration, mere consciousness raising and image control do little to uninscribe racism. Real change must come on a structural level. Hence my method in this chapter will be similar to my approach to gender. Rather than focus entirely on images of racialized subjects, I instead look at how race functions as a psychoanalytic category, and specifically at how Whiteness instantiates itself as a signifier of desire. As I did with gender, however, I focus on how books for children can reveal the tenuousness and conventionality of the constructions of race, thus pointing the way for displacing modernist narratives with more open and fluid dynamics. The reader will no doubt have noticed that most of my examples have been taken from canonical—that is, white Anglo—texts of the past century. This is part of my point of how Whiteness has inscribed itself in modernism as a place of desire, a norm against which any other way of thinking seems deviant or specialized, not applicable to everybody. Critical multiculturalists focus on how images affect our subjectivity; those specializing in Whiteness studies are especially concerned with how we can maintain positive depictions of what it means to be white while still emphatically displacing the hegemony of Whiteness in culture.[1] My argument attempts to uncover the logic of desire and signification that undergirds these projects.

So once again, I direct our attention beyond the content of images to the structures under which they are produced and valued. I would tentatively suggest that in every culture, individual subjectivities and desires are constructed, constrained, and contained within and through the stories the culture tells. But in Western culture in particular, the valorization of reading and film as our primary modes of storytelling results tangentially and significantly in the valorization of individuality and vision that come from replacing the communal nature of oral storytelling with the solitary reading subject, or the silent viewer in a darkened theater. Moreover, the iterability of the written signifier results in the reification of meaning, so that any attempt to take an antinormative stance generally ends by being taken up into the normative anyway, which is another way of saying that you can't be permanently avant-garde. But why must this be so? Why is the normative so consumptive, so eager to draw everything into itself?

The answer to this question lies in part in the nostalgic structure of subjectivity I have been outlining so far. We are split subjects, and we desire to overcome our split. At the level of vision, this takes place by metonymizing images, taking parts for wholes, filling in gaps in vision with conventional expectations. At the level of language, we attempt to overcome our finitude by installing what Lacan calls "master signifiers." These master signifiers work by suggesting plenitude; their signifieds are impossible concepts of wholeness. Though impossible, they hold our expectations under the blinding light of a fantasized perfectability, demanding that we continually move in a certain direction in an attempt to actualize the concept. The role of a master signifier is to cover over our status as split subjects; if we identify with the master signifier and can get others to validate our identity as such, then we can, conceivably, dupe both ourselves and others into its possibility. The problem, of course, is that our performance is never perfect, and in fact, *we don't desire it to be.* The master signifier founds a chain of signifiers and sets it in motion, each signifier establishing its meaning on the basis of its reference to the master signifier. But the master signifier itself is not part of the chain; it does not move. To be completely coincident with the master signifier would mean to leave the chain of signification altogether, and since it is only in that chain that we are subjects at all, we would be precisely nowhere. If it were possible, we would achieve something like Being itself and go out like Tweedledee's candle. Hence in a signifying economy dominated by a master signifier, we need the marker of difference, of failure, even, to maintain our distance from the ideal so that we may paradoxically continue to strive for it. If you will recall what happened when the character found his Missing Piece, you can see some of this logic at work. We need the master signifiers to activate desire, but we also need to maintain our distance from them to keep desire in play.

Whiteness functions as one of these master signifiers. According to Kalpana Seshadri-Crooks, "[T]he system of race as differences among black, brown, red, yellow, and white makes sense only in its unconscious reference to Whiteness, which subtends the binary opposition between 'people of color' and 'white'" (20). In the Western culture of modernity, anxiety is predicated on the presence of the material per se—the Cartesian error of "I think, therefore I am" has had the disastrous and monumental consequences of hegemonizing an impossibly detached, disembodied, rational perspective as the measure of human consciousness. I use the word "perspective" deliberately here, since such a measure of consciousness depends on what has been called "the hegemony of vision."[2] Vision, as I have said, has a metonymizing effect—it takes miniscule and disconnected bits of visual information and transmutes them into whole pictures. Thus it masks the pixilation or fragmentation of qualities in that which is observed. This is precisely the way a master signifier works—by offering itself as a whole, a complete and ideal Thing, without qualities, it supports a field of signifiers in which it does not participate but that define themselves in terms of their failure to attain its ideal wholeness. Under this hegemony of vision, Whiteness has attained the status of a master signifier. Consider, as a metaphor, the color of white light—we are taught in elementary school that white is comprised of every color, whereas individual colors are refractions, light perceived at a particular angle, rather than the purity of unrefracted light. Whiteness or any other color, for that matter, associated with a particular person or group of people can only ever function in this metonymous, nominal way, since it absolutely fails to describe anything objective about a person.

But as a master signifier, Whiteness acts as a nodal point of desire—not that we desire, as Seshadri-Crooks points out, to be Caucasian, but that we desire the ideal of Whiteness in its place as master signifier, its place of wholeness, the absence of difference and qualities. Indeed, Caucasians can be said to desire Whiteness just as much as anyone else, and it has been only through the conscious association of Caucasian peoples to the signifier Whiteness, mainly through vision and privileged access to the secondary signifiers that have attached themselves to it and that we will discuss presently, that they have been able to claim that signifier for themselves. But the system requires the visual markers of racial difference to keep Whiteness aloft as an unattainable but desirable ideal. Master signifiers set up the structural conditions for happiness itself: They name some ideal or other so that we can believe it exists, then set a chain of signifiers in motion that allow us to think that some people have better access to the ideal than others. Thus we are motivated to pursue the ideal as possible. This is of course a fiction, so we also need the fantasy of prohibition of the impossible, as we discussed in chapters 1 and 2. We need to believe that there are people preventing us from our own access to it, so that we don't have to acknowledge its impossibility. These factors keep our desire busily mobile; that the concept behind the master signifier doesn't exist would matter only if we were to achieve such a close approximation to it that we realized its inadequacy from there. Hence the notion that someone is actively preventing you from achieving your desire is a necessary hedge against the realization of its impossibility; prohibition is easier to swallow than radical impossibility, when it comes to desire. It should be evident that these conditions for happiness can turn also into the conditions for bitterness and despair, and unfortunately they have underwritten racial hatred in America in myriad ways. Hence we can see that Whiteness and difference are structural in nature but at the same time have been distinctly realized in historical and social constructions.

In a field such as children's literature that is obsessed by questions of multiculturalism, surprisingly little attention is paid to the social construction of Whiteness. Indeed, Whiteness studies as an area of inquiry has only a very recent history. As a master signifier, Whiteness is the screen against which any "other" culture is projected; it embodies the universal, making any other ethnicity the particular, the curious, the deviant. By unconsciously excluding Whiteness from the discourse of multiculturalism, scholars, teachers, and students cast Whiteness as the privileged ground upon which the term "multiculturalism" depends for its distinction. Indeed, Erving Goffman, in his 1963 study *Stigma: Notes on the Management of Spoiled Identity*, nuances the hegemony of Whiteness even further, suggesting that there is "only one complete unblushing male in America: a young, married, white, urban, northern, heterosexual, Protestant father of good complexion, weight, and height, and a recent record in sports" (128). Each of these qualities attaches itself to Whiteness as a secondary signifier, a signifier that is implied with every deployment of the master signifier of Whiteness. Valerie Babb, in her more recent book *Whiteness Visible: The Meaning of Whiteness in American Literature and Culture*, agrees that throughout American history, there has been a collective and self-conscious effort to make "white racial identity the 'authentic' American identity" (5). In the course of constructing this "unblushing male" as the American ideal, vagaries of race, religion, able-bodiedness, and sexual orientation have been socially and politically oppressed and psychologically repressed and/or abjected. Consider the unspoken binaries of Goffman's formula who are excluded from his norm: female, old, unmarried, nonwhite, rural, southern or western, homosexual, Catholic, Muslim, Jewish, Buddhist, atheist (etc.), mother, child, ugly, deformed, obese, disabled. These are characteristics that Goffman identifies as marks, or stigma, whereas the norm that he identifies goes unmarked, the ground against which the figure emerges.

Even with the advent of cultural studies on U.S. campuses, the content of Whiteness is rarely interrogated, not because it is too heterogeneous to classify, but because its hegemony is such that it absorbs the universal into itself. Babb notes: "Rarely do we consider that notions thought to have no racial content often do. It can be argued that Innocence, Freedom, and Individualism, concepts frequently used to characterize American culture and commonly deemed universal, are racialized through implicit exclusion" (15). The repeated associations of these characteristics with able-bodied white people, and their failure to regularly include people of other races and the disabled, "weds the racial to the universal, allowing the latter to disguise the former" (16). White identity requires the repression of the possibility of its own disability, and it requires the abjection of those who are racially, sexually, or ethnically different to establish its own boundaries. In that context, much multicultural discourse emerges as a return of the repressed, a mere symptom of Whiteness.

In the context of the European Enlightenment, Whiteness accrued to itself the secondary signifiers of rationality, achievement, innocence, freedom, individualism, and, even, human. It gathered unto itself the rights of conquest and colonization, since its claim on the former qualities did not extend to those who didn't meet the first condition of visual proximity to the master signifier. Babb argues that it is the continual and repeated association of characteristics with specific iconic figures (for instance, Shirley Temple as the embodiment of innocence, John Wayne as rugged individual) that constructs the content of racial stereotypes. But subtending these stereotypes is the master signifier of Whiteness itself. Now, we know from therapeutic observation and work that the way to release a subject from the domination of a master signifier is to dialecticize that signifier—to bring it into the play of signification. If that is the case in the clinic, then perhaps it offers a way to move us out from under the domination of Whiteness as a cultural master signifier as well. When Whiteness itself is opened to interrogation and theorization, when it is revealed to be historically and culturally grounded in specific qualities, then it can be mobilized as one signifier among many rather than as the unconscious support of a racist cultural system. But even if, because of the fundamentally nostalgic character of the subject, dialecticizing Whiteness itself turns out to be a utopic dream, it should at least be possible to disentangle the ideal of Whiteness as a thing without qualities from the secondary signifiers that have gotten attached to it. This work I find being done in Edward Bloor's widely read novel *Tangerine* and Louis Sachar's Newbery Award–winning *Holes*.

The Mysteries of Whiteness in *Tangerine*

Bloor's novel is tremendously popular because it is one of those books that, like the *Harry Potter* novels, has something for everyone. It is a Cinderella story, in which an undervalued younger brother comes into his own and gets revenge on those who have hurt him; a school story, in which relationships to peers play themselves out under the thumb of authority; a sports story, in which the underdog team emerges triumphant; a mystery, with clues artfully sifted along the way to its stunning revelation. It offers no challenge to conventional notions of right and wrong, and in fact the way justice is served up in the end makes the book fully satisfying. But more than this, it is a multicultural book in the true sense of that word, in that it not only features characters from cultures other than white upper-middle-class America, but also frankly encounters and interrogates the values of Whiteness.

Bloor settles us into the world of Tangerine County, Florida, by offering us no surprises.[3] For instance, we sense no disjunction in the fact that Latino characters Tino and Victor spend the majority of their time suspended from school, that they are violent and combative, and that their family depends for its living on agriculture and manual labor. Even their beat-up pickup truck, in which they ride in the back, makes good common sense to us, based on a long history of associative imagery. Latino/as in U.S. culture do not participate in Whiteness, in that they are perceived as emotional and passionate and thus prone to violence. They work with their hands, not with their minds, and hence miss the rationality and prosperity associated with Whiteness. Likewise, we sense the fitness of the black character Antoine's being both an exceptional athlete and a poor person doing something deceptive to beat the system; in the manner of a distinct cultural cliché about adolescent black males, his only way out of poverty, his only chance at a better life for himself and his family, is through an athletic scholarship. Betty Bright, another example of this stereotype, has returned to her hometown after a bittersweet sports career to help underprivileged youth toward that elusive better life through sports.

The white characters in *Tangerine* offer us no real surprises either. With the exception of one family, the white characters are all wealthy. The Fishers' moves from one unfinished development to another signify Mr. Fisher's career trajectory—ever upward and mobile, lacking the substance of history. Indeed, history is something Whiteness must suppress if it is to maintain its status as universal, immune to historical contingency. Fisher's son Paul emphasizes the sameness of the developments as well, suggesting that it doesn't matter where you are now any more than your history matters. The only thing that matters for Whiteness is progress. Mr. Fisher, as a civil engineer and public official, is, significantly, the one who controls that progress. When the lackadaisical practices of Mr. Fisher's boss, Charlie Burns, begin to reveal the holes in the system, Mr. Fisher is brought in to run the kind of damage control specific to Whiteness, that is, to preserve the fantasy that we can control everything from nature to our families to our own selves.

Mrs. Fisher's concern with the home and her proactive stance regarding Paul's schooling and the girls on his soccer team mark the kind of superficial feminism that characterizes upwardly mobile white women in America. She is not a female subject in the Lacanian sense precisely because she is too invested in the totalizing fantasy of Whiteness. Whiteness has come to be associated with a philosophical tradition of valorizing appearances and ideals over substance and materialism; it is more interested in the Symbolic than in the Real, which threatens it. Hence as long as Mrs. Fisher can maintain the appearance of a tidy, respectable home, it matters little whether or not the appearance is substantiated by anything real. In her work with the homeowners' association, she runs up against the paradox of individualism that characterizes Whiteness. Though one of the most important secondary signifiers of Whiteness is the myth of the individual autonomous subject, in practice more value is placed on homogeneity, the erasure of any sort of difference that might mark out an individual. This is because of the Kantian belief that an individual, left on his or her own, will come to a realization of an ideal or supreme good. Reciprocally, this transmutes to the belief that what we value as individuals must in fact be linked to that ideal good. Hence any deviation from the homogenizing aesthetic of the neighborhood shows a seam in the totalizing fantasy and must be eradicated.

This paradox is what marks Mrs. Fisher's feminism as well. She is so intent on asserting her ideal of feminist advocacy on behalf of her son and his female teammates that she fails to consider the individual circumstances of the people for whom she is advocating. Hence her intervention has disastrous effects for both Paul and Shandra, exactly the opposite of what she wanted. A more sinister reading of this would be that since she is advocating for the equality of people whose existence threatens the ideal of Whiteness (people with disabilities and nonwhite girls), her failure is secured from the outset by the very system that mandates it. Either way, she fails because she wants to value appearances over material conditions; these small failures foreshadow her crushing realization that this practice has destroyed her family.

Like those of their parents, Erik and Paul Fisher's concerns—moving to a new school, having a sports identity, developing the right kinds of friendships with both boys and girls—seem utterly typical and conventional; that is, they are unmarked in Goffman's sense. But Bloor's sustained and nuanced critique of these seemingly neutral values does indeed mark them, and his association of them with his white upper-middle-class characters enables us to see them as the concerns of economically advantaged people in a racist society, that is, as the values of Whiteness.

We don't get our first surprise until Paul teams up with a Latina classmate, Teresa, for their science project, and we find out that these Latino characters are not migrant workers but own their own groves, and that Teresa's older brother Luis is a scientist and an inventor. That is, he exemplifies some of the qualities so valued in the European Enlightenment—scientific investigation and manipulation of the natural world. And yet he is not white. This disjunction creates a wedge between the unquestioned association between white characters and Whiteness afforded by the hegemony of vision, thus denaturalizing the connection.

Bloor continues to systematically expose the flaws in many of the ideologies that have grown out of the quest for pure Whiteness: the sanitation and/or exclusion of the body, the exaltation of the individual, and notions of manifest destiny with regard to the environment. For example, with regard to manifest destiny and the environment, the white characters live in expensive new housing developments that are built on top of failed tangerine groves, which have simply been plowed under and covered with a layer of topsoil. As a result, the houses are subject to termites that have eaten their way through the trees and are starting on the houses, muck fires that result from the rotting vegetation, and lightning strikes that Paul speculates result from a kind of natural memory for rises in the landscape that have been bulldozed by people but not forgotten by the earth. Rather than heed these problems as symptoms of land misuse, the wealthy homeowners seek to cover them over. In a richly comic progression, they flood the muck fires, which results in an infestation of mosquitoes, which results in the need to spray the neighborhood with toxic chemicals. So the inhabitants of Lake Windsor Downs, which sounds like an outdoor paradise, cannot leave their climate-controlled homes. Another comic element that Bloor invents is the importation of expensive tropical koi to fill the man-made "lake." The brightly colored fish make attractive meals for natural predators, but the white homeowners insist that they are being stolen by the poor people of Tangerine.

The tangerine groves themselves suggest an insensitivity to the existing environment—Tangerine County is on the frost line, where the growing of citrus is a risky proposition at best. Nonetheless, someone tried to domesticate and cultivate this land in this particular way and failed. But instead of paying heed to what could be grown there, or even cleaning up the mess that the tangerine groves made, the developers simply covered them over. To highlight the wastefulness and insensitivity to the environment and show what might be done to honor Tangerine County's heritage, as well as its natural climate, Bloor shows his Latino characters working with their natural environment to create frost-hardy tangerines and to save their groves through long nights of freezing temperatures. These environmental problems act as metaphors for the ways Whiteness attempts to control its own image by covering over its history and ascribing problems to the work of outsiders—a move which ultimately fails.

Bloor offers other interconnected metaphors as well. We might consider, for instance, the sociocultural implications of football versus soccer. Whereas football is an exclusively male North American pastime, soccer represents those values that threaten the values of Whiteness. It is a team sport that relies heavily on interindividual cooperation. Football, on the other hand, has individual stars, and Erik's position as placekicker emphasizes his independence from the team. Soccer is open to anyone, male or female, and even, as in Paul's case, to people with certain kinds of disabilities. Hence its inclusive nature threatens the exclusivity that Whiteness is built on. In *Tangerine*, Bloor uses the football/soccer distinction to highlight the role of the favored son in sibling rivalry, another motif that Whiteness claims as its own—the elder son inherits, makes up for, or covers over the deficits of the father, while the younger challenges his right to do so. We know that Paul is afraid of his older brother, Erik, and that their parents do nothing to try to bring the boys together. But the real extent of the rivalry comes out in the Erik Fisher Football Dream that so consumes the boys' father that he doesn't come to even one of Paul's games, while he insists that the entire family sit through Erik's, rain or shine. Mr. Fisher believes that Erik will make good on his own failures. That Erik is so talented enables this fiction of the favored son as long as he is successful, but Bloor again uses comic hyperbole to expose the vacuity of the concept when Erik falls during a kick attempt. Moreover, Paul's disability challenges the father's ability to maintain his fiction of Whiteness as whole and perfect.

Bloor also exploits the football/soccer distinction to tell the story of Antoine and Shandra. When Antoine sacrifices his career so that Shandra can receive her due share of praise, we see an alternative story of siblings, one not predicated on the rivalry so favored in Whiteness ideology. Antoine has been playing out of his district, a common enough sin in contemporary high school sports, since economic inequities limit the potential of talented athletes in poorer school systems. Shandra has repeatedly been nominated to the all-county soccer team, but because she plays for Tangerine and Antoine plays for Lake Windsor, her success cannot be noted. Antoine's guilt gets the better of him, he owns up to the fact that he should not be playing for Lake Windsor, and the results are that every game in which he played will be stricken from the record. Hence any records set, including those by Erik Fisher, are unofficial. For the sake of his sister, Antoine jeopardizes not only his career, but also others'. In this alternate sibling story, the success of the family is valued over the success of the individual, exposing the myth of individualism as a distinct phenomenon of Whiteness.

In the case of the Costellos, another white family in Lake Windsor Downs, Joey undeniably loves his brother but is carefully taught that his grief over Mike's death has a season, and that season does not last beyond the funeral. His parents encourage him to go to the carnival immediately after Mike's funeral, and his behavior there does not show even a residue of the loss he must feel. When Erik and Arthur make fun of Mike, Joey marvels that they would be so cruel but does not react—the ideal, self-controlled, rational subject of Whiteness. Tino and Victor, on the other hand, openly grieve and avenge Tino's brother's death regardless of the consequences, again suggesting a different sort of family relationship, one not predicated on notions of self-control and containment.

The ideal of the individual is carried over even into the criminality that characterizes Whiteness. Erik's crimes are committed with a henchman, unlike the equally invested crimes of Victor and Tino. Moreover, Erik's crimes are unmotivated, or at least their motivation is nonrelational but comes more from that Cartesian autonomous subject that sees the world as nothing more than an instrumental extension of his own consciousness, a surface on which he can (literally, in Erik's case) write himself. Tino and Victor, on the other hand, fight to establish and maintain their sense of group identity or to avenge Luis's death. Their crimes are motivated by their relationships with people, whereas Erik's crimes are directly a result of his seeing people and the world as objects for his use.

Each of the problems in the book emerges from some sort of cover-up or deception, either literal or figurative, perpetrated by white people to maintain their hegemonic status and their attachment to Whiteness. If Whiteness depends for its power on a modernist regime of the visual, then it is through a refracted transmodern vision that it can begin to be dismantled. The reason Paul can see through the deception of Whiteness is precisely because his vision has literally been compromised ever since he was five and Eric sprayed paint into his eyes. Because Paul was so young and the doctor thought he might not remember the incident, his parents manufacture a lie in a vain attempt to keep Paul from hating and fearing his brother. But Paul sees through Erik, and as a result is punished at the level that makes the most sense of Whiteness—the level of its own hegemony. It is significant, I think, that Erik sprayed *white* paint into Paul's eyes. But it is also significant that the cover story Paul's parents concocted was that Paul became blind by looking at the sun during an eclipse. That is, he attempted to stare into the pure unrefracted light that is a metaphor for Whiteness and was blinded as a result. Paul's repressed memories then act as a kind of trope for the theorization of the relationship between Whiteness and multiculturalism. What Whiteness denies, represses, and abjects in order to constitute itself inevitably returns with violence and environmental and family crises. The satisfying ending of the book results from the demotion of Whiteness from its elevated, hierarchical status of patriarchal dominance to Tino's acceptance of Paul in a horizontal relationship as a "brother." In this move, Bloor manages to displace Whiteness as multiculturalism's privileged "Other," and to draw it into the circulation of cultural signifiers as one among many, creating a space for a genuinely multicultural discourse.

Throughout the book, Bloor has disturbed the status of Whiteness as a master signifier in two ways. First, he allows characters other than whites to embody some of the secondary signifiers attaching to Whiteness, which shows the contingency of the connection between white people and the values of Whiteness. Second, he shows the instability and undesirability of some of the secondary signifiers, which in turn challenges their neutrality and their status as universally valuable. But most important, he destabilizes the hegemony of vision on which they rest, so that, like Paul, in the end we are no longer blinded by the white.

The Color of Dirt

When Stanley Yelnats in Louis Sachar's *Holes* settles into his nightmare at Camp Green Lake, he notes that he is glad there are no racial tensions in the camp. Black, white, or Mexican, everyone on the lake is "the color of dirt" (Sachar, 84). It becomes clear, however, that Stanley is in denial. Specifically, Stanley is part of a larger conspiracy of white denial of the privilege that comes with being a white male. As does Bloor in *Tangerine*, Sachar conveys this sense of privilege through associating certain characteristics with certain characters, and letting metonymy do its work. At first, Stanley's privilege is hard to recognize. Accused of a crime he did not commit, he seems in an odd position for a white male subject. But it soon becomes apparent that Stanley's crime is linked to an entire history of both privilege and the denial of that privilege, and it is up to Stanley, in psychoanalytic terms, to assume responsibility for his position in the Symbolic order. In other words, although we are born into a world not of our own making, part of our making sense of that world is assuming responsibility for both our personal and our cultural histories.

The habit of Stanley's family when faced with misfortune is to blame it on their "no-good-dirty-rotten-pig-stealing-great-great-grandfather" Elya Yelnats. Elya, desperately in love with an empty-headed village girl, turns to his friend Madame Zeroni for help. She gives him a pig and instructs him to carry the pig up a mountain every day for a year to let it drink from a spring. At the end of the year, Elya would be nice and strong from carrying the pig back and forth, and he would also have a worthy pig to offer as dowry for his Myra. The only thing Madame Zeroni asks in return is that Elya carry her up the mountain so that she too can drink from the spring. Failing that, he and his descendants would be cursed forever. Of course, Elya does not carry Madame Zeroni up the mountain, not because he is ungrateful, but because he is heartbroken over Myra's rejection and sails off to America with his grief. Nonetheless, in thinking only of himself and in exercising the privilege of the white male to travel and make his way in the world, he has failed in his responsibility to the Other. It is this failure, this erasure or even mere forgetfulness of the debt to the Other for one's position as subject, that haunts Whiteness.

Jonathan Lear, in *Open-Minded*, goes so far as to offer this failure as an alternative reading for the oedipal problem. It is not that Oedipus wanted to sleep with his mother and kill his father. That is in fact precisely what he did not want. But Oedipus is nonetheless still the myth of white Western culture, in that Oedipus thinks he can escape his history, his destiny, his parentage, and his debt to the Other. When he solves the riddle of the Sphinx, he brags that he "hit the mark through native wit," rather than acknowledging the supernatural help of the goddesses who gave him the answer. It is the hubris of autonomy that marks him as the prototype of Whiteness, rather than his instantiation of the incestuous oedipal complex.

Stanley, while not denying his history, nonetheless does not actively take responsibility for it; it haunts him, but it isn't something he feels he can do anything about. And this is often the position of the subject of race. Neither the oppressor nor the oppressed is willing to take responsibility *now* for things that happened *then*. And yet both Sachar and Lacan require precisely that. According to Lacan, we all enjoy a certain level of *jouissance* in our positions as privileged or victims for which we must claim responsibility. Stanley is miserable; there is no doubt about that. But underlying his misery is a denial of his part in it. Once he begins to realize that he can in fact act, that he can claim his misery as his, his position begins to change. Even as he steals the water truck to go after fellow prisoner Zero, he realizes that he will have to come back. But he knows he will be coming back as a true criminal, a criminal who claims his crime as his own.

Stanley begins to assume his position of white privilege before he takes responsibility for it, however, when he starts to teach Zero to read. Because of the bargain that he and Zero make, that Zero will dig some of his hole for him in exchange for reading lessons, the latent racial tensions in the group surface. Stanley is in effect assuming the privileges of Whiteness—he can read, and he expects payment for services rendered. Zero, on the other hand, is assuming the position of a black subject in America. He perceives his exclusion from the privileges of Whiteness as lack and is willing to do what it takes to attain at least this secondary signifier of Whiteness—literacy. When he is ridiculed for doing this, he runs away. These boys are unconsciously reenacting the racist history of their society. Though they obviously had no part in crafting that history, they nonetheless reinscribe it in their present circumstances. And that is precisely why taking responsibility for that history becomes an ethical problem for both the black and the white subject. As controversial as this may sound, taking up a subject position in a racist society automatically entails taking up a racist position, for all of the reasons that I have outlined in previous chapters and will pursue in the chapters that follow. Our subjectivities are deeply implicated in the Other as culture; hence the history, traditions, and structure of the Other are our own.

Sachar demonstrates this and suggests further that if the subject position one assumes is coded white, the burden of that responsibility must include restoring one's honor, because the history of whites, like the history of Trout Walker (a particularly nasty resident of the original town of Green Lake) and Elya Yelnats, has been either maliciously or carelessly dishonorable. To effect reconciliation, Stanley must make good his grandfather's promise to Madame Zeroni by carrying her great-grandson, Zero, up the mountain. What makes this work so interesting is that Sachar quite unashamedly suggests that all of nature is under strain because of the failures of white honor. If we link Whiteness to the European Enlightenment, then Sachar's deeply irrational assertion that God punished the town of Green Lake for its racist murder of Sam the onion picker is nothing short of magical thinking. No rain has fallen on the town of Green Lake since the murder; rain does not return until Stanley and Zero effect their reconciliation. Further, the nonlinear presentation of the story suggests an approach to history and narrative that shows more carefully and precisely how we use history in our understanding of the present. Hence by disturbing imposed structures of linear thinking and progress, as well as by reintroducing magic as a vital force in present experience, Sachar, like Bloor, attempts to pry apart and revalue the reified relationship between the secondary and master signifiers of Whiteness.

Whiteness is only one of the master signifiers we use to structure our subjectivities, but it has the unfortunate consequence of grounding a race-based, and thus racist, social structure as well. The intervention that is most likely to be effective in counteracting that effect includes a conscious assumption of our position as raced subjects combined with a conscious challenging and displacement of the secondary signifiers of Whiteness. When this happens, when Whiteness is revealed to be a site of specific, historicized qualities rather than a privileged access to being, the master signifier will be replaced in its position by the split subject operating as a nexus of discourses that includes race but is not fully determined by it.

Unfortunately, the dislodging of a master signifier often results, not in the satisfying closure and reconciliation shown in the two examples I've given, but in an outbreak of violence. This is because of the tremendous investment we make in the master signifiers themselves as they hold out the hope that we might overcome our status as split subjects. The following chapter explores in detail the logic of abjection that results from our reliance on these master signifiers to cover over our lack.

CHAPTER SEVEN

Abjection and Adolescent Fiction

Ways Out

In previous chapters, I have discussed the various ways the child subject uses literature to negotiate his passage from the Real to the Symbolic. Crucial to this passage is the formation of a coherent sense of a potential self through the Imaginary—that is, the child uses fictional small others to mirror back to him his own possibilities for identity construction. This is an ongoing process that persists throughout the life of the subject, but beyond the initial critical period of oedipalizing, the process tends to become re-formative rather than formative.[1] In the preoedipal period, the subject has quite a bit of work to do to flesh out the Imaginary features of his Ideal ego—that image of himself that will remain relatively constant throughout variations undertaken through Symbolic processes. In chapter 2, we envisioned him, in the time for looking, as an indiscriminate collector of images and representations. But all the while, his collection is narrowing itself in important ways. One way is through his assumption of a gendered, raced position and the relationship to the Symbolic that entails. This position is built on an exclusionary logic; the reader will recall that it is built as much on specifying what it is not, as on what it is. Yet as the subject becomes fully oedipalized, that is, enters into a phallic economy, he finds himself faced with yet another crisis of identity. We call this crisis "adolescence."

The literature written for adolescents suffers from a bit of an identity crisis itself. It boasts no consistent canon, since books of this genre tend to become dated very quickly. In fact, one of the key features of young-adult fiction is its currency, its absolute synchronicity with the concerns of the audience to whom it is marketed. Characterized by the material expressions of dress, drugs, music, language, and sexuality, most young-adult novels have a relatively short shelf life. But it is precisely because of their currency that we might find it useful to explore contemporary young-adult novels in order to better understand the contours of "coming of age" in today's society. Authors of this effervescent genre must find tropes adequate to engage the psychic preoccupations of contemporary readers on both conscious and unconscious levels to remain viable in this highly market-driven field. One such element that is becoming more prevalent is the condition of social and psychological abjection that Julia Kristeva describes as something that "disturbs identity, system, order" (*Powers of Horror* [PH], 4). While Roberta Seelinger Trites argues persuasively in *Disturbing the Universe* that issues of power are what characterize and even define the genre, I will be exploring the psychoanalytic component of abjection that underwrites the social structures of power and domination so prevalent in the genre.

The shootings at Columbine High School in 1999 mark one of those watershed moments when the terms of how we understand adolescence are profoundly changed. Two boys, Dylan Klebold and Eric Harris, operating at the social rim of their environment, targeted people whom they perceived as "plugged in" to some group or some identity—Christian, athlete, popular crowd, and so on. These are precisely the kinds of connections that elude the abject person; as an outsider, he or she has an intensely ambivalent relationship toward the walls that prevent him or her from fitting in. The tension between despising people for whom such connections work and being desirous yet unable to forge those connections themselves erupts in violent and aggressive acts toward the others who make it look so easy. The media is quick to call the perpetrators "monsters" and to configure such outbreaks of teenage violence as isolated events, even as news reports map their occurrence all over the country. This kind of media attention serves to further isolate people who have already constructed themselves as outsiders, people who cannot seem to fit in with any particular crowd. These teens are living out the condition of abjection. Adolescent fiction that deals with abjection offers us a means of understanding abjection and its contribution to violent behavior, as well as some strategies for dealing with abjection that might reduce violence.

In its social context, "abjection" means to operate at the social rim. Adolescence is a time of cultivating group identity; socially abject figures cannot seem to manage either the material conditions and habits or the identifications necessary to sustain a position in a social group. Certainly this kind of abjection is a fundamental problem in adolescent literature and cul-ture and has been a significant factor in recent school shootings. But in-finitely more subtle and complex is the psychologically abject character, whose abjection defines his or her way of being in the world, and whose presence haunts both the narrative and the actual world of the reader. Both social and psychological abjection precipitate violence in the narratives of young-adult fiction and hence offer suggestive ways of thinking about the increasing violence of adolescent society. In what follows, I explore the workings of abjection in its various guises in adolescent literature, begin-ning with an exploration of why and how abjection has become such a dis-tinctive feature of contemporary adolescent culture.

Abjection and Its Relation to Adolescence

Julia Kristeva's focus throughout her work has been to understand the pro-cesses whereby the subject is constituted as a desiring being in language. Working within a Lacanian frame, she both challenges and complements Lacanian theory in her focus on how preoedipal processes continue to bear on the oedipalized subject. In *Powers of Horror,* she looks specifically at the types of corporeal exclusions that the subject undertakes, those things that he or she must abject to constitute his or her "clean and proper" body. As we have seen through multiple examples, the Lacanian theory of subject formation has the infant unable to reconcile the experience of a fragmented body with the visual coherence it finds in the mirror. The body lived by the baby is incompetent and uncontrollable compared to what the baby imag-ines about its visual counterpart in the mirror. Hence the baby is alienated from his lived body in favor of an Imaginary anatomy constituted in large part by the Symbolic interventions and physical handling of his caregivers. Caregivers pay more attention to certain parts and processes than to others, and they code those parts and processes as dirty and untouchable or as pretty and acceptable, according to the patterns of their culture. In West-ern culture, for instance, products of elimination (waste, vomit, menstrual blood) are accompanied by disgust, and breasts generate images of eroti-cism rather than of sustenance. Since a child's primary caregiver is usually a mother, the mother, who through giving birth and feeding is already in-timately connected with the body, is also, Kristeva emphasizes, the first ar-biter of cultural convention and law, the first embodiment of the other that the child has to contend with. Her body literally enabled the baby's corporeal existence in the first place, but she also mediates its displacement from the Real into an Imaginary anatomy coded through Symbolic conventions. Hence the Real of her own body is what must first be excluded for the baby to achieve autonomy. For the baby to become a subject, the mother must become an object. This isn't an easy transition by any means; both the mother and the child fight against it by turns. But the child must expel as abject those things that violate the purity and stability of his subjective boundaries—among other things, feces and the maternal breast. As the reader will recall from chapter 1, it is precisely these two objects that Lacan discusses in relation to demand. Before the child becomes a fully desiring subject, he or she is caught in the attempt to satisfy the demand of the Other—through the presentation of feces as a gift in toilet training, and through the detachment of the maternal breast from the body of the child into the interstitial space "in which, beneath a veil, lies the Mother's desire" (Lacan, "Introduction to the Names-of-the-Father Seminar" [NF], 85). In other words, the preoedipal position of demand is dominated by the abject. As we have seen, normal development proceeds with the instantiation of the third term, the Name of the Father, as an effective intervention in the dual relationship between the mother and the child. The child must learn to transform his demand for the maternal body, which is a death instinct—a nostalgic movement toward the inertia of presence—into the mobilized desire for the ever elusive *objet a*. The paternal presence, because of its prohibitions against the incestuous union and also because of our attraction to its phallic power, along with the baby's recognition that the maternal presence can smother as easily as it can anchor and secure, enables separation to occur; the maternal body as Thing is repressed, and the baby begins the process of becoming an oedipalized subject.

Kristeva is interested in the interplay between the Real body and the Imaginary body insofar as subjectivity itself is constituted by excluding the lived body as abject. Abjection is the process of expulsion that enables the subject to set up clear boundaries and establish a stable identity. Implicated in that expulsion is the subject's exclusion of corporeality as such. This exclusion forms the basis of Cartesian duality, a split between mind and body, between being and meaning, between subject and object. It is a sacrificial logic that lays the foundation for identity. Abjection, as Kristeva defines it, marks a stage in the preoedipal development of the subject. In order for the child to organize her boundaries with respect to inside and outside, subject and object, self and other, she must first expel as abject that which is not part of her "clean and proper" ego. This includes incestuous attachments to the mother, as well as bodily secretions that persist as reminders that our subjectivity is in fact dependent on, indebted to, corporeality.

The constitution of an inside and an outside of bodies also lays the foundation for the social body. Just as we abject the unclean and improper evidences of the body's physicality in order to constitute a clean and proper body, so in the social realm we abject the unclean and the improper, again often on the basis of physicality in order to constitute the boundaries of community and nation. This is, as Elizabeth Grosz points out, not an original insight on Kristeva's part. Freud indicates that civilization as we know it is founded on such exclusions, specifically the exclusion of incest and polymorphous pleasures and perversions (Grosz, 86–87). Throughout social history, the exclusions of peoples based on race, sexuality, and disabilities have established and bolstered both personal and national identities. Kristeva's primary insight is that what we have expelled as abject does not simply and finally disappear. Identities, communities, and nations are "permanently brittle" constructs because they are built on abjection, which haunts their borders. "The more or less beautiful image in which I behold or recognize myself rests upon an abjection that sunders it as soon as repression, the constant watchman, is relaxed" (Kristeva, PH, 13).

To achieve oedipal stabilization, then, the subject must find some way to subdue the abject; she must find a way to keep the abject in its proper place outside the functioning of everyday life in the Symbolic. In an idealized oedipal economy, she would find support for this project in a number of areas. One such support comes from a univocal superego. In a Symbolic order where God, country, and family speak with one patriarchal voice, the repression of maternal desire and polymorphous perversity would find its strongest support in the Symbolic mandate. It is clearly the duty of the subject to break free from the dual (mother/child) relationship and come under the sway of the Law. There she will establish a kind of autonomy supported by the structure of her Symbolic position, and she will be beholden to the social rule of law regarding what is clean and proper in terms of sexuality and identity. Her duty as a citizen will be clear—to stand against sexual deviance, to practice benevolent but distant tolerance of the disabled, and to protect the nation's interests and borders against the encroachment of foreign ideas and organized, recognizable enemies. An alternative way of protecting herself from psychic abjection would be to displace her fear of the abject through religious rituals and practices that establish a clear boundary between the sacred and the profane. In the case of Christianity, for instance, abjection is held at bay through the various implications of the sacrifice of the God made flesh. On the one hand, the Christ became himself incarnate to redeem the body as such. Thus corporeality itself need not be regarded as abject. He then abjected sin through that body in his death, with his resurrection displacing abjection altogether in that it, first, provides the conditions for a corporeality beyond sacrifice and, second, demands our encounter with the subjectivity of the victim. In other words, in a properly understood Christian economy of subjectivity, we needn't sacrifice the body, and we must take into account the particularity of the Other rather than simply use him as our abject support. Yet another cultural support for the maintenance of the abject in its proper place is sublimation. Artistic endeavor transforms the (death-) drive energies responsible for abjection into poetic language, image, or dance that articulates affects beyond the codes of the Symbolic. Repression, displacement, and sublimation, then, are three ways that the Symbolic has traditionally maintained the exclusion of the abject.

Proper exclusion of the abject can be read as a stage along the way toward oedipal stabilization. What, then, could its role be in the contemporary experience of adolescence? In a conference dedicated to her work in 1987, Kristeva defines adolescence as an "open psychic structure," a time of psychic reorganization where, "[i]n the aftermath of the oedipal stabilization of subjective identity, the adolescent again questions his identifications, along with his capacities for speech and symbolization" ("The Adolescent Novel" [AN], 9). Considering this conceptualization of adolescence as a time of reopening and rethinking questions of identity, and also considering the proximity of its publication date to *Powers of Horror* (1982), it is surprising that Kristeva doesn't link the concepts of adolescence and abjection in her work. They are structurally and logically compatible for several reasons. At the level of the social, we think of adolescence in terms of the way it, like abjection, breaches and challenges boundaries. It is an in-between time, a time where what we know and believe about children is challenged, and where what we hope and value about maturity is also challenged. Adolescents are both more and less sophisticated and knowing than we want them to be. They challenge the borders of identity, trying to become adult without becoming adulterated. Striving for social recognition but not wanting to stand out, locating with specificity their status as sexual subjects and objects, seeking the terms of individuation within affiliative groupings, adolescents are intensely involved in the construction of social boundaries and in reaffirming their distance from the socially abject.

The psychoanalytic terms of abjection's connection to adolescence are even more compelling. Adolescence begins with a reassertion of the Real body. Kristeva indicates three categories of bodily abjection—oral, anal, and sexual—as in the markers of sexual difference. Grosz further reminds us that "[t]he objects generating abjection—food, feces, urine, vomit, tears, spit—inscribe the body in those surfaces, hollows, crevices, orifices, which will later become erotogenic zones—mouth, eyes, anus, ears, genitals" (88). The Imaginary anatomy of the subject has until the point of adolescence been gendered but not consciously sexualized. The anticipated but always unexpected emergence of abject fluids—nocturnal emissions for boys and menses for girls—signals the need for a conscious reinscription of that Imaginary anatomy, a movement from disgust to eroticism. Social and cultural contexts for this reinscription more often take the form of competitive and conflictual messages regarding sexuality, masturbation, and maternity than of simple prohibitions. Since contemporary culture no longer supports repression of teenage sexuality but has yet to come to terms with its own conflictual attitudes regarding exploration and polymorphous expressions of that sexuality, the subject is as likely to topple into the abyss of abjection, which includes such material expressions of the death drive as eating disorders and predatory sexual behavior, as he or she is to develop a healthy body image.[2]

In addition to the reassertion of the body, the adolescent's identity is destabilized by the reintensification of conflict between paternal law and maternal desire. And here I think Kristeva gets it wrong, or at least she is operating under anachronistic assumptions regarding the superego, when she attributes the questioning of adolescent identity to a "tremendous loosening of the superego" (AN, 9). Certainly adolescence is a time of loosening parental control, but the relationship between parents and superego formation has changed in our (arguably) postoedipal economy. The structural function of the superego—to curb and limit the subject's access to his desire—remains intact. But the cultural content and the place from which the superego issues its mandates have changed significantly. The failure of absolutes or even agreement among church, family, and state has precipitated a diffusion of superegoic injunctions; conflicting demands and prohibitions come from everywhere all the time rather than being focalized through a paternal presence functioning within and bolstered by a master discourse. The superego is thus rendered multivocal. Moreover, its perverse mandate "Enjoy!" is felt more insistently than its prohibition. Hence the more common experience of the superego for today's adolescent is as a diffuse ubiquity rather than a loosening—a net above and on all sides, rather than a jail cell with a temporarily open door. Abjection emerges as a result of this ambiguity caused by "*[t]oo much strictness on the part of the Other*, confused with the One and the Law," and the "*lapse of the Other*, which shows through the breakdown of objects of desire" (PH, 15). If the objects break down, so does the ego; where the superego permeates the culture as its inescapable unrelenting noise, the abject emerges. "To each ego its object, to each superego its abject" (2).

Another important part of the structural upheaval of adolescence which Kristeva doesn't mention is the reassertion of a maternal-type desire, a desire to fuse with the Other rather than to individuate. Despite the fact that many authors use the dead or dying mother as a trope to represent this problem (and indeed, the genre is littered with the corpses of mothers), the proposed partners in this adolescent repetition of the dual relationship are not the mother and the child anymore, but the teen and his peer group, or the teen and a media hero who functions for him as an ideal image, or the teen and another teen. The adolescent moves back in developmental time to the mirror stage, when questions of alienation and identification, separation and the establishment of boundaries between the me and the not-me, need to be resettled. The visual position is always already one of alienation; I always look from the outside. As the adolescent looks around, he fantasizes that the disconnection he feels toward the group, reminiscent of his experience of the fragmented body, is not felt by the visually coherent others that he wishes to mirror. Much of that fantasizing is due to the increased prevalence of the media image as the site of the "clean and proper" body. Artistic sublimation of abjection requires an image that merges the perfect with the imperfect but maintains the tension between the two. Digitally enhanced media images are impossibly perfect, bodies without secretions or imperfections. Rather than assert himself against them or even identify with their symbolic position of power, as a paternal logic would specify, the adolescent longs to dissolve into them. He sees in-crowds, sports teams, and media stars that appear to him as what Lacan calls "unweaned brother[s] [that] provoke a special aggression only because [they] repeat for the subject the imago of the maternal situation and, together with it, the desire for death" ("The Family Complexes" [FC], 17). It is as if the adolescent, having emerged from the initial battle between maternal desire and paternal Law wherein he established his subjectivity, must return to fight again, must reabject specifically his incestuous desire for the mother and the fusion she represents.

Structurally speaking, then, adolescence is a time of apocalypse, a last battle to establish one's place (or not), finally and irrevocably, within the Symbolic order. Considering the tantrums and aggressive behaviors of the toddler initially negotiating this stage, it should not be surprising that violence would accompany this second battle. What seems to be at issue in contemporary society, however, is why the violence is increasingly being acted out, rather than repressed, displaced, or sublimated. As I have indicated, it is partly because we have lost the social and cultural supports for those processes needed to keep abjection at bay. In the absence of such supports, the abject figure never gets to that point where drive energies are sublimated into the substitutive logic of the Symbolic. Abjection is by definition an expelling of what cannot be contained, of that which is not-me, but it does not provide for the introjection of paternal imagoes or representations of morality, religion, or law as Imaginary ideals. For that one needs Symbolic support. Abjection is a "vampire in the mirror" trick—one can see only what surrounds but is not part of the self. The results are a truncated, atrophied Imaginary and an inability to symbolize the losses one undergoes in becoming a subject. The problem is experienced as an absence of subjectivity itself—the abject figure never becomes a signifier for another signifier. Usually this would mean that the individual is psychotic. But Kristeva's notion that there are some people—the abjects—who are neither subject nor object finds expression in certain characters of young-adult fiction. They do not disavow the terms of subjectivity itself; they know precisely that accession to the Symbolic comes only through being subjected to the Name of the Father. They know, too, as Lacan points out, that "once the subject comes into being, he owes it to a certain nonbeing upon which he raises up his being" (*Seminar II* [SII], 192). They simply choose (and "choose" is perhaps a more active word than I mean here) to organize their existence around the pole of that nonbeing—the unsublimated expression of the death drive—rather than to organize it around the pole of the Name of the Father and desire. Indeed, it seems to me that the most useful way to think about these figures of abjection is to say that they refuse to or cannot sublimate the death drive and hence are compelled to enact and reenact it. In other words, according to Kristeva, it is possible to have a psychic structure not founded on desire but rather to persist as the "fascinated" and "willing" (PH, 9) victims of abjection.

Abject Heroes in Adolescent Fiction

Among the writers of adolescent fiction, the one who approaches abjection with the most appropriate brutality is Robert Cormier. The postoedipal diffusion of the superego that precipitates abjection is readily apparent in his novel *The Chocolate War*. In both family and school, the paternal presences of Jerry Renault's life are ineffectual; his father is sleepwalking through life after losing his wife, and the headmaster of the Catholic high school is gone due to an extended illness. But rather than a loosening of the superego such absences might portend, the operations of the superego fall to the hands of Brother Leon, a cruel, sadistic man, and the Vigils, an unofficial group of students whose activities, which include pranks meant to frighten and control both the underclassmen and the teachers, keep Trinity High School under constant internal pressure. Archie Costello, the most heinous member of the Vigils, knows exactly the group's role and its power: "It [the Vigils] was there because it served a purpose. The Vigils kept things under control. Without the Vigils, Trinity might have been torn apart like other schools had been, by demonstrations, protests, all that crap" (*The Chocolate War* [CW], 25). Archie devises "assignments" that require the students to strike random victims, and he occasionally switches loyalties. For instance, in order to discombobulate a new teacher, he instructs the students to stand and dance a silent jig whenever the teacher uses the word "environment." As the game wears on and he gets bored, he tells the teacher what's going on, so that the teacher can use the word more frequently to torture the boys. Thus Archie, who is the feared embodiment of the Law for the students at Trinity, is perceived as a random, unpredictable, sadistic figure. But as a literary figure, he is foil and counterpart for protagonist Jerry Renault—the abject hero, as it were, of this book.

Jerry's assignment from the Vigils is to refuse, for the first ten days, to participate in the school fund-raising effort. Each student is supposed to sell fifty boxes of leftover Mother's Day chocolates. The success of the sale will solidify Brother Leon's position as the official head of the school; its failure will likely result in his dismissal. It is significant for our purposes that the chocolates are related to the mother. These chocolates, twenty thousand boxes meant to honor the mother, did not find their rightful market.

Hence Brother Leon's power is dependent on the dishonoring of the maternal. Moreover, their status as candy and their failure to sell as Mother's Day gifts renders them abject—they represent an oral rejection of the maternal body, a weaning, as it were. Jerry's mother is dead, a circumstance he has yet to come to terms with. When she died, he was overcome with an anger "so deep and sharp in him that it drove out sorrow. He wanted to bellow at the world, cry out against her death, topple buildings, split the earth open, tear down trees. And he did nothing" (48). Jerry's mandated refusal to sell the chocolates suggests in a powerful way the assertion of superegoic power in the face of his refusal to accept his mother's death in the form of a prohibition of the already lost. He *must* dishonor and discharge his connection to his mother's body by refusing to participate in the sale. When he continues to refuse beyond the assignment, however, the reading of his refusal changes. When he says no the day after his assignment ends: "Cities fell. Earth opened. Planets tilted. Stars plummeted. And the awful silence" (89). Instead of responding to a prohibition, he is in fact refusing to participate fully in the weaning process. In his locker, he has a poster that quotes T. S. Eliot: "Do I dare disturb the universe?" His simple refusal to abject the body of his mother profoundly disturbs the Symbolic universe of Trinity.

The Vigils, and more specifically, Archie, embody the perverse superego against which Jerry sets himself. Archie as superego has his own explicit relation to the abject: "He hated the secretions of the human body, pee or perspiration. . . . He couldn't stand the sight of greasy, oozing athletes drenched in their own body fluids" (106). Jerry as abject bleeds, vomits, and sweats his way through the book. As his refusal to sell the chocolates threatens to make him a folk hero, the Vigils begin a campaign of torture and violence, first by physically abusing him in the halls, but then by completely ignoring him, refusing even to acknowledge his existence. "And yet, from its place of banishment, the abject does not cease challenging its master" (Kristeva, PH, 2); Jerry persists in his refusal to sell the chocolates. It is tempting to see his act of refusal as a heroic assertion of agency and individualism. In fact, many of his classmates read it this way. But for Jerry, it is an utterly passive resistance. He takes no energy or joy from his refusal, feels no satisfaction in it. Rather, it is as if he cannot help what he is doing. The unconscious connection between his mother's body and the chocolates is far too strong, far too taken up with death-drive energy, for him to sublimate the connection and expel it. Unable to abject his mother's body, then, he becomes himself abject. He falls into the abyss that gapes at the boundary of his subjectivity, the abyss of abjection that ultimately leads to his getting beaten almost to death. The community at Trinity, despite the ambivalence of some of its members, expels Jerry as abject. But insofar as Jerry refuses to cede the conditions of his existence, even his abject existence, to the desire of the Other, he is acting the part of the Lacanian hero.

Cormier creates other abject characters in other novels. Some are in fact psychotic or monstrous as they knowingly refuse to take up a subjective position through the agency of the Name of the Father, but most are ordinary kids like Jerry, the conditions of whose existence render them abject. Buddy Walker, the protagonist in *We All Fall Down*, is one such character. The novel begins: "They entered the house at 9:02 on the evening of April Fool's Day. In the next forty-nine minutes, they shit on the floors and pissed on the walls and trashed their way through the seven-room Cape Cod cottage" (Cormier, *WAFD*, 1). Buddy, one of the trashers, finds himself in the room of Jane Jerome, a girl his own age. He pees on her walls, cuts his finger on the glass from a broken picture frame, and vomits on the floor. When Jane returns home, she is overwhelmed with disgust at Buddy's abject bodily residue, and even after the room has been gutted and repainted, she is still haunted by the Imaginary smell of his vomit. Cormier goes out of his way from that point to create Buddy as a sympathetic, indeed almost pathetic, character, a boy hurt by his parents' divorce who turns to alcohol and questionable friendships to assuage his pain. The loss of his family stability results in a loss of his own oedipal stability; he no longer desires to identify with his father, and he cannot bear the weight of his mother. The aftermath of the trashing causes Jane to enter a period of abjection herself. The randomness of the crime and her status as victim disturbs her relationship with her friends; the social cannot bear a reminder of the abject at its borders. After losing her friends and having her general sense of security unsettled by the trashing, she loses her subjective bearings. She begins to wander the mall, unknowingly haunted and pursued by Buddy. When the two meet and fall in love, the reader considers the possibility of forgiveness for Buddy. Their romance is sweet and exhilarating, an Imaginary union with the full Symbolic sanction of first love. But the Real, that abject beyond of bodies and residual corporeal debt, intrudes and destroys any hope of absolution. When Jane learns that Buddy is one of the trashers, she excludes his presence from her life through her own vomit—she rejects, abjects, Buddy as her Imaginary ideal lover. Cormier's treatment of abjection reveals the fragility of the social construction of identity, especially adolescent identity, and forces the reader to confront the abject at the thin borders of ordinary existence.

Cormier is certainly not the only author to treat abjection in this way. The main characters in Walter Dean Myers's *Monster*, Gary Crew's *Strange Objects*, Mel Glenn's *Who Killed Mr. Chippendale?* and *The Taking of Room 114*, to name but a few, all fall into the category of abject hero—ordinary people who refuse to reintegrate into society under its terms but instead haunt and disrupt its borders. In Virginia Walter's unfortunately prescient novel *Making Up Megaboy*, Robbie Thomas shoots and kills a Korean shop owner for no apparent reason. Nor does he offer one. Robbie chooses to remain silent throughout the novel, which consists of a variety of documents— police reports, psychological profiles, interviews with family and acquaintances, drawings made by Robbie, and photos of Robbie growing up. Through her nonlinear narrative strategy, Walter accomplishes several things. She decentralizes Robbie as a subject, she destabilizes the categories of victim and perpetrator, and she emphasizes Robbie's status as abject. Robbie never comes to his own defense but rather draws a comic in which a human boy is waiting in a tree for Megaboy to come and return him to his home planet. Since Robbie has seemed to imagine himself as Megaboy in other comics, this one confuses Robbie's status—is he Megaboy or the human boy, subject or object? Or is he neither one, being instead the movement of the abject at the borders between the two? And what does Robbie's story, told wholly through the eyes of those around him, suggest about the role of the social in the construction of the abject hero?

Social Abjection and Cultural Complicity

It is telling that one of the first young-adult novels to be categorized as such was called *The Outsiders* and was written by a teenager in 1967. S. E. Hinton tells the story of a group of socially abject boys who are defined by the way they wear their hair: They are Greasers. Hair grease is one of those substances that Western culture, with its soaps and shampoos, tries to expel from the "clean and proper body," but for these characters, it is a mark of identity. The attempt to control the social boundaries of their world leads the Socs (short for Socialites, the rich kids from the South Side) to fight two of the boys—Ponyboy and Johnny—for the crime of talking to Soc girls. Johnny kills Bob in order to save Ponyboy, and the two escape to a hideout in the country, where tragedy again finds them as their hideout burns to the ground when some little kids find their cigarettes and matches. Johnny and Ponyboy heroically save the children, but Johnny is badly burned over much of his body. As the Socs and the Greasers have it out in a final rumble, Johnny dies in the hospital. The final tragedy of the book occurs when Dallas, the hardest delinquent in the novel, cannot accept Johnny's death and challenges the police with an unloaded pistol. What is interesting in this novel in terms of abjection is that the Greasers who die are those without family support. Johnny's parents are abusive and neglectful, and Dallas is portrayed as simply on his own. Ponyboy's parents are both dead, but he has strict, loving brothers. The other boys in the book have at least mothers who care for and support them. Johnny and Dallas are the only truly abject characters, the only absolute outsiders. That they die suggests that abjection is an unsustainable social position. That they die violently, one in an attempt at heroic action and one at the hands of the Law, suggests something more sinister from a psychoanalytic perspective. Hinton is making a rather obvious commentary here on the cost of setting up exclusive social boundaries and on the power of connectedness and understanding. But the unconscious truth of her 1967 text is that figures like Johnny and Dallas must be expelled from a clean and proper society. Ponyboy's successful adult identity is contingent upon his ridding himself of his associations with these abject figures. With them in his life, he will always have the option to stray, to remain an outsider, a deject. But their deaths establish for him the value of his own submission to his brothers' harsh authority and his place in society. Significantly, Ponyboy sublimates the loss of his friends by turning to literature as a productive iteration; he is the narrator of this story, which begins and ends with the repetition of the same line.

As does *The Outsiders*, novels for this age group have traditionally supported the normative development of the ego by following the trajectory of a rite of passage—there is a preliminal stage that ends with separation from family or community, a liminal experience of individuation, and a rite of reincorporation. In fact, the bildungsroman represents the most common plot structure of the genre, and certainly acts as wish fulfillment not only for the adolescent reader but also for adult society, as it relates a narrative of successful integration into one's role as a fully oedipalized adult subject in the Symbolic order. In this type of narrative, abject characters act as foils for main characters. They bolster the protagonist's claim on his or her position in the Symbolic order by being themselves excluded from it; they define the abject in their status as sacrificial, cast off. In the case of *The Outsiders*, their sacrifice is heartwrenching. Their status as abject is not their fault; they have done nothing to deserve their fate.

More contemporary versions of that pattern, however, pose more complex questions, especially as they respond to actual events in contemporary culture. Anne Fine's *The Tulip Touch* can be read as an exploration of the cultural complicity of abjection. Natalie, the protagonist, lives with a loving but busy family. She meets Tulip, an unusually cruel and powerful girl her own age whose father is verbally abusive and whose mother is ineffectual. As their friendship grows, the boundaries between the two girls' egos are breached: Natalie comes to feel Tulip's presence inside her head, directing her thoughts and actions. Tulip is obviously jealous of Natalie's family, seeing Natalie as the unweaned sibling that augments her aggressive behavior. Natalie begins to realize that she is what her principal calls a "hold-your-coat merchant," someone who likes to see others get into trouble and encourages their aggression by volunteering to hold their coats while they fight. She understands that in order to rescue herself, she has to reestablish her own boundaries. In other words, she must abject Tulip. When Natalie rejects Tulip, Tulip enacts a bizarre ritual: She repeatedly goes to the home of a girl who has drowned and asks the girl's mother if her dead daughter can come out and play. Natalie realizes that her rejection has prompted Tulip's act of brutality, but she also blames her own father and other adults for not intervening in Tulip's obviously abusive home life. Her father openly admits the necessary use of Tulip as abject in Natalie's identity construction: "You've let down Tulip and you've saved yourself" (Fine, 135). But Natalie knows that it should not be that simple. Tulip should have the same rights to subjectivity as herself, and not be merely a prop on which to establish the clean and proper workings of her family and herself.

The abject characters thus act as foils and props for establishing the clean and proper identity of the normal protagonists, suggesting that one way out of abjection is the successful oedipalization of identity. Reincorporation into adult society requires leaving such figures behind. It's a parasitical move, but a self-preserving one, which makes it distasteful to theorize. It suggests that, in one sense at least, anyone who has successfully integrated into clean and proper society is complicit in the creation of abject figures. Society needs the abject to constitute itself and to establish order and boundaries. But as our culture emerges as less willing to define itself in dualistic terms, we begin to see the problems of such sacrificial logic in human terms.

What, we begin to ask, is the cost of our success in becoming atomized individuals? The question is not posed out of altruistic or philanthropic urges or out of a disinterested desire to know the other, but out of fear. In the school libraries and lunchrooms across our country, the abject is starting to assert itself. Are we in fact hold-your-coat merchants for the Dylan Klebolds and Eric Harrises of the world, building our group and individual identities on the sacrifice of these people as abject? That which we have previously found too distasteful to explore is forcing itself into our conscious awareness, and it is prompting profound ethical questions regarding the logic of abjection itself as a way of solidifying social and individual identities.

The Ethics of the Imaginary versus the Ethics of the Real

The preferred method of working one's way past the abjection of adolescence has traditionally been to repeat the process of repression that stabilized the oedipal identity in the first place. This has created as many problems for the social as it has solved for the individual. When the choice is so stark as to reject outright the maternal structure of connection and corporeality in favor of the paternal structure of independence and transcendence, we can have only a subjectivity that represses its debt to embodiment and its possibility for the creation and sustenance of worlds. But on the other hand, the rejection of the paternal in this context can lead only to psychosis, as in the cases of Robbie in *Making Up Megaboy*, and Steven Messenger in *Strange Objects*.

There are, however, successful cases in adolescent fiction where the subject has emerged from the ashes of the abject, as it were, and it is useful to explore these for possible alternatives. Paul Fleischman's *Whirligig* combines the socially abject with the psychologically abject in the character of Brent Bishop. Brent is materially abject, in that he is a stray, a victim of a succession of parental career moves that have left him continually in doubt as to where he is. With every move, he checks to make sure the proper ear is pierced, the proper clothes available, the proper hairstyle effected. He has no inner aesthetic, suggesting that his imaginary ideational representations are ephemeral, unstable. He has even chosen a girl from his new school to complete his latest wardrobe transformation, but his attempts to woo her at a party prove disastrous. Here he is confronted with what for him represents a visual image of his outsider status among the unweaned brothers—

the organizer of the party has asked everyone to dress in all white or all black to enact a human chess game. Nobody told him of the requirement, so his red shirt and khaki pants immediately establish his status as outsider. His inability to join the game he frankly despises brings to the surface all his conflictual emotions—he hates to stand out in a crowd, but this crowd is weirdly organized with respect to superegoic diffusion of authority. A game played with humans as the pieces? And he desires to join such a game? When he is publicly rejected by the girl he has chosen, he reaches his limit and decides to kill himself by closing his eyes and letting his car drift off the highway into oblivion.

He lives, but he has killed a girl his own age—a complete stranger named Lea, whose car he hit when he crossed the median strip. As restitution, her mother requests that he make four whirligigs and place them at the four corners of the United States. In the process of completing this odd task, Brent consciously decides to assume his status as abject, rather than let others define him as such. He seeks out coastal areas, borderlands, where he can imagine what Lea must have been like, and he transforms his thoughts of her into the whirligigs he creates. He also connects imaginatively to the previous owner of a book on whirligig construction that he uses, adding his marginal notes to the ones he finds there in a tentative dialogue of artist to artist. At first he makes a simple representational model of Lea as a mermaid, but his designs become more complicated and integrated, more like ideational representations of emotions. As he works through his atonement, he senses her forgiveness and adopts as his own her desire to be involved in the human community. He ends his journey by sharing his story, for the first time, with an artist, and he joins a contra dance, a human whirligig, that is taking place in the local town. He thus uses art, work, and finally dance as the means of reclaiming his connection to a corporeality he wanted to destroy; he has sublimated the experience of that corporeality by turning death into art.

Fleischman is a master of metaphors for abjection and its resolution through artistic sublimation, revisiting the theme in both *Mind's Eye* and *Breakout*. In both books the main characters feel the abjection of having no stable family. Courtney's mother is dead and her stepfather is not interested in her, and Del has been bounced from foster family to foster family until she has had enough. Each of the girls becomes further abject: In *Mind's Eye*, Courtney becomes paralyzed in an accident, and in *Breakout* Del fakes her own death so that she can start over. Courtney ends up in a nursing home, and Del in a traffic jam on her way out of town, both metaphoric spaces of liminality and immobility, of being stuck in the pushed-off, in-between spaces of culture. Courtney finds her way through abjection, however, through an imaginary journey to Italy, where she rejects the body-celebrating art of the Renaissance, which would emphasize her abject status, for the more contemplative, static art of the Medievalists, which offers her a new mirror and a new ideal in which to find herself. Del discovers stand-up comedy and uses it to establish a new identity and to make connections with the strangers around her. Though the arts are different for each character, the function of sublimation is the same for each.

Another "way out" of abjection can be found through spiritual experience that displaces abjection. In David Almond's *Skellig* and Annette Curtis Klause's *The Silver Kiss*, the main characters encounter supernatural but nonetheless material embodiments of their own abject conditions. Skellig is a wonderfully disturbing and ambiguous character—a filthy, disgusting, embodied angel who eats mice, bugs, and Chinese food when he can get it. And yet he is beautiful under his filth, and his supernatural intervention combines with Michael's love to preserve the life of Michael's newborn sister. In *The Silver Kiss*, Zoe can come to terms with her dying mother's body only by abjecting her own. She stops eating and begins to contemplate a substitutionary, sacrificial, abject logic—her life for her mother's. But Simon, a vampire, helps her to see that there are things worse than the death of the body. In order to accept the death of her mother, she has to be willing to kill Simon's brother, a child vampire who preys on the maternal sympathies of strangers. By killing the deathless child, Simon and Zoe achieve the ability to separate themselves from the maternal bodies that haunt them, and they are able to release their own abject bodies—Zoe's mom's and Simon's own—to a peaceful death.

Strategies of sublimation and displacement, like repression, are reworkings of traditional Symbolic and Imaginary approaches to dealing with abjection. As such, they participate in an ethics of the Imaginary—that is, an ethics founded on the binary logic and ideal images of the Imaginary, rather than one that takes into account the Real of bodies. Maire Jaanus points out that society has always had such an ethics (Jaanus, 2). Notions of love, freedom, equality, democracy, tolerance, and respect are set in counterpoint to their opposites—hate, domination, inequity, totalitarianism, and intolerance—and these define the conscious goals of ethical interaction in the

Symbolic. The problems of such an ethics can be located in both its cultural contents and its structure. As we noted in chapter 5, those ideal notions—freedom, respect, equality, democracy—are not universally enacted or even understood. They are racialized by the people who have access to them, and their very definitions are contingent on social and cultural conditions of power. Tolerance, for instance, can exist only from a place of perceived superiority.

Moreover, these ideals depend on a structurally binary logic of abjection. Such logic is built on haves and have-nots; it is undermined by the very notion that all might be haves, or, in more precisely Lacanian terms, have-nots. That is, a logic of abjection is effective because it allows for the expulsion of what is not clean and proper; I can push it away and thus establish my own completeness, rather than confronting, every minute of every day, that I too have bits that are unclean and improper, and that what I have excluded is not purely and simply gone. Socially speaking, under a logic of abjection, my identity depends on gathering to me those who bolster my illusion of totality (that is, those who are like me), and pushing away those people who remind me of my difference, my lack. Insofar as I might have a fully functioning body, for instance, I will push away, either psychically through pity or actually through disgust, those bodies that remind me of the fragility of embodiment itself. As long as I can disidentify with them as the not-me, I can maintain a benevolent distance. But if I begin to realize that I too have a body that could, at any minute, become disabled, I have to readjust my distance, my benevolence, my pity, my Imaginary ideals themselves, because of the intrusion of the Real.

This is an obvious example; less obvious is that we are each related to our own *jouissance* in distinct ways that determine our idiosyncratic calls of concern, and this reveals to us the fundamental unknowability of any other. Jane and Buddy in *We All Fall Down* offer an example of this: Their Imaginary relationship of first love can be maintained only as long as it disavows the origin of their relationship in the Real, that is, in the smell of Buddy's vomit on Jane's carpet. An ethics of the Imaginary seeks to live on the surface of this problem, to disavow that bodies or idiosyncratic kernels of desire matter in questions of ethics.

A clear illustration of this problem can be found in Francesca Lia Block's Weetzie Bat books. These postmodern fairy tales are highly stylized versions of the problem novel; playing between magic and reality, they show young adults trying to find love and to create families in the face of parental neglect, drug addiction, AIDS, environmental crises, and consumer culture. If one strips away Block's fanciful descriptions of gingerbread houses and fairy godmothers, one finds the stark reality of a girl and a boy who are desperately trying to find love in the mosh pits of Los Angeles. In the first of five books that focus on the same constellation of characters, these teens make a home together through the granting of Weetzie's three wishes: a "duck" (slang for a cute gay boy) for Dirk, a Secret Agent Lover Man for herself, and a house for them to live happily ever after in. The death of Dirk's grandmother provides them with the house, and Weetzie and Dirk both find their loves, oddly enough named My Secret Agent Lover Man and Duck, respectively.

The fact that Weetzie called these things into being more than suggests their Imaginary character, which is reinforced by the way Weetzie and Dirk treat their lovers. They absorb them into their lives as extensions of themselves, and at crucial moments openly disregard their lovers' pain and frustration because it does not correspond to their own desires. Against My Secret Agent Lover Man's wishes, Weetzie sleeps with both Dirk and Duck in order to have a baby. Dirk is more sensitive to Duck's pain, but Duck nonetheless feels the need to run away from Dirk rather than toward him when he is struck by the impact of AIDS on the people he knows. Shortly after Weetzie's baby, Cherokee Bat, is born, another baby appears on their doorstep; My Secret Agent Lover Man, terribly hurt by Weetzie's disregard for his wishes, has fathered a child with another woman. This child, Witch Baby, is brooding and serious like her father, whereas Cherokee Bat is blond and light-hearted like her mother. But Weetzie's response to them, as to all of the members of her household, is to play on the surfaces of their relationships, to draw everyone into her "love current." Rather than respond to their otherness, she seeks to assimilate everyone into her perfect world, aestheticized and anesthetized by music and flowers and feathers and vegetarian cuisine.

But Witch Baby continually resists being drawn in. She prefers to face the pain of the world, to keep traumatic wounds open so that they can do their ethical work of reminding us of our separateness and the way we fail one another. Weetzie glosses over Witch Baby's preoccupation with disaster, thinking that all will be well if Witch Baby joins the dance that Weetzie self-consciously crafts out of their lives. As a result, Witch Baby runs away, and Weetzie realizes that she has in fact been using Witch Baby to contain her own pain. As long as Witch Baby looks at the dark side of things, Weetzie doesn't have to; through Witch Baby, Weetzie has an externalized social conscience that she needn't pay any mind to. Thus, Weetzie is operating under the logic of abjection, and Witch Baby is merely a container for that which she abjects. But Witch Baby's refusal to play Weetzie's game exposes it for what it is—a failed ethics of the Imaginary.

One would think that Witch Baby would understand, then, that you can't simply use people as your objects, and yet we find that she too must learn that lesson. In *Missing Angel Juan*, Witch Baby must face losing the boy that she needs in the same way that Weetzie needs her. She sees Angel Juan as an extension of herself rather than as a person in his own right. He exists for Witch Baby as her complement, as the container of her pain. When he goes off to New York, she obsessively follows him. As she looks for him, though, she encounters the ghost of Weetzie's father, Charlie Bat, who helps her to see that you have to honor the otherness of the other, to face your lack squarely without trying to cover it over with identification or incorporation of that which you think might fill you. When Witch Baby finds Angel Juan, he has been kidnapped by a serial killer who makes plastic mannequin models of his victims in which he encases them so that he can keep them forever caught in an image he has made of them. Witch Baby and Angel Juan both realize that this horror is the metaphorical equivalent of Witch Baby's desire for Angel Juan, and Witch Baby understands that she must let him be himself, other from her, in order for them to achieve a mature love. The separateness they afford each other thus strengthens the selves they have to offer one another in love by paradoxically allowing space for each other's brokenness.

There are some very recent novels for young adults that suggest similar strategies in enacting a Lacanian ethics of the Real. These novels articulate the problems of bodies and the nature of *jouissance* that cannot be ameliorated by Imaginary solutions. An ethics of the Real "examines the movements beyond the pleasure barrier and the barrier of anxiety, towards all types of morbidity" (Jaanus, 1). Obviously, Cormier's texts push those boundaries. His novels specifically refuse the Imaginary solace of a benevolent big Other that requires only the subject's complicity to be complete. Adam in *I Am the Cheese* and Ben in *After the First Death* must confront the fact that they are tools for their government. But rather than that government representing a seat of disinterested justice, they find that they are the victims of its corrupt and ineffectual systems of power and control. Significantly, they find this out through an encounter with the Real, when their bodies are pushed to a point of failure and they cannot maintain their Imaginary or Symbolic façades. Both boys end up dead or nearly so, like Jerry Renault in Cormier's *The Chocolate War.* Thus, Cormier's texts, while laudable in their refusal to cover over Real problems with Imaginary solutions, nevertheless point only to a failure of the ethics of the Imaginary and miss the chance for a productive encounter with an ethics of the Real.

Other novels push "beyond the pleasure barrier . . . towards all types of morbidity" and yet maintain some hope, suggesting that an ethics of the Real may have some exigency. Annette Curtis Klause's *Blood and Chocolate* is the story of a young female werewolf. The stirrings of her adolescent body prompt her to explore the possibility of connecting sexually with a human. He has written a poem that suggests he might understand the beauty of her werewolf body, the pleasures of a body that embraces and celebrates its animality rather than attempting to deny or ignore it. When she transforms in front of him, she realizes that what for her is the site of *jouissance* is for him a place of horror and abjection, no matter what his poetry says. His gesture of sublimation is an attempt to hold the abject at bay, whereas her response is to recast the terms of abjection—*she* abjects *him* for his denial of his own corporeal, animal nature. Significantly, it is her father, the former leader of the pack, who is dead in this novel, while her mother remains an active, sexual presence. Recasting the terms of abjection in this context means to reject the lawful, disembodied, patriarchal Symbolic in favor of the embodied law of the pack that honors the joy of the body.

Recasting the terms of abjection, and learning instead to bear the abject rather than to ignore or dissolve into it is also the solution proposed in Nancy Werlin's *The Killer's Cousin.* Seventeen-year-old David has been acquitted of the murder of his girlfriend, but his acquittal and the accidental nature of her death do nothing to negate the fact that he killed her; a beloved human being is dead at his hand. Likewise, his eleven-year-old cousin Lily is responsible for the death of her sister. Lily forces David to admit to the feelings of power, desire, and *jouissance* that accompanied his act, and to acknowledge that because they have done it once, they could do it again. David makes a pact with Lily that, unlike the other people in their lives, they will not try to erase, ignore, deny, or forget the abject condition that grounds their existence. They will not participate in the ethics of the Imaginary that presumes them innocent. Instead, they will bear their condition of otherness together.

Fleischman's *Breakout* argues eloquently for a logic beyond abjection that realizes the otherness within the self. The text presents an extreme situation with Del faking her own death to literally claim her abject status as morbidity, but her epiphany in the traffic jam works its way out into an ethics of the Real. The traffic jam might be seen as an intrusion of the Real into her fantasy of rebirth. But whereas other drivers attempt to ascribe personal reasons for the jam, as "*a sign that the speaker is really too sick to go to work, as a punishment for a second bowl of ice cream, as a chance to review anger management techniques, as a warning against a romantic tryst, as a sign that the brakes aren't safe*," (Fleischman, *Breakout*, 86), and so on, Del realizes that this is a silly way to approach the problem. In our terms, it is an attempt at Imaginary closure, rather than an openness to a genuine encounter with the Real. Del, after a few false starts, refuses to see the jam as some great cosmic message addressed to her, choosing instead to open herself to the encounter with Otherness. "*I think of all the people I saw in the jam. They're all so strange. We're all so strange. I am one of the Other People*" (122), she realizes, referring to and undermining Sartre's definition of hell as other people. But there is more to be gained than self-realization from an encounter with the Real. She continues: "*It's not just other people we have to accept. It's Otherness. Things we have no control over, didn't ask for, don't deserve. History. Earthquakes. Cancer. Family. Traffic jams. 'It is what it is'*" (122).

An ethics of the Real, then, acknowledges and attempts to work through abjection, acknowledges but does not despair at the sure and certain knowledge, every day, that what is unthinkable can return, that death can infect life, even at the hands of a child. In fact it is our children who are teaching us that we must bear the weight of this knowledge, rather than continue to build our lives on its exclusion. Working through the ethical problems and solutions proposed in young-adult literature helps teens become aware of their complicity in the construction of insiders and outsiders, and they are led to see how such exclusionary practices lead to violent behavior. But they may also be confronted with their complicity in the construction of themselves as outsiders. By exploring the inner lives of abject characters, they may well be led to understand that it is possible to connect to others; indeed, they may make their first affective links with the characters themselves, thus beginning the process of developing a more fully realized Imaginary on which to build stable yet flexible Symbolic identities without disavowing the presence of the Real. Knowing that they are not alone in their abjection, and knowing that there are alternative ways to deal with abjection, may in fact point the way toward a Symbolic exchange, whether of sublimation, displacement, or forbearance, that preempts the violent acting out of aggression.

Postmoderns at the
Gates of Dawn

I have argued throughout this book that most of the literature read to and by children and adolescents tends to participate in the construction and reinforcement of a modernist subjectivity. Alasdair MacIntyre argues in *After Virtue* that "man is in his actions and practice, as well as in his fictions, essentially a story-telling animal," but he adds that "I can only answer the question 'What am I to do?' if I can answer the prior question 'Of what story or stories do I find myself a part?'" (216). This study has been an attempt to answer that prior question at the level of how we become a part of those stories which shape us. In *The Novel as Family Romance*, Christine van Boheemen says that the "significance of our stories derives from their relation to the models of signification operative in our society—causality, centrism, linearity, and teleology—which are our inescapable unconscious heritage" (13). Underlying her claims of an "inescapable unconscious heritage" is the assumption of both a novel form and a subject that have fairly stable structures. But what happens if the models of signification she lists are no longer operative or are articulated as malleable rather than inescapable? If we take subjectivity to be constructed on the model of the narrative, we are called upon to inquire into any significant changes in the form of narrative that might work themselves out as changes in the structures or at least in the contents of subjectivity itself. This is an especially important inquiry when it regards children's literature, as the child is much more vulnerable to the vicissitudes of language than is the adult. When postmodern narrative forms are presented to adults, they may be regarded as interesting, weird, unsettling, or liberating, but they will rarely change an adult's fundamental outlook on the relations between, say, language and the world, representation and authority, meaning and interpretation. The adult tends to approach the text with an eye toward whether it matches his version of reality (in which case it is true or insightful) or doesn't (in which case it is false or wrongheaded). But for the child, that "prodigiously open" creature who is using the textual Other to organize his inner as well as his outer world, everything the text tells him about the world is at some level true, because it is what generates the conditions for truth.

By way of conclusion, then, I briefly outline some trends in postmodern children's literature that may have a significant impact on the kinds of subjects our children become. To further clarify the terms presented in my introduction, I will note that most of the literature I have discussed bears the mark of the modernist subject. Where the traditional subject is thought to be whole, transparent to himself, and oriented toward some external standard of good or evil, the modernist subject is split. She has an unconscious that is inaccessible, and she regards this with a great deal of angst. Not to know herself is a violation of the traditional Aristotelian maxim, and she experiences guilt and anxiety over not being able to live up to it. Her fantasy is therefore directed toward the goal of self-knowledge. Implicit in that aim is the goal of being *known* by the Other, or especially by one or two privileged others with whom she has developed intimacy and trust. She values closure, even if it is fantasmatic. She insists on the possibility of a stable referent, even if it is ultimately unknowable. She believes in the world and yet represses the fact that it is a belief. Yet because of her split she can imagine a world other than the one she believes in, and she can produce that world in her arts, making them the carriers of her unconscious residue.

The truly postmodern subject is, at this point in time, only a postulate. Part of the reason for this, I think, is because children's literature has only recently begun to adopt the narrative conventions of postmodern literature. Perhaps the ambivalence felt by many writers toward postmodern techniques has prohibited them from enacting those techniques for an audience we feel deserves our protection from undue stress and anxiety. On the other hand, could it be said that the child's perceived delight in and celebration of the multivalence of the world his imagination presents to him makes him a perfect viewer for the postmodern aesthetic, a sort of prototypic postmodern? To give a definitive answer would be to construct a kind of child who may have no bearing on current reality. Certainly the child is open to the world as it is presented to him. Perhaps that openness does have certain affinities with, or could be said to be one of the conditions for, postmodernity. But the child reared on predominantly modernist texts will come to structure himself around modernist concerns. Childlike openness is unsustainable; it necessarily closes around the sum of the child's experiences. Nonetheless, openness in the postmodern sense could be cultivated as the dominant feature of those experiences. This seems to be the direction that much contemporary children's literature is taking.

I turn now to three emergent trends that correspond to the central issues I have discussed in previous chapters: the nature of language, the relation of the subject to the Law, and, finally, the construction of a moral universe.

The Nature of Language: Children's Alphabet Books

I have argued elsewhere that alphabet books seem to be undergoing a shift in the way language is related to its referent, and the way the reemergence of the image serves to challenge the linearity of phallocentric discourse.[1] I will briefly recapitulate the first part of that argument here. In 1962, J. L. Austin published a series of lectures under the title *How to Do Things with Words* in which he inaugurated something called speech-act theory, which has been taken up, used, misused, critiqued, and discarded by any number of influential critics and theorists, including John Searle, Paul de Man, Stanley Fish, Jacques Derrida, and J. Hillis Miller. Judith Butler's work makes extensive use of Austin's theories; in fact, I would venture to say that if one wants to understand any of the more difficult postmodern thinkers of our time (and I would include in that list Homi Bhabha, Richard Rorty, and Lacan, as well as Butler herself), a good place to start is with an informed reading of Austin. Or, perhaps, with a comparative reading of Chris van Allsburg's *The Z Was Zapped*.

Austin begins his elaboration of speech acts by distinguishing between constative utterances, which describe an existing state of affairs, and performative utterances, such as promises, bets, or warnings, which bring a state of affairs into being. Practitioners of speech-act theory, particularly Austin's student John Searle, have created elaborate taxonomies to explain the conditions of success for specific kinds of performative utterances, but that is only one direction in which one might develop Austin's project. And in fact, it is one way of reading Austin that could conceivably participate in a profound misreading of Austin, because in the end, Austin admits that the distinction between constatives and performatives doesn't necessarily hold, or that it holds only within a certain way of viewing language.

That way of viewing language is largely unconsciously under the sway of the Descriptive Fallacy. Austin says: "It was for too long the assumption of philosophers that the business of a 'statement' can only be to 'describe' some state of affairs, or to 'state some fact,' which it must do either truly or falsely"(1). As noted in chapter 1, in this way of thinking, authority rests in an outside referent, and truth is measured by the perceived degree of correspondence to that referent.

This view of language underwrites the traditional alphabet structure of "*a* is for apple." George Bodmer, in his essay "The Post-Modern Alphabet: Extending the Limits of the Contemporary Alphabet Book, from Seuss to Gorey," looks at some of the ways the genre of the alphabet book has strained at its borders in recent years, and indeed, one can only ever look at some of the ways this is taking place, given the incredible proliferation of the genre. His purpose is to point out certain postmodern techniques at work in contemporary alphabet books, noting especially the antididactic and parodic strains in postmodern texts. But I would like to suggest that one of the markers of a truly postmodern alphabet book lies less in its technique or presentation than in the way it views language. Despite the heterogeneity of artistic techniques, an alphabet book participates in either a constative view of language, where *a* is always for something else, or a performative view of language, where *a* is a thing all by itself, so to speak.

The vast majority of alphabet books operate under the constative view of language and hence participate in the Descriptive Fallacy Austin spoke of. But in recent years, the changing view of the relationship of words to world has reached the alphabet book. Dr. Seuss, in *On Beyond Zebra*, offers us a way of viewing the transition from a constative view of language, where the "direction of fit," to use Searle's terminology, is words to world, and language is a way of knowing reality, to a performative view, where the direction of fit is world to words, and language becomes a means of constructing reality. For Seuss, the view that language is a way of knowing reality gives rise to the feeling of a sort of dead end.

Said Conrad Cornelius o'Donald o'Dell
My very young friend who is learning to spell:
"The A is for Ape. And the B is for Bear.

"The C is for Camel. The H is for Hare.

"The M is for Mouse. And the R is for Rat.

"I know *all* the twenty-six letters like that . . .

". . . through to Z is for Zebra. I know them all well."

Said Conrad Cornelius o'Donald o'Dell.

"So now I know everything *any*one knows

"From beginning to end. From the start to the close.

"Because Z is as far as the alphabet goes." (n.p.)

The narrator of the story challenges the idea that knowledge of the world has to stop with Z and, in so doing, sets the stage for challenging the epistemological nature of language as a way of knowing existing reality. He still insists that language has a referential quality, but he evokes the power of language to perform realities that exist outside the traditional order. We could say that this is a similar position to the one that E. B. White takes in *Charlotte's Web*. Charlotte uses the performative power of language to recreate Wilbur, but Wilbur still must become the existential referent of her words.

The shift from a constative view of language to a performative one has become evident in the past several years in children's alphabet books. Austin himself suggests the temporal dimension of the shift when he says that the constative and the performative may not be "really two poles, but rather an historical development" (146). In a postmodern view, *a* is no longer referential, it is no longer *for* something, but rather it *is* a something all by itself. Language becomes material; it acts and, in acting, produces material effects. In becoming material, it also becomes playful, autonomous, and vulnerable.

Chicka Chicka Boom Boom is an alphabet book which shows the joy that is one possible outcome of the liberation from reference. In this rhythmic, playful alphabet book, "A told B and B told C, 'I'll meet you at the top of the coconut tree,'" and on and on until all of the lowercase letters climb the tree. The tree bends over and they all fall out. Though the "real world" (as represented by the coconut tree) collapses under their collective weight, the letters are picked up and dusted off by their own uppercase letters— language is pictured here as a self-sufficient, self-authorizing structure. It doesn't need propping up by outside referents, and in fact outside referents cannot bear its weight. This represents a profoundly different world-view than one in which language must be found that will correspond more closely to the world in order to express truth. Language is not about knowing in

Chicka Chicka Boom Boom; rather it is about enjoying, acting, performing. It may get scuffed and bruised in the process—black-eyed P and loose-toothed T being but two examples—but it is ultimately unstoppable in its playful effects.

What happens in the shift from constative to performative is a sea-change in the direction of fit from referent to sign. Consider books like *Alphabet City*, where instead of a letter corresponding to an object, the photo-realistic paintings depict objects that conform to letters. The same is true of a book for toddlers called *Let's Play ABC*, where there are pictures of toddlers contorting their bodies into the shapes of the letters, and the opening text encourages children to imitate the pictures. It's a standard feature on *Sesame Street* for a group of children to make the letter of the day with their bodies, and if not the children, then William Wegman's mournful-looking dogs. This encouragement of active participation in the making of letters reinforces the material nature of the letter, its autonomous existence that enables the letter itself to become an object for representation rather than a transparent instrument of representation. Letters become performers in and of reality rather than simply pointers to something outside themselves.

But the performative view of language is not all about play and freedom from reference. It has its sinister possibility as well, as evidenced in Chris van Allsburg's eerie alphabet book *The Z Was Zapped*. That his book represents the performative view is most clearly and conveniently demonstrated by each of the letters appearing on a stage, with each appearance called an Act. But it is not the performative as play. Instead, as the book jacket obliquely points out, it is not without "great personal sacrifice" that language reveals its status as performative. For if language is a thing in the world rather than an epistemological tool, Van Allsburg seems to be saying, then it is vulnerable to the dangers common to all things. It can outgrow itself, be devoured, disappear.

Van Allsburg portrays quite vividly the angst produced by a performative view of language for those of us brought to consciousness through a constative view. Herein I think lies the major difficulty in reading thinkers such as Butler, Rorty, Foucault, and Lacan, whose work on subjectivity proceeds from and presupposes the performative view of language. For I suspect that for everyone who embraces this view, there are others who, while granting it some validity, nonetheless experience a kind of vertigo in the face of the loss of an ultimate referent *outside* of language. We might call it a crisis of authority, a succumbing to moral relativism, a failure of faith in absolutes. But what we are really talking about is the abandonment of an overly simplified notion of the correspondence of words to world. What will be interesting to track is how our own postmodern children will locate, or more precisely relocate, the foundations and conditions of truth and authority as they grow up, having learned from their constative *and* their performative alphabet books that language not only allows them to know and order the world, but also works to make that world.

The Relation of the Subject to the Law: Interactive Texts

A second notable trend in children's literature is the tremendous growth and diversity of interactive texts. Crafting your own ending to a story is certainly not a new impulse. Stories told and retold over time bear the marks of the individual teller's experience and desires, as well as the needs of the community. How a story ends is very important, since the ending confers the moral, settles out who was the hero and who was the villain, and restores order to the mayhem introduced through the story's conflict. If the ending is changed, the entire sense of the meaning of each of the story's elements changes with it. L. M. Montgomery tells of her propensity in childhood to write new endings to many of the stories she read, usually making the wimpy female into a strong heroine who saves the day. We can see in this example the subversive potential of rewriting the ending. Oral stories tend to preserve their fluidity, but a story written down tends to reify. Whole academic careers are built on authenticating "original" texts and ferreting out authors' original intentions before their works underwent outside editing. The written word constitutes its own authority. It establishes its rightness simply by being in print, as Charlotte reminds us. When a child undertakes to rewrite an ending to suit her, she is challenging an authoritative structure. As the Montgomery example suggests, that authoritative structure is male dominated, an agent of the Name of the Father. Part of the satisfaction of the rewriting comes from the desire to transgress the Name of the Father.

Interactive texts resituate that authority. They come in all sorts of guises, from picture books that pose mysteries to solve, Waldos to find, or everyday objects recontextualized into "look-alikes," to series of the *Choose Your Own Adventure* and *You Be the Jury* nature, to computer texts. Interactive texts give the reader the authority, and the responsibility, for crafting an ending.

Whereas books with fixed endings emphasize (unconsciously) the desirability of an ending, and the necessity of the particular ending the author has chosen, interactive texts replace inevitability with contingency. Herein lies the practical fruition of the theoretical notion of the "death of the author"—the reader really does become the writer of the text. Consider this then: Instead of seeing himself mirrored in a text as a totality, the postmodern subject sees himself mirrored as an openness, a site for the proliferation of possibilities. In his essay "What Is an Author?" Foucault says that the role of the author function is to shut down the proliferation of possibilities. By attaching a proper name, or even a common but definable noun, to a subject, we establish certain boundaries between what is that person and what is other. Endings play a large role in this construction, because they close down, at least temporarily, possibilities. But the way interactive texts work is to allow the reader to work through different scenarios, so the story never ends. Even if you die, you can go back and get another life to start all over with. What does this do to the authoritative mandates to choose a sexual position, a moral position, an ethical position, and to stick with it?

Lacan's answer is that the proliferation of subjective possibilities is always limited by the way the subject's desire has been canalized. But as we have seen, much of that work is done by poetic and literary language. In interactive texts, the language is largely functional. It is meaning driven, with little thought to its phonemic resonance or beauty. The question to ask then is what becomes of the psychoanalytic use of language, especially literary language, to mourn loss and reclaim *jouissance*, when narrative is reduced to a set of instructions or the posing of a problem. The phonemic resonances are lost in the computer-generated noise and mechanized vocal tones of the interactive text. In addition, what becomes of the child's capacity for empathy, especially empathy for the victim, if he or she is always, so to speak, the one aiming the weapon?

The Construction of the Moral Universe:
Series without Subjects

In traditional series books, the series is defined by a person or a group of people. The Hardy Boys, Nancy Drew, Anne of Green Gables, the Baby-Sitter's Club, Harry Potter, and countless others star in book after book. We get to know the characters and the author's methods, and we can then predict or at least judge the behavior of the characters, which is almost always on the side of the good. Hence we form a view of the total world of the series. We know who the good guys are—they are the title characters. Even if they do something wrong or stupid, they learn a lesson, and all is put right in the end. There is a consistency of conventional virtue in the worlds of these series. There is nothing sinister, for instance, in the world of the Baby-Sitter's Club. It is simply suburban life at its most idyllic and innocent. There is also a sense of the knowableness of the world in these books. L. M. Montgomery's Prince Edward Island is so carefully and consistently depicted that a visit to the actual province confirms the realism of the books and even evokes a sense of homecoming. And even in the criminal-filled world of the young-detective series, we come to know certain things. We know, for instance, that nothing really horrible is going to happen to the main characters. Nancy Drew is not going to get raped. No matter what dangers they encounter, they will emerge relatively unharmed. Moreover, we trust the formula that they will "win" in their encounters with villains. Evil just doesn't go unpunished, and it certainly never triumphs at the expense of the hero or heroine. We are also assured that any loose ends are left loose only for the sake of creating a sequel. Most often, however, the case is closed, or the adventure or mishap is resolved, at the end of the book.

Not so with certain contemporary series fiction. R. L. Stine's wildly successful Goosebumps books have almost nothing in common with conventional series fiction. The only mark of consistency is their inconsistency. First, they are not organized around a person or group of people who returns in each book. We might link this trend to the poststructural notion of the end of man or the death of the subject, and extend it to other contemporary series fiction where the series is linked by place—as in Stine's Fear Street series for adolescents, or even Cormier's novels, which aren't properly series fiction but are still connected by virtue of taking place in the same cluster of towns—or by genre, as in Christopher Pike's horror series or the burgeoning genre of vampire series books. Personalities are no longer as important as positions. In Stine's work, the position of the protagonist is generally, but not always, the position of the unwitting victim of some horrific and supernatural villain. But there is no consistency even in this. In one Goosebumps book, for instance, the protagonist is the daughter of a scientist whose project has gone horribly wrong, and while she is in some danger, her main concern is to rescue her father. In another, the protagonist herself is the stalker. In still another, the protagonist thinks she is in danger of being victimized by a monster, but when she confides her fears to her parents, they invite the monster over, turn into monsters themselves, and eat him as an object lesson for their daughter.

Because of this inconsistency in the status of the protagonist, there is no sense of how the story will or should end. The stories have no predictable moral center that allows us to desire one outcome over another based on a prevailing sense of an ordered and just universe. In one case, the main character, who seems harmless enough, is turned into a bird by her enemy. In another, a more predictable outcome prevails: The children save themselves and their parents from being turned into zombies by their dead neighbors. In the case of the monster parents cited above, the lesson to be learned by the main character is that you have to keep the monster population down if you want to be able to live normal lives among people who are not monsters. Otherwise, your community becomes either a circus or a witch hunt. In short, in the world of *Goosebumps*, sometimes evil wins, sometimes evil loses, sometimes evil gets run over by a random bulldozer. Most often, however, it's hard to sort out who is evil, who is good, and who is simply gross. Since most of the books are written in first person, evil is often located in a Lacanian Imaginary sense as that which is farthest from the main character, regardless of his or her moral status considered from an extradiegetic position.

The most striking feature of these books, however, is their lack of diegetic closure. Again, the individual books are inconsistent. Some have very definite narrative closure. But most do not. When the evil ventriloquist gets run over by the bulldozer, the book ends with the formerly inanimate and seemingly harmless dummy congratulating the girls on getting rid of his rival. The children who escape the zombies cannot stop the next family from moving in to Dead House. Some of the books simply end with an unanswerable question. Despite the fact that Stine comes out with one of these books a month, there are relatively few that pick up these open-ended strands and continue them as sequels. But that doesn't seem to bother the young readers who devour these books. In fact, they seem to relish the technique, giving the lie to such nostalgic constructions of childhood that write children as craving closure. Series fiction has always played to that part of the child that wants the story to continue. Stine steps up that effect by offering the openness without the answering sequel.

There is, then, no sense of the "ultimate" in the postmodern series. Good and evil are contingent upon the status or position of the character. Justice is local and specific to situations that change in surprising ways, undoing what seemed to be just moments before. Not even death is final. In fact, many of the newer series focus specifically on the realm of the undead. It is no wonder that, in 2002, one of the common teen slang words was "random," applied seemingly without any attachment to a consistent reference. The categories Boheemen suggests are inescapable—"causality, centrism, linearity, and teleology"—are (un)systematically dismantled and revealed to be contingent formations of modernism. Other formations emerge instead —randomness, diffusion, relativity, and contingency. The question then: Will these formations become our children's "inescapable unconscious heritage"? When the stories of which we find ourselves a part undergo significant structural change, what will be the effect on our ethics, our desires, our actions, and our subjectivities themselves?

NOTES

Introduction

1. To cite but a few examples: Peter Brooks's *Reading for the Plot: Design and Intention in Narrative*; James M. Mellard's *Using Lacan, Reading Fiction*; Christine van Boheemen's *The Novel As Family Romance: Language, Gender, and Authority from Fielding to Joyce*; Marshall W. Alcorn, Jr. and Mark Bracher's "Literature, Psychoanalysis, and the Re-Formation of the Self: A New Direction for Reader-Response Theory."

2. McGillis offers a reading of *The Root Cellar* that touches on many of the important features of Lacan's theory of subjectivity in his "Another Kick at La/can: 'I Am a Picture.'" Nodelman and Reimer and Bosmajian present succinct introductions to Lacanian theory that briefly hint at possible implications for interpretation in, respectively, *The Pleasures of Children's Literature*, and "Reading the Unconscious: Psychoanalytical Criticism." Other psychoanalytic readings of children's texts can be found in Lucy Rollin and Mark I. West's *Psychoanalytic Responses to Children's Literature*, and Margaret Rustin and Michael Rustin's *Narratives of Love and Loss: Studies in Modern Children's Fiction*. These latter studies are not Lacanian in their orientation.

3. Ashraf H. A. Rushdy, for instance, in "'The Miracle of the Web': Community, Desire, and Narrativity in *Charlotte's Web*," evokes Lacanian theory with respect to what he calls a "'reflective model' of interpellation," using Lacan's famous essay on the mirror stage in the service of Rushdy's own model of text as reflective of society. Focusing his attention on a straightforward reading of the metaphor of the mirror, Rushdy evokes Lacan's work only to dismiss it, stating that "Lacan, in the end, can represent only the model of desire as reflection" (41). In this study, I hope to show how unwise it is to say of such a complex thinker, "Lacan, in the end . . ."

4. For a clear articulation of these problems, see *Girls, Boys, Books, Toys: Gender in Children's Literature and Culture*, edited by Beverly Lyon Clark and Margaret R. Higonnet. The introduction is especially useful for understanding the ways gender has been studied in children's books.

1. How to Save Your Life

1. This project is a psychoanalytic reading. I aim to explore many of the less generally understood concepts of Lacanian thought, but I will nevertheless assume a familiarity on the part of the reader with certain overdetermined "truths" of psychoanalysis. Among these, phallic symbols loom large.

2. Although this discussion may seem to leave out those disenfranchised children whose access to books is compromised by economic or social class or disability, I would contend that those children are still surrounded by the swirl of language, image, and story. Their access to representation and cultural imagery may be limited to public advertisement and television, but they can do little to avoid that access, which is ubiquitous. Moreover, their status as disenfranchised is regarded as such precisely because our culture values the book so much; literacy is such an object of desire and a method of empowerment that its very lack compromises their success in attaining certain subject positions in our culture. My own experience with rearing a disabled child has taught me that those children who can't or don't read are in fact the ones most likely to be captivated by images. Unfortunately, the emphasis on traditional alphabetic literacy, the cultural prejudice in favor of which I have indicated, works to exclude certain potentialities, most importantly the potential for developing subjectivities that others will recognize as complex and multivalent, for disenfranchised children.

2. A Time to Mourn

1. I must admit that explanations of the solutions to logic problems make my eyes go blurry. The reader who enjoys that sort of thing is referred first to Lacan's text itself, and then to several very good explanations of the text, including alternate solutions, offered by Bruce Fink in "Logical Time," 356–386, and "Notes on Temporal Tension," 23–28).

2. I am, of course, ignoring that class of "activity" or "busy" books that invite interaction through textures and manipulatives. They also tend, I think, to reinforce the materiality of the signifier.

3. An anecdotal example of this kind of learning came to my attention when the child of a friend asked his mother if she was Diane, then was she his mother, and did she have two cats? The mother was shocked and dismayed, thinking that her child had developed amnesia and didn't know who she was. As it turned out, the child had just realized that his mother's name was Diane. He had a friend named Diane, and she had two cats. If, by associational logic, his mother was called Diane, then she couldn't also be his mother, and she must then have two cats.

4. See Anne Anlin Cheng's study *The Melancholy of Race* for an excellent discussion of these issues.

5. A violence in the phallic function is suggested here that is reminiscent of *Bambi*, *Dumbo*, *Babe*, *The Story of Babar*, and others, and is very different, it seems to me, from the mother voluntarily turning away from the child to pursue her desire

elsewhere. It lets the mother off the hook in a way, and allows her to be eulogized into a symbolic function like the dead mother in fairy tales who returns as the fairy godmother. This is often, but not always, the case in these sorts of stories.

3. Mourning into Dancing

1. See chapter 4 for a detailed description of the functioning of the *objet a*.
2. More about *jouissance* in chapter 4.
3. A dialectic movement between the excess of syntax and the lack of semantics is not a bad way of describing the unconscious, though to thoroughly flesh it out would require a separate study. Briefly, we may say that the unconscious is the storehouse of syntactic knowledge, of what Lacan calls the "know-how" of language, without any semantic content. In that sense, we can adjust Lacan's famous maxim "The unconscious is structured like a language" to the more specific "The unconscious is structured like a nonsense text."

4. Looking Glasses and Neverlands

1. It is important to note that not everyone's Alice is the one Carroll wrote. As I mentioned in the last chapter, very few people have actually read the original Alice stories. But the idea of her has persisted and proliferated in all sorts of media, so even children who are not bookish, or even literate, have some sense of who Alice is.
2. James Kincaid has authored a very important study that takes up the issue of pedophilia in Victorian and contemporary culture—*Child-Loving: The Erotic Child and Victorian Culture*. As with my discussion of *The Story of Babar* and *Curious George*, the following discussion should be read as a supplement to work that has come before, tracing the specifically psychoanalytic mechanisms that undergird the political and sociocultural fantasies at work in these texts.
3. "Desire is the desire of desire, desire of the Other, we have said, be it subject to the Law." Where possible, I have used the English versions of Lacan; however, translations in the notes are mine unless otherwise noted.
4. "It is therefore rather the assumption of castration that creates the lack upon which desire is instituted."
5. Kincaid articulates this idea this way: "In this sense, the child is constructed as a mirror that is also a window, reflecting back to the adult viewer a child, a true child. The child, then, is at the same time alien and familiar, that which is different and that which can pass for the self. . . . The child performs as a complex narcissistic image offering entry into a vision of play" (195–196).
6. This absence of a mirror image is in keeping with Lacan's assertion that the *objet a* is "nonspecularizable."
7. This is, of course, part of a larger cultural fantasy that children can somehow access the Real through faith or belief. As they grow, the myth goes, they lose this ability. This myth is enacted through and in this story—Wendy, John, Michael,

and the Lost Boys eventually lose their ability to fly because they lose their ability to believe. In the play, the real children in the audience are asked to assert their belief in fairies by clapping their hands. It is as if adults need to believe that children believe.

5. "I Never Explain Anything"

1. For a full account of the performativity of gender, see Judith Butler's *Gender Trouble*.
2. But, one might argue, what stops us from simply reversing the binary? If female is nothing more than not male, then why is male anything more than not female? Structurally speaking, this is a valid question, but history and culture tend to reify the content within the structures on which they are built. The animation of the structural binaries by human subjects has more often than not validated the dominant term through the annihilation of its other.
3. Phallocentrism is here to be understood in an Irigarayan sense as the problem of the eclipse of difference caused by the structure of binary oppositions described above. Phallocentrism is the discourse of the one, the discourse that represents difference as "a/not a" rather than "a/b." This sort of representation, according to Irigaray, is an inherent feature of all modern discourses, making them all, consciously or unconsciously, phallocentric. For further discussion, see Irigaray's *An Ethics of Sexual Difference*.
4. And yet, it is important to remember that in *Seminar XX*, Lacan writes, "the apparent necessity of the phallic function turns out to be mere contingency" (94), that is, it is a phenomenon that appears in this particular culture at this particular time, with no claims to either universality or atemporality.
5. I am deeply indebted for this reading to the work of these writers, who include Gilbert Chaitin, Joan Copjec, Bruce Fink, Robert Samuels, and Slavoj Žižek. I sense that the move toward schematic formulae and symbolic logic, on Lacan's part, as well as on the part of his commentators, results at least in part from a frustration with the limits of ordinary language to describe something that is, ultimately, uninscribable. My approach will be to lay out a series of metaphors with the hope that one or more of them will resonate with and prove useful to the reader.
6. I rely on the reader's subjective experience to bear out the way signifiers function to "name" this lack. Also, Fink offers a detailed explanation of this process in *The Lacanian Subject* (114–115).
7. I am using the Walt Disney movie version of *Mary Poppins* for several reasons. First, the movie, more than the book, is an icon of modern American childhood. Second, the screenplay, especially the songs, lends itself aptly to a Lacanian reading. And lastly, I like the character as portrayed by Julie Andrews much better than her textual counterpart. Good cultural and theoretical reasons, as well as a very sound subjective reason, I think.
8. Slavoj Žižek examines the anal father, his differences from the Symbolic pater-

nal function, and the effects he has in *Enjoy Your Symptom! Jacques Lacan in Hollywood and Out*, especially 124–128.

9. It is interesting and important to note that the books I have examined, all written by women, are read mostly by girls. However, since structure is not predetermined by anatomical sex, it is possible for boys who read these books to find themselves interpellated by the feminine structure, just as it is possible for girls reading *Charlotte's Web* to be interpellated by a masculine structure. The problematic of gendered "reading" is undertaken most insightfully by film theorist D. N. Rodowick in *The Difficulty of Difference: Psychoanalysis, Sexual Difference, and Film Theory*.

6. Blinded by the White

1. See, for instance, *White Reign: Deploying Whiteness in America*, edited by Joe L. Kincheloe, Shirley R. Steinberg, Nelson M. Rodriguez, and Ronald E. Chennault, and *Displacing Whiteness: Essays in Social and Cultural Criticism*, edited by Ruth Frankenberg.

2. *Modernity and the Hegemony of Vision*, edited by David Michael Levin, is the title of a collection of essays exploring the ocularcentrism of modernism.

3. Throughout this section, I use the words "us" and "we," as if my audience were monolithic. I do so deliberately, because I want to emphasize that these values are available to and get internalized by anyone with access to a television set, which is the primary conveyor of images in contemporary culture, and which works especially, by the associative logic I have been describing, to attach certain types of qualities to certain types of people.

7. Abjection and Adolescent Fiction

1. There is certainly no consensus as to when the structuring process stops for any given subject. In fact, some subjects probably never achieve anything like a fixed structure, whereas others become fixed in their structure very early. In any event, literature written for adolescents, with which this chapter is concerned, seems to assume a psychic structure open to modification, either in a formative or reformative capacity.

2. Roberta Seelinger Trites makes this point very convincingly in chapter 4 of *Disturbing the Universe*.

Conclusion

1. See my "P Is for Patriarchy: Re-Imaging the Alphabet."

BIBLIOGRAPHY

Alcorn, Marshall W., Jr., and Mark Bracher. "Literature, Psychoanalysis, and the Re-Formation of the Self: A New Direction for Reader-Response Theory." *PMLA* 100 (1985): 342–54.

Allsburg, Chris van. *The Z Was Zapped.* Boston: Houghton Mifflin, 1987.

Almond, David. *Skellig.* New York: Delacorte, 1999.

Althusser, Louis. *Lenin and Philosophy.* Translated by Ben Brewster. New York: Monthly Review P, 1971.

Anderson, Celia Catlett, and Marilyn Fain Apseloff. *Nonsense Literature for Children: Aesop to Seuss.* Hamden, Conn.: Library Professional Publications, 1989.

Austin, J. L. *How to Do Things with Words* (2d. ed.). Cambridge: Harvard UP, 1962.

Babb, Valerie. *Whiteness Visible: The Meaning of Whiteness in American Literature and Culture.* New York: NYUP, 1998.

Babe. Based on the book by Dick King-Smith. Screenplay by George Miller and Chris Noonan. Directed by Chris Noonan. Universal, 1995.

Barrie, J. M. *Peter Pan* (1911). New York: Puffin, 1986.

Bell, Elizabeth, Lynda Haas, and Laura Sells, eds. *From Mouse to Mermaid: The Politics of Film, Gender, and Culture.* Bloomington: Indiana UP, 1995.

Belsey, Catherine. *Critical Practice.* New York: Routledge, 1980.

Benveniste, Emile. *Problems in General Linguistics.* Translated by Mary Elizabeth Meek. Coral Gables: U of Miami P, 1971.

Bettelheim, Bruno. *The Uses of Enchantment: The Meaning and Importance of Fairy Tales.* New York: Penguin, 1978.

Block, Francesca Lia. *Dangerous Angels: The Weetzie Bat Books.* New York: Harper-Collins, 1998.

Bloor, Edward. *Tangerine.* New York: Scholastic, 1999.

Blum, Virginia, and June Cummins. "Lost and Found: Transitional Objects and the Adult-Child Relationship in *Something from Nothing* and *Owen.*" Paper presented at the Modern Critical Approaches to Children's Literature Conference, Nashville, Tenn., 20 April 1995.

Bodmer, George. "The Post-Modern Alphabet: Extending the Limits of the Contemporary Alphabet Book, from Seuss to Gorey." *Children's Literature Association Quarterly* 14.3 (Fall 1989): 115–117.

Boheemen, Christine van. *The Novel As Family Romance: Language, Gender, and Authority from Fielding to Joyce.* Ithaca: Cornell UP, 1987.

Bosmajian, Hamida. "Reading the Unconscious: Psychoanalytical Criticism." In *Understanding Children's Literature*, edited by Peter Hunt, 100–111. London: Routledge, 1999.

Brooks, Peter. *Reading for the Plot: Design and Intention in Narrative.* New York: Knopf, 1984.

Brown, Margaret Wise. *Goodnight Moon* (1947). Illustrated by Clement Hurd. New York: Harper and Row, 1975.

Burnett, Frances Hodgson. *A Little Princess* (1905). New York: Signet, 1990.

Butler, Judith. *Gender Trouble: Feminism and the Subversion of Identity.* New York: Routledge, 1990.

———. *The Psychic Life of Power: Theories of Subjection.* Stanford: Stanford UP, 1997.

Cannon, Janell. *Stellaluna.* New York: Scholastic, 1993.

Carroll, Lewis. *Alice in Wonderland* (1897). Edited by Lewis Gray. New York: Norton, 1971.

Chaitin, Gilbert D. *Rhetoric and Culture in Lacan.* Literature, Culture, Theory, vol. 18. Cambridge: Cambridge UP, 1996.

Chambers, Aidan. *Booktalk: Occasional Writings on Literature and Children.* London: Bodley Head, 1985.

Cheng, Anne Anlin. *The Melancholy of Race: Psychoanalysis, Assimilation, and Hidden Grief.* Oxford: Oxford UP, 2001.

Cixous, Hélène. "Introduction to Lewis Carroll's *Through the Looking Glass* and *The Hunting of the Snark.*" *New Literary History* 13.2 (winter 1982): 231–251.

Clark, Beverly Lyon, and Margaret R. Higonnet, eds. *Girls, Boys, Books, Toys: Gender in Children's Literature and Culture.* Baltimore: Johns Hopkins UP, 1999.

Coats, Karen. "P Is for Patriarchy: Re-Imaging the Alphabet." *Children's Literature Association Quarterly* 25.2 (Summer 2000): 88–97.

Copjec, Joan. *Read My Desire: Lacan against the Historicists.* Cambridge: MIT Press, 1994.

Cormier, Robert. *After the First Death.* New York: Pantheon, 1979.

———. *The Chocolate War.* New York: Dell, 1974.

———. *I Am the Cheese.* New York: Knopf, 1977.

———. *We All Fall Down.* New York: Delacorte, 1991.

Coward, Rosalind, and John Ellis. *Language and Materialism.* London: Routledge and Kegan Paul, 1977.

Crew, Gary. *Strange Objects.* New York: Simon and Schuster, 1993.

Cummins, June. "The Resisting Monkey: *Curious George*, Slave Captivity Narratives, and the Postcolonial Condition." *ARIEL: A Review of International English Literature* 28.1 (January 1997): 69–83.

Cuomo, Chris. "Spinsters in Sensible Shoes: *Mary Poppins* and *Bedknobs and Broomsticks.*" In *From Mouse to Mermaid*, edited by Elizabeth Bell, Lynda Haas, and Laura Sells, 212–223. Bloomington: Indiana UP, 1995.

deBrunoff, Jean. *The Story of Babar* (1931). New York: Random House, 1960.

Desmond, William. *Desire, Dialectic, and Otherness: An Essay on Origins.* New Haven: Yale UP, 1987.

Dr. Seuss. [Theodor Seuss Geisel]. *The 500 Hats of Bartholomew Cubbins*. Eau Claire, Wisc.: E. M. Hale for Vanguard Press, 1938.

———. *And to Think That I Saw It on Mulberry Street*. New York: Random House, 1937.

———. *The Cat in the Hat*. New York: Random House, 1957.

———. *Dr. Seuss's ABC*. New York: Random House, 1963.

———. *Green Eggs and Ham*. New York: Random House, 1960.

———. *Horton Hatches the Egg*. New York: Random House, 1940.

———. *How the Grinch Stole Christmas*. New York, Random House, 1957.

———. *The King's Stilts*. New York: Random House, 1939.

———. *On Beyond Zebra*. New York: Random House, 1955.

———. *One Fish, Two Fish, Red Fish, Blue Fish*. New York: Random House, 1960.

Dusinberre, Juliet. *Alice to the Lighthouse: Children's Books and Radical Experiments in Art*. London: Macmillan, 1987.

Eastman, P. D. *Are You My Mother?* New York: Random House, 1960.

Egan, Michael. "The Neverland of Id: Barrie, *Peter Pan*, and Freud." *Children's Literature* 10 (1982): 37–55.

Evans, Dylan. *An Introductory Dictionary to Lacanian Psychoanalysis*. London: Routledge, 1996.

Feldstein, Richard, Bruce Fink, and Maire Jaanus, eds. *Reading Seminars I and II: Lacan's Return to Freud*. Albany: SUNY Press, 1996.

Felman, Shoshana. *Jacques Lacan and the Adventure of Insight: Psychoanalysis in Contemporary Culture*. Cambridge: Harvard UP, 1987. (JLAI)

———. *The Literary Speech Act: Don Juan with J. L. Austin, or Seduction in Two Languages*. Translated by Catherine Porter. Ithaca: Cornell UP, 1983. (LSA)

Fine, Anne. *The Tulip Touch*. Boston: Little, Brown, 1997.

Fink, Bruce. *The Lacanian Subject: Between Language and Jouissance*. Princeton: Princeton UP, 1995. (LS)

———. "Logical Time and the Precipitation of Subjectivity." In *Reading Seminars I and II: Lacan's Return to Freud*, edited by Bruce Fink, Richard Feldstein, and Maire Jaanus, 356–386. Albany: SUNY Press, 1996.

———. "Notes on Temporal Tension." *Newsletter of the Freudian Field* 2 (1988): 23–28.

Fleischman, Paul. *Breakout*. Chicago: Cricket, 2003.

———. *Mind's Eye*. New York: Holt, 1999.

———. *Whirligig*. New York: Holt, 1998.

Fletcher, John, and Andrew Benjamin, eds. *Abjection, Melancholia, and Love*. New York: Routledge, 1990.

Frankenberg, Ruth, ed. *Displacing Whiteness: Essays in Social and Cultural Criticism*. Durham, N.C.: Duke UP, 1997.

Freud, Sigmund. "The Ego and the Id." In *Standard Edition*, vol. 19, 3–66. London: Hogarth Press, 1961. (SE 19)

———. *Jokes and Their Relation to the Unconscious*. In *Standard Edition*, vol. 8. London: Hogarth Press, 1960.

————. "Mourning and Melancholia." In *Standard Edition*, vol. 14, 239–258. London: Hogarth Press, 1957.

————. *The Standard Edition of the Complete Psychological Works of Sigmund Freud*. 24 vols. Edited and translated by James Strachey. London: Hogarth Press, 1952–74.

————. "Three Essays on the Theory of Sexuality." In *Standard Edition*, vol. 7, 125–243. London: Hogarth Press, 1953

————. "The Uncanny." In *Standard Edition*, vol. 17, 217–256. London: Hogarth Press, 1955.

Friedenberg, Edgar Z. *The Vanishing Adolescent*. New York: Dell, 1962.

Gagnon, Laurence. "Webs of Concern: *The Little Prince* and *Charlotte's Web*. *Children's Literature* 2 (1973): 61–66.

Gattégno, Jean. *Lewis Carroll*. Translated by Rosemary Sheed. New York: Thomas Y. Crowell, 1976.

Gaudrat, Marie-Agnes, Thierry Courtin, and Tony Mitton. *Let's Play ABC*. London: Orion, 1994.

Giddens, Anthony. *Modernity and Self-Identity: Self and Society in the Late Modern Age*. Stanford: Stanford UP, 1991.

Gilman, Phoebe. *Something from Nothing*. New York: Scholastic, 1992.

Glenn, Mel. *The Taking of Room 114: A Hostage Drama in Poems*. New York: Lodestar, 1997.

————. *Who Killed Mr. Chippendale? A Mystery in Poems*. New York: Lodestar, 1996.

Goffman, Erving. *Stigma: Notes on the Management of Spoiled Identity* (1963). New York: Simon and Schuster, 1986.

Grams, Armin. "Understanding the Adolescent Reader." In *Young Adult Literature: Background and Criticism*, compiled by Millicent Lenz and Ramona M. Mahood, 18–26. Chicago: American Library Association, 1980.

Griffith, John. "*Charlotte's Web*: A Lonely Fantasy of Love." *Children's Literature* 8 (1979): 111–117.

Grosz, Elizabeth. "The Body of Signification." In *Abjection, Melancholia, and Love*, edited by John Fletcher and Andrew Benjamin, 80–103. New York: Routledge, 1990.

Gubar, Marah. "'Where is the Boy?': The Pleasures of Postponement in the *Anne of Green Gables* Series." *Lion and the Unicorn* 25.1 (January 2001): 47–69.

Heidegger, Martin. *Being and Time*. Translated by John Macquarrie and Edward Robinson. San Francisco: Harper and Row, 1962. (BT)

Hinton, S. E. *The Outsiders*. New York: Dell, 1967.

Hollindale, Peter. "The Adolescent Novel of Ideas." *Children's Literature in Education* 26.1 (1995): 83–95.

Holt, John. *How Children Learn*. Rev. ed. New York: Dell, 1983.

Hunt, Caroline. "Young Adult Literature Evades the Theorists." *Children's Literature Association Quarterly* 21.1 (1996): 4–11.

Hunt, Peter, ed. *Understanding Children's Literature*. London: Routledge, 1999.

Irigaray, Luce. *An Ethics of Sexual Difference*. Translated by Carolyn Burke and Gillian C. Gill. Ithaca: Cornell UP, 1984.

Iskander, Sylvia Patterson. "Readers, Realism, and Robert Cormier." *Children's Literature* 15 (1987): 7–18.

Jaanus, Maire. "The Ethics of the Real in Lacan's Seminar VII." *Literature and Psychology* 43 (1997): 1–18.

Jan, Isabelle. *On Children's Literature*. New York: Schocken, 1969.

Julien, Philippe. *Jacques Lacan's Return to Freud: The Real, the Symbolic, and the Imaginary*. Translated by Devra Beck Simiu. New York: NYUP, 1994.

Kincaid, James R. *Child-Loving: The Erotic Child and Victorian Culture*. New York: Routledge, 1992.

Kincheloe, Joe L., Shirley R. Steinberg, Nelson M. Rodriguez, and Ronald E. Chennault, eds. *White Reign: Deploying Whiteness in America*. New York: St. Martin's Press, 1998.

Klause, Annette Curtis. *Blood and Chocolate*. New York: Delacorte, 1997.

————. *The Silver Kiss*. New York: Delacorte, 1990.

Kohl, Herbert. *Should We Burn Babar? Essays on Children's Literature and the Power of Stories*. New York: New Press, 1995.

Kristeva, Julia. "The Adolescent Novel." In *Abjection, Melancholia, and Love*, edited by John Fletcher and Andrew Benjamin, 8–23. New York: Routledge, 1990. (AN)

————. *Powers of Horror*. (1980). Translated by Leon Roudiez. New York: Columbia UP, 1982. (PH)

Lacan, Jacques. *Ecrits*. Paris: Editions du Seuil, 1966. (Ec)

————. *Ecrits: A Selection*. Translated by Alan Sheridan. New York: Norton, 1977. (E)

————. "The Family Complexes." Translated by Carolyn Asp. *Critical Texts* 5 (1988): 12–29. (FC)

————. *Feminine Sexuality*. Edited by Juliet Mitchell and Jacqueline Rose. Translated by Jacqueline Rose. New York: Norton, 1982.

————. *The Four Fundamental Concepts of Psychoanalysis*. Translated by Alan Sheridan. New York: Norton, 1978. (FFC)

————. "Introduction to the Names-of-the-Father Seminar." In *Television: A Challenge to the Psychoanalytic Establishment*, 81–95. Translated by Denis Hollier, Rosalind Krauss, and Annette Michelson. New York: Norton, 1990. (NF)

————. "Kant avec Sade." In *Ecrits*. Paris: Editions du Seuil, 1966.

————. "Logical Time and the Assertion of Anticipated Certainty." Translated by Bruce Fink and Marc Silver. *Newsletter of the Freudian Field* 2 (1988): 4–22. (LT)

————. *The Seminar of Jacques Lacan Book I: Freud's Papers on Technique, 1953–1954*. Translated by John Forrester. New York: Norton, 1988. (SI)

————. *The Seminar of Jacques Lacan Book II: The Ego in Freud's Theory and in the Technique of Psychoanalysis, 1954–1955*. Translated by Sylvana Tomaselli. New York: Norton, 1988. (SII)

————. *The Seminar of Jacques Lacan Book III: The Psychoses, 1955–1956*. Translated by Russell Grigg. New York: Norton, 1993. (SIII)

————. *The Seminar of Jacques Lacan Book VII: The Ethics of Psychoanalysis.* Edited by Jacques-Alain Miller. New York: Norton, 1992. (SVII)

————. *The Seminar of Jacques Lacan Book XX: Encore, 1972–1973.* Translated by Bruce Fink. New York: Norton, 1998. (XX)

————. *Television: A Challenge to the Psychoanalytic Establishment.* Translated by Denis Hollier, Rosalind Krauss, and Annette Michelson. New York: Norton, 1990. (TV)

Laplanche, J., and J.-B. Pontalis. *The Language of Psychoanalysis.* Translated by Donald Nicholson-Smith. New York: Norton, 1973.

Lasch, Christopher. *The Culture of Narcissism.* New York: Norton, 1979.

Lear, Jonathan. *Open-Minded: Working Out the Logic of the Soul.* Cambridge: Harvard UP, 1998.

Lecercle, Jean-Jacques. *Philosophy of Nonsense: The Intuitions of Victorian Nonsense Fiction.* New York: Routledge, 1994.

Lefort, Rosine. *Birth of the Other.* Translated by Marc Du Ray, Lindsay Watson, and Leonardo Rodriguez. Chicago: U of Illinois P, 1994.

Lemaire, Anika. *Jacques Lacan.* Translated by David Macey. London: Routledge and Kegan Paul, 1977.

Lenz, Millicent, and Ramona M. Mahood, eds. *Young Adult Literature: Background and Criticism.* Chicago: American Library Association, 1980.

Levin, David Michael, ed. *Modernity and the Hegemony of Vision.* Berkeley: U of California P, 1993.

Lindgren, Astrid. *Pippi Longstocking* (1950). New York: Puffin, 1978.

MacCannell, Juliet Flower. *Figuring Lacan: Criticism and the Cultural Unconscious.* Lincoln: U of Nebraska P, 1986.

MacIntyre, Alasdair. *After Virtue* (2d. ed.). Notre Dame: U of Notre Dame P, 1984.

Martin, Bill, Jr., and John Archambault. *Chicka Chicka Boom Boom.* Illustrated by Lois Ehlert. New York: Simon and Schuster, 1989.

Mary Poppins. Based on the book by P. L. Travers. Walt Disney Productions. Burbank, Calif., 1964.

McGillis, Roderick. "Another Kick at La/can: 'I Am a Picture.'" *Children's Literature Association Quarterly* 20 (1995): 42–46.

Mellard, James M. *Using Lacan, Reading Fiction.* Urbana: U of Illinois P, 1991.

Montgomery, L. M. *Anne of Green Gables* (1908). New York: Bantam, 1983.

————. *Emily of New Moon* (1923). New York: Bantam, 1983.

Mukherjee-Blaise, Bharati. "Mimicry and Reinvention." In *The Commonwealth in Canada,* edited by Uma Parameswaran, 147–157. Calcutta: Writer's Workshop, 1983.

Myers, Walter Dean. *Monster.* New York: HarperCollins, 2000.

Nodelman, Perry. "The Eye and the I: Identification and First-Person Narratives in Picture Books." *Children's Literature* 19 (1991): 1–30.

————. "Text As Teacher: The Beginning of *Charlotte's Web.*" *Children's Literature* 13 (1985): 109–127.

————. *Words about Pictures: The Narrative Art of Children's Picture Books.* Athens: U of Georgia P, 1988.

Nodelman, Perry, and Mavis Reimer. *The Pleasures of Children's Literature.* 3d. ed. New York: Allyn and Bacon, 2003.

Parish, Peggy. *Amelia Bedelia* (1963). Illustrated by Fritz Siebel. New York: HarperCollins, 1992.

————. *Amelia Bedelia Goes Camping.* Illustrated by Lynn Sweat. New York: Greenwillow Wm. Morrow, 1985.

————. *Come Back, Amelia Bedelia* (1971). Illustrated by Wallace Tripp. New York: HarperCollins, 1995.

————. *Teach Us, Amelia Bedelia.* Illustrated by Lynn Sweat. New York: Wm. Morrow, 1977.

————. *Thank You, Amelia Bedelia* (1964). Illustrated by Barbara Siebel Thomas, based on original drawings by Fritz Siebel. New York: HarperCollins, 1993.

Patrick, Denise Lewis. *What Does Baby Hear?* New York: Western, 1993.

————. *What Does Baby See?* New York: Western, 1990.

Ragland-Sullivan, Ellie. *Jacques Lacan and the Philosophy of Psychoanalysis.* Urbana: U of Illinois P, 1986.

————. "The Magnetism between Reader and Text: Prolegomena to a Lacanian Poetics." *Poetics* 13 (1984): 381–406.

Rajchman, John. "Lacan and the Ethics of Modernity." *Representations* 15 (Summer 1986): 42–56.

Rey, H. A. *Curious George.* Boston: Houghton Mifflin, 1941.

Rodowick, D. N. *The Difficulty of Difference: Psychoanalysis, Sexual Difference, and Film Theory.* New York: Routledge, 1991.

Rollin, Lucy, and Mark I. West. *Psychoanalytic Responses to Children's Literature.* Jefferson, N.C.: McFarland, 1999.

Rose, Jacqueline. *The Case of Peter Pan; or, The Impossibility of Children's Fiction.* London: Macmillan, 1984.

Rushdy, Ashraf H. A. "'The Miracle of the Web': Community, Desire, and Narrativity in *Charlotte's Web.*" *Lion and the Unicorn* 15 (1991): 35–60.

Rustin, Margaret, and Michael Rustin. *Narratives of Love and Loss: Studies in Modern Children's Fiction.* London: Verso, 1987.

Sachar, Louis. *Holes.* New York: Farrar, Strauss and Giroux, 1998.

Samuels, Robert. *Between Philosophy and Psychoanalysis: Lacan's Reconstruction of Freud.* New York: Routledge, 1993.

————. *Hitchcock's Bitextuality: Lacan, Feminisms, and Queer Theory.* Albany: SUNY P, 1998.

Say, Allen. *Allison.* Boston: Houghton Mifflin, 1997.

Sendak, Maurice. *Where the Wild Things Are.* New York: Harper and Row, 1963.

Seshadri-Crooks, Kalpana. *Desiring Whiteness: A Lacanian Analysis of Race.* New York: Routledge, 2000.

Silverman, Kaja. *The Subject of Semiotics.* New York: Oxford UP, 1983.

Tafuri, Nancy. *Have You Seen My Duckling?* New York: Wm. Morrow, 1984.

Taylor, Alexander L. *The White Knight*. Edinburgh: Oliver and Boyd, 1952.

Trites, Roberta Seelinger. *Disturbing the Universe: Power and Repression in Adolescent Literature*. Iowa City: U of Iowa P, 2000.

Waddell, Martin. *Owl Babies*. New York: Candlewick, 1992.

Walter, Virginia. *Making Up Megaboy*. New York: DK, 1998.

Weitzman, Lenore, Deborah Eifler, Elizabeth Hokad, and Catherine Ross. "Sex-Role Socialization in Picture Books for Preschool Children." *American Journal of Sociology* 77 (1972): 1125–1150. Rpt. in *Sexism and Youth*, edited by Diane Gersoni-Stavn, 174–195. New York: Bowker, 1974.

Werlin, Nancy. *The Killer's Cousin*. New York: Delacorte, 1998.

White, E. B. *Charlotte's Web*. New York: Harper and Row, 1952.

Widmer, Peter. "The Imperative of Perversion: Lacan's Understanding of the Superego." Translated by Elizabeth Stewart. *Literature and Psychology* 43 (1997): 19–46.

Wilder, Laura Ingalls. *Little House on the Prairie*. New York: Harper Trophy, 1971.

Wolf, Tim. "Imagination, Rejection, and Rescue: Recurrent Themes in Dr. Seuss." *Children's Literature* 23 (1995): 137–164.

Žižek, Slavoj. *Enjoy Your Symptom! Jacques Lacan in Hollywood and Out*. New York: Routledge, 1992. (ES)

———. *For They Know Not What They Do: Enjoyment as a Political Factor*. London: Verso, 1991.

———. *The Indivisible Remainder*. London: Verso, 1996. (IR)

———. *Looking Awry: An Introduction to Jacques Lacan through Popular Culture*. Cambridge: MIT Press, 1992. (LA)

———. *The Ticklish Subject: The Absent Centre of Political Ontology*. New York: Verso, 1999.

INDEX

abject hero, 146–148, 149
abjection, 7–8, 126, 138–146; defined, 140; social, 138, 149–152
adolescence, 137, 138, 142–143, 145
adolescent literature, 137–138, 139
After the First Death. See Cormier, Robert
alienation, 19, 24, 26, 73, 99
Allison. See Say, Allen
Allsburg, Chris van, 163; *The Z Was Zapped*, 163, 166
Almond, David, 154; *Skellig*, 154
Alphabet City, 166
Amelia Bedelia, 64, 67, 87
anal stage, 53, 60
Anderson, Celia Catlett, 65
Apseloff, Marilyn Fain, 65
Are You My Mother? See Eastman, P. D.
Austin, J. L., 163–164; *How to Do Things with Words*, 163, 165

Babb, Valerie, 125, 126
Babe: A Little Pig Goes a Long Way. See King-Smith, Dick
Barrie, J. M., 77–79; *Peter Pan*, 77, 89–95
Block, Francesca Lia, 155; *Dangerous Angels: The Weetzie Bat Books*, 155–157
Blood and Chocolate. See Klause, Annette Curtis
Bloor, Edward, 126; *Tangerine*, 126, 127–133
Blum, Virginia, 61
Bodmer, George, 164
Boheemen, Christine van, 161, 171

Bosmajian, Hamida, 5
Breakout. See Fleischman, Paul
Burnett, Frances Hodgson, 110; *A Little Princess*, 110
Butler, Judith, 9, 70, 71, 72, 74

Cannon, Janell, 72; *Stellaluna*, 8, 49–54, 62, 70, 71, 73, 75
Carroll, Lewis, 65, 77–89; *Through the Looking Glass*, 9, 79–89
castration, 60, 94; Symbolic (linguistic), 64, 80, 84, 91, 99, 103
Chaitin, Gilbert, 62, 65–66, 69–70, 100, 102–103, 109
Charlotte's Web. See White, E. B.
Chicka Chicka Boom Boom (Martin), 165–166
Chinaberry, 43
Cixous, Hélène, 79, 84, 87, 88
Copjec, Joan, 22, 45
Cormier, Robert, 146, 157; *After the First Death*, 157–158; *The Chocolate War*, 146–148; *I Am the Cheese*, 157–158; *We All Fall Down*, 148–149, 155
Coward, Rosalind, 26
Cummins, June, 63, 70
Cuomo, Chris, 105–106
Curious George. See Rey, H. A.

death drive, 95, 140, 142, 143, 145
deBrunoff, Jean, 72; *The Story of Babar*, 8, 70, 71, 72, 73–74, 75, 112
demand, 28, 140
desire, 29, 54, 77–82, 84–86, 140; cause

of, 38; feminine, 108; normative, 21; relation to master signifier, 123, 124–125; transgressive, 63, 78

Desmond, William, 112–113

Disney, 103, 106; *Bambi*, 71; *Mary Poppins*, 9, 101–110, 112; *Peter Pan*, 93

Dr. Seuss, 64, 67; *And To Think That I Saw It on Mulberry Street*, 68; *The Cat in the Hat*, 67, 69; *Dr. Seuss's ABC*, 66; *The 500 Hats of Bartholomew Cubbins*, 68; *Green Eggs and Ham*, 4, 67, 68–69; *Horton Hatches the Egg*, 68; *How the Grinch Stole Christmas*, 66; *The King's Stilts*, 68; *On Beyond Zebra*, 164–165

Dusinberre, Juliet, 2

Eastman, P. D., 48; *Are You My Mother?*, 48

ego, 24, 38, 45–46, 141, 150

ego psychology, 68

Ellis, John, 26

Evans, Dylan, 40

existentialism, 16, 17

fantasy, 49, 52, 62, 65, 128; Lacanian formula for, 49, 53, 61; male, 103, 106; traversal of fundamental, 32, 99; wish-fulfilling, 52

father, 18, 94, 109; primordial, 18, 103, 105, 112, 117–118; symbolic function, 113

Felman, Shoshana, 20, 31

feminist critiques of Lacan, 98–99

Fine, Anne, 151; *The Tulip Touch*, 151

Fink, Bruce, 20–21, 67, 89, 101; *The Lacanian Subject*, 21, 22, 24, 32, 45, 90, 100–101

Fleischman, Paul, 152; *Breakout*, 153–154, 159; *Mind's Eye*, 153–154; *Whirligig*, 152–153

Foucault, Michel, 9, 168

Freud, Sigmund, 38, 65, 90, 98, 103; "The Ego and the Id," 38

Gagnon, Laurence, 16, 24, 29, 31

Gattégno, Jean, 77

gender, 9, 97–99

Gilman, Phoebe, 60; *Something from Nothing*, 60–63, 68

Goffman, Erving, 125, 129

Goodnight Moon, 47

Green Eggs and Ham. See Dr. Seuss

Griffith, John, 15

Grosz, Elizabeth, 141, 143

Gubar, Marah, 111

Have You Seen My Duckling?, 49

Heidegger, Martin, 31

Hinton, S. E., 149; *The Outsiders*, 149–151

Holes. See Sachar, Louis

Holt, John, 44

I Am the Cheese. See Cormier, Robert

ideal(s), 5, 6, 38, 44, 121, 123, 124, 128, 145; ego, 27, 137; images, 6, 19, 108

identification, 19, 20, 34, 47, 63

identity, 4–5, 65, 140

Imaginary, 20, 23, 26, 84, 86, 121, 137, 140; body, 139–140, 143; ethics of, 10, 154–155, 157; support for Symbolic, 20, 53, 159–160

Irigaray, Luce, 98, 118

Jan, Isabelle, 80–81

jouissance, 9, 59, 64, 89–95, 134

Kincaid, James, 175n2, 175n4

King-Smith, Dick, 34; *Babe: A Little Pig Goes a Long Way*, 34

Klause, Annette Curtis, 154; *Blood and Chocolate*, 158; *The Silver Kiss*, 154

Kohl, Herbert, 70

Kristeva, Julia, 138–141, 143–144, 145; "The Adolescent Novel," 142, 143; *Powers of Horror*, 138, 139, 141, 142, 144, 146

Lacan: *Ecrits*, 79; *Ecrits: A Selection*, 18, 53; "The Family Complexes," 144; *The Four Fundamental Concepts of Psychoanalysis*, 81, 100; "Introduction to the Names of the Father Seminar," 140; "Kant avec Sade," 83; "Logical Time and the Assertion of Anticipated Certainty," 39–40, 46, 47, 50; *Seminar I*, 4, 45; *Seminar II*, 145; *Seminar XX*, 102, 176n4

lack, 47, 79–80, 82–83, 105, 114; in the Other, 66, 100–101

language, 17, 87; performativity of, 30–31, 61, 163–164, 165–167; relation to desire, 79–80, 110; relation to subjectivity, 2, 4, 16, 30–31, 35, 65

Laplanche, J., 18

Law of the Father, 7, 18, 94, 112. *See also* Name of the Father, paternal metaphor, third term

Lear, Edward, 65

Lear, Jonathan, 134

Lecercle, Jean-Jacques, 66–67

Lefort, Rosine, 20, 43

Lemaire, Anika, 80, 85, 86

Let's Play ABC, 166

Lewis, Denise Patrick, 42; *What Does Baby Hear?*, 42, 44; *What Does Baby See?*, 43, 44

Lindgren, Astrid, 99, 110; *Pippi Longstocking*, 9, 101, 110–116

Little House on the Prairie. See Wilder, Laura Ingalls

A Little Princess. See Burnett, Frances Hodgson

logical time, 8, 39; for comprehending, 40, 41, 46–57; for concluding, 40, 41, 49, 51, 63–70; for looking, 40, 41, 42–46, 51

love, 37–38, 105

MacCannell, Juliet Flower, 86

MacIntyre, Alisdair, 161

Mary Poppins. See Disney

master signifiers, 103, 109, 118, 126, 135–136; defined, 123; Whiteness as, 8, 9, 56, 124, 126, 132, 135

McGillis, Roderick, 5

melancholy, 37, 44

Mind's Eye. See Fleischman, Paul

mirror stage, 6, 27, 46–47, 84, 144, 173n3; defined, 19

The Missing Piece. See Silverstein, Shel

modernism, 6, 7, 8, 30, 44, 50, 112, 122, 171. *See also* subject, subjectivity

Montgomery, L. M., 99, 111, 117, 167; *Anne of Green Gables*, 111, 117; *Emily of New Moon* trilogy, 116–119

mother, 19, 20, 45, 46, 51, 141; as abject, 139–140, 147; as Other, 46; dyadic relationship with child, 19, 20, 23, 46, 51, 53, 76, 140; exclusion of, 28, 29, 38, 46, 65, 69, 140; incorporation of, 37; loss of, 47, 48, 55, 64–65; phallic, 29, 33; relation to *jouissance*, 90, 94

mother's desire, 19, 21, 29, 52, 140, 144; barred, 20, 23, 25

mourning, 37, 65

Mukherjee-Blaise, Bharati, 115

Name of the Father, 21, 25, 28, 32, 99, 113, 114, 140, 145; defined, 20. *See also* Law of the Father, paternal metaphor, third term

narcissism, 18

neurosis, 8, 20, 28, 70, 75–76

Nodelman, Perry, 5, 15; "Text as Teacher," 26, 27, 29, 31, 33; *Words about Pictures*, 54

nonsense, 64–70

objet a, 9, 61, 81–83, 101, 104, 140; defined, 61, 81

oedipalization, 7, 10, 95, 113, 137, 139–142

On Beyond Zebra. See Dr. Seuss

oral stage, 42, 44, 45, 71

orality, 67, 113

Other, 53, 84, 104, 111, 142; as constitutive of self, 27, 100, 133–134, 135; defined, 17; desire of, 24, 54, 70, 89; as feminine, 103, 105; lack in, 66, 67, 78, 100–101, 102, 104, 108, 109, 110, 117; as language, 4, 40; relation to subject, 28, 62–70, 74–76, 97; relation to unconscious, 50, 69, 79

The Outsiders. See Hinton, S. E.

Owl Babies, 49

paternal metaphor, 21, 25, 53, 105, 107, 114. *See also* Law of the Father, Name of the Father, third term

perversion, 8, 20, 70, 74–75, 89

Peter Pan. See Barrie, J. M.

phallic stage, 42

phallus, 18, 29, 87, 106, 114–115, 116; as signifier, 98–99, 100–101, 103, 108, 117

Pippi Longstocking. See Lindgren, Astrid

Pontalis, J.-B., 18

postmodernism, 10, 55, 162. *See also* subjectivity

preoedipal, 71, 72, 137, 139, 140

psychic structure, 70. *See also* neurosis, perversion, psychosis

psychosis, 8, 70, 73–74, 112, 114

queer, 110–111, 114, 115–116, 118

Ragland-Sullivan, Ellie, 17, 23, 26–27

reading, 59, 64, 69, 122

Real, 26, 81, 104, 105, 114; and body, 100, 140, 143; defined, 22, 99; ethics of, 10, 157–160; ex-sistence, 108; and mother, 46, 94

repression, 21, 52, 61, 126, 132

Rey, H. A., 72; *Curious George*, 8, 70, 71, 72, 73, 74–75, 112

Sachar, Louis, 126; *Holes*, 126, 133–135

Say, Allen, 56; *Allison*, 56

separation, 25, 39, 47, 71, 140

Seshadri-Crooks, Kalpana, 123

sexual difference, 97–98

sexuation, 99, 100–110

signifier, 24, 104, 109; logic of, 20, 43–44, 100; materiality of, 43, 69; movement of, 23, 63, 126; relation to subjectivity, 40, 55, 62; and signified, 80, 81, 87–88, 121. *See also* master signifier

The Silver Kiss. See Klause, Annette Curtis

Silverman, Kaja, 82

Silverstein, Shel, 81; *The Missing Piece*, 81–83

Skellig. See Almond, David

Stellaluna. See Cannon, Janell

Stine, R. L., 169–170

Story of Babar. See deBrunoff, Jean

structuralism, 16

subject: defined, 3–4; as effect of language, 2, 16, 30, 35; female, 105–110, 118; split, 47, 81, 83–84, 100, 122, 135–136, 162. *See also* subjectivity

subjectivity, 5, 24, 71, 113, 122, 135, 140, 142; absence of, 89, 145; female, 118; modernist, 5–6, 7, 17, 21, 30, 110, 162; opposed to subjection, 62, 68, 73; performativity of, 32–33, 115; postmodern, 10, 162

sublimation: artistic, 144, 153–154

superego, 141, 143–144, 146; as perverse, 147

Symbolic: defined, 99; mandates, 97; as modernist, 9; as patriarchal (male-order, phallic), 83, 102, 111, 114, 115, 118, 141, 158; performativity of, 107–108; relation to Imaginary, 20, 86, 139–140; relation to Name of the Father, 27; relation to unconscious, 90–91

Tangerine. See Bloor, Edward

Taylor, Alexander L., 86

third term, 20, 25, 52, 99, 113, 140. *See also* Law of the Father, Name of the Father, paternal metaphor

Through the Looking Glass. See Carroll, Lewis

Travers, P. L., 99, 102. *See also* Disney

Trites, Roberta Seelinger, 138

The Tulip Touch. See Fine, Anne

unconscious, 6, 66, 69, 90, 105; closing of, 62; difference between Freudian and Lacanian, 90–91; instantiation of, 50–51, 52

Walter, Virginia, 149; *Making Up Mega-boy*, 149

We All Fall Down. See Cormier, Robert

Weetzie Bat. See Block, Francesca Lia

Werlin, Nancy, 158; *The Killer's Cousin*, 158

What Does Baby Hear? See Lewis, Denise Patrick

What Does Baby See? See Lewis, Denise Patrick

Where the Wild Things Are, 37–38

Whirligig. See Fleischman, Paul

White, E. B., 15; *Charlotte's Web*, 4, 15–34, 51, 61, 111, 114

Whiteness, 8, 9, 10, 56, 122, 127, 128–133, 134, 135; and feminism, 128; as master signifier, 123–126, 132–133

Wilder, Laura Ingalls, 5; *Little House on the Prairie*, 5

Wolf, Tim, 67–68, 69

The Z Was Zapped. See Allsburg, Chris van

Žižek, Slavoj, 42, 51, 74, 81, 114, 115; *Enjoy Your Symptom*, 115; *The Indivisible Remainder*, 41, 51; *Looking Awry*, 42, 54, 81–82, 83, 89; *The Ticklish Subject*, 74